"*Speech Is My Hammer* seamlessly weaves together poignant personal reflections, historical narrative, literary theory, and critical race theory to address the question of what it means to become fluent in a language and literary tradition that is dedicated to erasing you. This is a must-read for anyone who is interested in thinking carefully about what it means to decolonize the canon and our relationship to it. Bravo!"

—**MICHAEL E. SAWYER**
Author of *Black Minded: The Political Philosophy of Malcolm X*

"In prose that is equally percussive and probing, Max Hunter has done something I hadn't thought possible. He has dutifully explored his ambivalent relationship with African American literature while literally exploring the abundance of 'ambivalence' in African American literature. . . . Hunter's patient rumination on his experience with the literature is beyond brilliant. . . . This work is stunning. I can't wait to teach it."

—**KIESE LAYMON**
Author of *Heavy: An American Memoir*

"The challenge of Hunter's *Speech Is My Hammer* is also its chief gift: contemplating black male literacy ambivalence reveals the pervasive and subtle ways racism corrupts the reader (and writer) who isn't careful. . . . But the power in these pages goes beyond diagnosing a problem. Hunter reveals a way through."

—**R. DWAYNE BETTS**
Author of *Question of Freedom: A Memoir of Learning, Survival, and Coming of Age in Prison*

"*Speech Is My Hammer* is . . . both astoundingly astute and authoritatively grounded in Hunter's personal experience. It is precisely the kind of book that black men need to challenge generations of harmful indoctrination regarding literacy, and what others need to comprehend our historically ambivalent relationship to reading and writing."

—**MITCHELL S. JACKSON**
Author of *Survival Math: Notes on an All-American Family*

# SPEECH
### Is My HAMMER

# SPEECH
## Is My HAMMER

*Black Male Literacy Narratives
in the Age of Hip-Hop*

## Max A. Hunter

 CASCADE *Books* · Eugene, Oregon

SPEECH IS MY HAMMER
Black Male Literacy Narratives in the Age of Hip-Hop

Cascade Books
An Imprint of Wipf and Stock Publishers
199 W. 8th Ave., Suite 3
Eugene, OR 97401

www.wipfandstock.com

PAPERBACK ISBN: 978-1-6667-0307-8
HARDCOVER ISBN: 978-1-6667-0308-5
EBOOK ISBN: 978-1-6667-0309-2

*Cataloguing-in-Publication data:*

Names: Hunter, Max. author.

Title: Speech is my hammer : black male literacy narratives in the age of hip-hop / Max A. Hunter.

Description: Eugene, OR : Cascade Books, 2022 | Includes bibliographical references.

Identifiers: ISBN 978-1-6667-0307-8 (paperback) | ISBN 978-1-6667-0308-5 (hardcover) | ISBN 978-1-6667-0309-2 (ebook)

Subjects: LCSH: African American young men—Education. | Reading—United States. | African American young men—Books and reading.

Classification: LC2731 .H86 2022 (paperback) | LC2731 .H86 (ebook)

VERSION NUMBER 081922

I dedicate this book to Grandmother
—the matriarch of the Walker clan,

**Bennie Jewel Walker**

How has it happened that so many people have come to take up this strange attitude of hostility to civilization?

It was discovered that a person becomes neurotic because he cannot tolerate the amount of frustration which society imposes on him in the service of its cultural ideals, and it was inferred from this that the abolition or reduction of those demands would result in a return to possibilities of happiness.

—Sigmund Freud, *Civilization and Its Discontents*

"I too have become acquainted with ambivalence," I said. "That's why I'm here."

"What's that?"

"Nothing, a word that doesn't explain it."

—Ralph Ellison, *Invisible Man*

Which is to say, that the discourse of mimicry is constructed around *ambivalence*; in order to be effective, mimicry must continually produce slippage, its excess, its difference. The authority of that mode of colonial discourse that I have called mimicry is therefore stricken by an indeterminacy: mimicry emerges as the representation of a difference that is itself a process of disavowal.

—Homi Bhabha, "Of Mimicry and Man"

# Contents

## RACE, EDUCATION, AND POVERTY:
# THE WIRE

## CHID 250 C | T/Th 2:30–4:20

W UNIVERSITY *of* WASHINGTON

DR. MAX HUNTER

"THE WIRE IS DISSENT. IT ARGUES THAT OUR SYSTEMS ARE NO LONGER VIABLE FOR THE GREATER GOOD OF THE MOST, THAT AMERICA IS NO LONGER OPERATING AS A UTILITARIAN AND DEMOCRATIC EXPERIMENT. IF YOU ARE NOT COMFORTABLE WITH THAT NOTION, YOU WON'T AGREE WITH SOME OF THE TONALITIES OF THE SHOW. I WOULD ARGUE THAT PEOPLE COMFORTABLE WITH THE ECONOMIC AND POLITICAL TRENDS IN THE UNITED STATES RIGHT NOW — AND THINKING THAT THE NATION AND ITS INSTITUTIONS ARE EQUIPPED TO RESPOND MEANINGFULLY TO THE PROBLEMS DEPICTED WITH SOME CARE AND ACCURACY ON THE WIRE (WE REPORTED EACH SEASON FRESH, WE DID NOT WRITE SOLELY FROM MEMORY) — WELL, PERHAPS THEY'RE PLAYING WITH THE TUNING KNOBS WHEN THE BACK OF THE APPLIANCE IS IN FLAMES." —DAVID SIMON

If you're interested in engaging a dissenting and unsettling view on the traditional academic and journalistic perspectives that analyze and describe the issues of race, identity, education, and poverty in urban America, then CHID 250 is the course for you. In this course, we will use The Wire (often described as a masterpiece of American Television) and readings from diverse academic perspectives investigate the cleavages in narratives and perceptions about disparities in racial experiences and urban realities.

INTRODUCTION

# Black Intellectual Swagger
## African-American Literacy and Its Discontents

MANY AMERICANS TAKE IT for granted that African-American males, especially those who identify with hip-hop or street culture, are antagonistic to gaining academic literacy. Yet, on occasion, American media portrays the ambivalent black male. The film *Finding Forrester* provides a stunning cultural and historical illustration that counters our common sense on black male literacy. Jamal Warner is a sixteen-year-old African-American male residing in the Bronx. The protagonist is a standout basketball player and gifted student, a voracious closet reader who downplays his intelligence and interest in literature. In an opening scene, Jamal's English literature teacher, Ms. Joyce, introduces a lesson on Edgar Allan Poe. The African-American educator uses culturally-appropriate teaching practices when describing the author Poe as a cocaine addict obsessed with death, who penned "The Raven" in 1845 at the bottom of his depression. After reciting a few lines— "Once upon a midnight dreary, while I pondered weak and weary"—Ms. Joyce calls on Jamal to discuss his reading of the poem. He feigns ignorance to avoid disclosing his literary prowess. Jamal is not alone in his literary closet. Over lunch, Damon, a member of his neighborhood crew, played by the rapper Lil' Zane, transforms Poe's "The Tell-Tale Heart" into an urban myth—and Jamal recognizes that he's not alone in his closeted literacy.

The narrative provides Jamal an opportunity to pursue his hidden literacy aspirations unencumbered by black male anti-academic cultural norms found in urban public schools. Because Jamal had scored high on a standardized exam, the school principal convinces Jamal's mother to send him to a prestigious independent school. Of course, Jamal fears crossing

1

the cultural border between his 'hood and the elite Manhattan college-preparatory school world. In this privileged environment, coaches, teachers, and other students will judge Jamal based on his ability to conform to their norms in the classroom and on his ability to adapt to elite conduct in competition, including class-defined sportsmanship on the basketball court.

Jamal serendipitously discovers William Forrester, a reclusive literary figure, holed up in a stuffy neighborhood flat filled with books. Jamal's friends have developed a Poe-esque narrative about the mysterious inhabitant in the apartment overlooking the neighborhood basketball court. The instigating Damon dares Jamal to enter the apartment to prove a sinister occupant does not haunt it. Once in the dim and musky apartment, the solitary author startles his unexpected guest, causing Jamal to drop his backpack in which he has hidden notebooks filled with his notes on the literary works that he has read and several of his literary efforts. When returning to the apartment to retrieve his bag, Jamal discovers that Forrester has read his notebooks and commented on their content. The street-savvy Jamal grasps the opportunity to approach and convince Forrester to help him improve his writing to support his private-school academic aspirations. Robert Crawford, a recalcitrant and feared English teacher who doesn't trust Jamal's code-switching between ghetto-inflected black vernacular and literary savant swagger, has questions about his student's literary prowess. When Crawford accuses Jamal of plagiarizing an essay he submitted in a campus-wide writing competition, the predicament forces Jamal to confront and convince Forrester to overcome his unexplained phobia to confront the suspicious teacher with the truth about their literary friendship. This seemingly improbable hip-hop-inflected tale was a hit at the American box office.

The American public's broad acceptance of this tale suggests that our society expects African-American males to struggle outwardly with our educational system and inwardly with their literacy anxieties. However, what is less recognized is that Jamal's literacy ambivalence has been present in African-American males' historical and literary canon from slavery to the present day. Beginning with Olaudah Equiano's slave narrative, *The Interesting Narrative of the Life of Olaudah Equiano* (1789), and moving forward to contemporary stories—Wes Moore's *The Other Wes Moore: One Name, Two Fates* (2011); R. Dwayne Bett's *A Question of Freedom: A Memoir of Learning, Survival, and Coming of Age in Prison* (2010); André Robert Lee's film *The Prep School Negro* (2012); and Jeff Hobbs's *The Short and Tragic Life of Robert Peace: A Brilliant Young Man Who Left Newark for the Ivy League* (2014)—African-American male biographies, memoirs, and films such as these have constructed a genre of literature that portrays a heretofore unrecognized ambivalent resistance to socialization into mainstream culture and the appropriation of suitable literacy and speech.[1]

By studying African-American "literacy narratives," based on methods developed in literacy studies to understand attitudes regarding English mastery in fiction in the past, we can discover historical attitudes among black males toward literacy and, by comparison, much about our own attitudes and beliefs in respect to ambivalence.[2] Janet Carey Eldred explains:

> Fiction [and other genres in literature] revels in specificity, in particular places and characters that are constructed out of the language of a given place and time. All fiction historicizes problems of socialization, including literacy; it dramatizes conflicts between characters from specific language communities and highlights differences between dialects and usage. With its compact form, the short story tells a particular kind of narrative, a narrative of arrested socialization that ends with characters who, having glimpsed new language and cultural possibilities, find their speech inadequate and the new speech problematic. In the end, these characters remain suspended between languages; in such endings, short fiction "freezes" or crystallizes the problem of literacy.[3]

But the "problem of literacy" is more fact than fiction. I, too, have experienced a similar ambivalence as I traveled on a school bus from a palm tree-lined government housing project to a new middle school near the white sands of La Jolla, California. During my early childhood, my mother had moved our family from Los Angeles, California, to a ghetto minutes away from the Mexican border. My black, almost hippie mother, who was eclectic in all things—art, films, food, and friends—did not seem affected by the move. Moms's creativity and resilience informed the culinary delights, books, and company that flowed into our apartment. Even as a young bagel-and-chop-liver-eating child, as we moved from calling her Mommy to the less colloquial Moms for Mamma, I recognized the irony of our welfare-funded existence beneath the white-hot sun and beautiful palm trees in America's finest city.

Once in San Diego, my doting and barely literate grandmother took on a second job to help pay my tuition at St. Rita's, a local Catholic school, and then encouraged me to devour books with abandon. Grandma had shelves of classic texts in the Western canon. This part of the story is a bit

1. Eldred, "Narratives of Socialization," 686–700.
2. Eldred and Mortensen, "Reading Literacy Narratives," 512–39.
3. Eldred, "Narratives of Socialization," 686.

hackneyed. Growing up in Southern California in the sixties and seventies, I had absorbed a black nationalist ethos that promoted an urban black cultural aesthetic in all things. I resisted the mandate to choose an essentialist approach to my blackness during these formative years in South Central Los Angeles, and I'd hang out with teenage extended family members as they listened to James Brown, Stevie Wonder, and other black musicians. My family in San Diego chose a lifestyle that cherished Soul food and music, but not without spending weeks at my polyamorous uncle's summer apartments on the beach listening to jazz and rock and my mother's excursions to small restaurants in the city's gay district. On my own, I entered the streets and the suburban enclaves, moved towards manhood to embrace neo-black nationalism in the academy while dabbling in art film, new wave music, and burgeoning hip-hop culture. On the brink of manhood, my colleagues and I developed a deep-seated ambivalence regarding cultural assimilation based on a clash that divided black and white culture.

As a youth, I had no idea that our emerging politics of black authenticity had a long genealogy. A servant in William Wells Brown's novel *Clotel* (1853) lays bare the black authenticity politics deep in African-American history. The enslaved Pompey declares, "Dis nigger is no counterfeit; he is de genewine artekil."[4] The braggadocios slave appears as the first *real nigga* in American literature. As a mature scholar interested in ambivalence among black males regarding literacy, Pompey's claim suggests that African Americans have been bantering about the terms of authenticity (a coherent, impervious, and no-acquiescent black identity) since their enslavement in the Americas.

The defining elements of black authenticity have been fluid and contingent upon class and historical context.[5] "Long before the rapper Ice-T insisted upon being called a nigger, my father declared that he was proud to be a 'stone nigger'—by which he meant a black man without pretensions who was unafraid to enjoy himself openly and loudly despite objections of condescending whites or insecure blacks," according to Harvard Law Professor Randall Kennedy.[6] In *American Hunger*, Richard Wright captures this sentiment among his youthful peers. He describes his pubescent recognition of their racial impunity,

> Having grown taller and older, I now associated with older boys and I had to pay for my admittance into their company by subscribing to their racial sentiments. The touchstone of fraternity

4. Brown, *Clotel*, 12.

5. Hohle, *Black Citizenship*, 82–102.

6. Kennedy, *Nigger*, xviii.

was my feeling toward white people, how much hostility I held toward them, what degrees of value and honor I assigned to race. None of this was premeditated, but sprang spontaneously out of the talk of the black boys who met at the crossroads. . . . We had somehow caught the spirit of the role of our sex and we flocked together for common moral schooling. We spoke boastfully in bass voices; we used the word "nigger" to prove the tough fiber of our feelings; we spouted excessive profanity as a sign of our coming manhood; we pretended callousness toward the injunctions of parents; and we strove to convince one another that our decisions stemmed from ourselves and ourselves alone. Yet we frantically concealed how dependent we were upon each other.[7]

Wright's narrative presages future changes one might now perceive in the relationship between black masculinity and literacy among African-American males. Yet, Malcolm X ushers the black male reader into the stage where literacy's connection becomes more legible. Malcolm X embodied black authenticity's next iteration (with implications for both black masculinity and erudition).

Michael Sawyer's text, *Black Mind: The Political Philosophy of Malcolm X*, examines, among other considerations, Malcolm's moving beyond ontological blackness (i.e., blackness as a biological fact) to epistemological blackness (i.e., blackness as cultural and political praxis). Ossie Davis's eulogized Malcolm X in Harlem in a manner that rendered the connection between literacy, masculinity, and racial identity inescapable. He mused,

[Harlem a] nonetheless proud community has found a braver, more gallant young champion than this Afro-American who lies before us, unconquered still. I say the word again, as he would want me to: Afro-American. Afro-American Malcolm, who was a master, was most meticulous in his use of words. Nobody knew better than he the power words have over the minds of men. *Malcolm had stopped being a "Negro" years ago.* It had become too small, too puny, too weak a word for him. Malcolm was bigger than that. *Malcolm had become an Afro-American and he wanted so desperately that we, that all his people, would become Afro-Americans, too.*[8]

Later, I will discuss Malcolm's approach to his literacy politics. Here, I want to underscore his identity politics, as Davis alludes to his being Afro-American and Sawyer who is concerned with "understanding of what Davis

7. Wright, *Black Boy*, 78.
8. Davis, "Our Shining Black Prince," xi–xii; emphasis mine.

means by marking the 'manhood' of Malcolm X, what he understands as 'our living, black manhood.'"[9] He explains, "As Ossie Davis proposed, this is a mindset. To exceed the boundaries of the marginalized subjectivity of the Negro, Malcolm X embarks on a complex intellectual project that I suggest is best labeled by his own framework, Black Minded."[10] George Frederickson's history of black ideologies illuminates this emerging mindset that,

> This repudiation of a strictly genetic view of blackness paralleled a subtle and little noticed difference of the 1960s and the earlier variants. . . . As we have seen, these forerunners were men of dark complexions who distrusted mulattoes and at times openly disparaged them. But in the 1960s, the foremost champion of blackness could be light-skinned and red-haired Malcom X. The implicit message was . . . one was as black as one felt, and that people of African-Ancestry who retained integrationist view that white culture was superior to black culture continued to be "Negroes" rather than "blacks," however dark complexioned they happened to be. . . . Whether or not the new American affirmation of a non-genetic blackness influenced the racial thinking of Black Consciousness, there can be no doubt that [independent black thinkers] innovated significantly in making race consciousness more a matter of existential choice and political awareness than of biological determination.[11]

Sawyer's read on Frederickson's thesis lays bare "malleability" in the emerging notion of blackness in late-twentieth-century black nationalism.[12] Malcolm's black mindedness "is a way of knowing about the self, and in so doing, understanding [that malleable] self to be a necessarily radical political subject as the threshold condition of that knowing."[13] According to Sawyer, this "epistemological tendency and . . . radical political subjectivity" summonses Negroes, as defined in the black political imagination informed by white supremacy, to abandon their *de facto* marginalization and embrace a revolutionary black self-awareness "is a cry for true subjectivity in the form of Being Human."[14] However, after Malcolm X's assassination, young black nationalists responded by defining blackness in biological and ideological terms.

9. Sawyer, *Black Minded*, 6.

10. Sawyer, *Black Minded*, 8.

11. Frederickson, *Black Liberation*, 302.

12. Sawyer, *Black Minded*, 14.

13. Sawyer, *Black Minded*, 10.

14. Sawyer, *Black Minded*, 10.

At the moment between the civil rights movement and the height of urban decay in the American inner-cities that gave birth to hip-hop culture and music, young black nationalists redefined the terms of blackness along this line of reasoning. These young Turks had happened upon Melville Herskovits's idea about African recidivisms in African-American culture and music in *Myth of the Negro Past* (1941), which allowed them to redeem disparaged ideas about lower-class black culture, language, music, and romantic relationships. Whereas the liberal project drew from idealized citizenship to move blacks into the core of American society,

> the black nationalists made claims of authenticity to distinguish themselves from the center. Black authenticity refers to the embodied idea of [culturally and] racially pure racial identity based in opposition to whiteness and deracializing strategies. The idea behind authenticity is that it is exclusive and limited to a certain population. For [young black nationalists], the bourgeoisie created authenticity through "distance" or the social gap between them and the [lower classes] . . . black authenticity was unattainable to whites because whites could never understand the black lived experience. Black authenticity was a [multi-faceted] embodied practice exclusive to blacks.[15]

This approach to policing the boundaries of blackness led to oversimplification in defining black culture among black youth, which had implications for black masculinity conceptions. "Performances of Black masculinity often reflect cultural stereotypes rather than biological and psychological realities," according to Strayhorn and Tillman-Kelly.[16] Black males adhere to rules from a hidden curriculum referred to as "The Brother Code" to avoid being labeled "acting white" or "acting gay," etc.[17] "In some black families where reading is encouraged in girl children, a boy who likes to read is perceived on the road to being a "sissy," according to feminist scholar bell hooks.[18] Parents with aspirations to raise either hyper-masculine and/or patriarchal black males within the African-American community, writ large, interpreted the behavior of the boys and men who chose to perform their identities as intellectuals, law-abiders, or schoolboys might consider code violators among their peers due to their acting white or *acting* gay, which is the opposite of authentic blackness.[19]

15. Hohle, *Black Citizenship*, 9.
16. Strayhorn and Tillman-Kelly, "Queering Masculinity," 89.
17. Dancy and Hotchkins, "Schools for Better Making of Men?," 9.
18. hooks, *We Real Cool*, 40.
19. Strayhorn and Tillman-Kelly, "Queering Masculinity," 90.

The trope of the *real nigga* is a double-edged sword revealing the paradox of black authenticity. The attempt to redeem the "N-word" among certain African Americans has unintentionally led to a cultural straitjacket's fashioning. According to Brian Keith Alexander,

> The trap [of the trope] is that the complicated cultural construc-
> tion of the "nigga" both acknowledges the problematic historical
> origins of the reference, while engaging in radical reappropria-
> tion of that term—suggesting family, familiarity, and affiliation.
> The dubious reference when directed by blacks to blacks both
> signals a desired and affective performative identity, while also
> establishing a particular evaluative [criterion] on which such
> embodied and enacted performances are measured.[20]

This paradox is ubiquitous in African-American culture. "The difference," Alexander asserts, "is whether the phrase is used as affirmation or discon-firmation of identity and racial membership."[21] Its effect vacillates between empowerment and marginalization due to internalized racism and strate-gies to advance an imagined African-American political and social agenda. More importantly, we must be clear about how polarizing masculinities create "the expectations and possibilities of being a black man" and conflate masculinity "into a limited series of performative displays—you are and you are not—as if performative displays somehow transcend physical beings."[22]

In the seventies, black activists invoked narratives about Africanisms within African-American culture. This response reveals the "polyvalent mobility" of racism—its inherent ability to recover and recast sedimented knowledge in prior racial discourses in efforts to provide resistant represen-tations—informing the emerging anti-black discourse(s) that led to earlier strategies for opposition. In the past, bourgeois blacks invoked respectabil-ity politics, and then many shifted to a more defiant black self-presentation since Malcolm X's assassination. Foucault's terminology lays bare the "co-productive" or "mutually constitutive" nature of racial discourse, leading to an unintended reenactment and recreation of racist tropes. We co-produce in discursive spaces and generative processes that produce different, some-times unanticipated, conclusions. Our innate ability to influence one anoth-er (even those with contrary opinions) leaks into efforts towards knowledge production, values clarification, and social relations interpretation.

As a theory, co-production further illuminates the polyvalent nature inherent in racist ideology and racism (acts and social structure). This lens

20. Alexander, *Performing Black Masculinity*, 65.

21. Alexander, *Performing Black Masculinity*, 65.

22. Alexander, *Performing Black Masculinity*, 74.

suggests that constraining, contemptuous, and racist opinions impact black males regarding their literacy and masculinity through leaking into and permeating their oppositional responses—ideological, political, and practical—to these limiting narratives. Hence, Foucault concludes that focusing on black males struggling to resist racist ideas and structures reveals the tactile mobility and promiscuous nature of these discourses and ideas. He argues,

> First, I would like to stress the fact that it would be a mistake to regard this discourse on race struggle as belonging, rightfully and completely, to the oppressed, or to say that it was, at least originally, the discourse of the enslaved, the discourse of [black] people, or a history that was claimed and spoken by [black] people. It should be . . . obvious that it is a discourse that has a great ability to circulate, a great aptitude for metamorphosis, or a sort of polyvalence.[23]

Foucault requires us to focus less on divergent and contestatory counter-narratives that struggle to rupture the dominant racial assumptions about black male literacy and masculinity and to concentrate more on the re-articulation of racist narratives in our counter-narratives and efforts to resist racism(s). He argues for a more complicated process that "includes the simultaneous 'reinscription,' 'encasement,' and 'recovery' . . . of older racial discourses as they are reshaped into new ones, understood as a layering sedimented hierarchal forms."[24] Both activism and oppression are grounded in negative historical discourses about black intelligence and language capacity. Consequently, one discovers within black and white racial discourses the authors, so to speak, regardless of their identity, co-producing and conforming to racist narratives. The latter's influence over the former is entirely unintended. Consequently, we can now perceive how black males who invoke counternarratives involving black authenticity to resist black bourgeois or middle-class white cultural expectations inadvertently reproduce a hidden racist discourse that reifies archaic racist ideologies. Both authenticity politics and black counternarratives unintentionally lead to literacy ambivalence among African-American males.

My childhood coincides with the era in which cultural relativism shaped black authenticity among adherents to black power politics as resistance to middle-class norms and white supremacy. During this era, one finds the reappropriation of African identity, and the N-word emerges from the tension between our democratic aspirations and the unpleasant racial

23. Foucault, *Society Must Be Defended*, 76.
24. Stoler, *Carnal Knowledge*, 148–49.

realities African Americans face. I grew up in a community where young black men and women would use the term *nigga* to reveal their "disdain for dressing up their colloquial language. They [did] not even attempt to put their best foot forward [to impress whites or erode] stereotypes because they [intuitively perceived] such mission as a lost cause."[25] During this period in the seventies, the street gangs emerging in Los Angeles began to stake a claim on the invisible ghetto in Southeast San Diego—hidden, that is, to those who only visited the tourist-packed beaches, Sea World, and the zoo.

Throughout my earliest childhood years in Southern California, the black power ideology's regime influenced black children's racial formation. My generation witnessed a shift in urban black culture among underclass African Americans aspiring to participate in class mobility based on the politics of respectability espoused by civil rights leaders to soulful black essentialism and then onto an urban-ethos grounded in "the code of streets" and the underground economy. This cultural shift informed the attitudes of antagonistic and ambivalent black youth whom society forced to learn to "code-switch"—a bimodal linguistic strategy that revealed my awareness of the demeaning narratives regarding black English. According to Deric M. Greene and Felicia R. Walker,

> In response [to the need to move across social boundaries], African Americans, for the most part, engage in the almost "unconscious and reflexive" practice of code-switching as a means of adapting to or negotiating various communication contexts. Used to convey social information and for stylistic purposes, code-switching allows African Americans "to identify what language is acceptable in different situations and modify their speech to the appropriate style."[26]

Although my family members expected children in our clan to code-switch, many of my homies refused to do so because it signaled acquiescence to dominant perceptions about black English and behavioral standards. I, too, discovered my cheeky proclivity to resist aspirational black bourgeoisie social norms and hyper-masculine posers. My ambivalent tendency to both embrace and resist code-switching has historical antecedents.

Psychoanalysts constructed the concept of *ambivalence* to explain a continuous fluctuation in one's desire or attraction and repulsion toward a material object, individual, or act. In the nineties, Homi Bhabha began to draw on the idea to describe colonial domination and resistance with the

25. Kennedy, *Nigger,* 39.
26. Greene and Walker, "Recommendations to Public Speaking," 435.

terms "mimicry,"[27] "ambivalence,"[28] and "in-betweenness."[29] He started with the posit that ambivalence emerges in colonial discourse due to a feigned effort to produce "compliant subjects who reproduce [the dominant group's] assumptions, habits, and values—that is, 'mimic' the colonizer."[30] Hence, Bhabha modifies the psychoanalytical framework to describe "the complex mix of attraction and repulsion that characterizes the relationship between colonizer and colonized."[31] He begins by explaining that "mimicry is the desire for a reformed, recognizable Other, *as a subject of difference that is almost the same, but not quite.*"[32] There is, however, an unintended consequence for both parties—the dominator and the dominated.

On the one hand, "mimicry is constructed around an *ambivalence*; in order to be effective [for the colonizer], it must produce its slippage, its excess, its difference."[33] On the other hand, "mimicry is . . . stricken by an indeterminacy: mimicry is, thus, a representation of difference that is itself a process of disavowal." Hence, one finds two valences: partial domination and mocking insubordination. Bhabha writes, "mimicry is, thus, a sign of double articulation; a complex strategy of reform, regulation, and discipline." This colonizer's commitment to reform is incomplete (or ambivalent) "because it never wants colonial subjects to be exact replicas of the colonizers—this would be too threatening."[34] This ambivalence or duality

> turns from mimicry—a difference that is almost nothing but not quite—to mimic—a difference that is almost total but not quite. And in that other scene of colonial power, where history turns farce and presence to "a part," can be seen [cognitive dissonance or Du Boisian double-consciousness in] the twin figures of narcissism and paranoia that repeat furiously, uncontrollably.[35]

In the end, one might expect from a historical relationship based on racial domination and submission "between the white presence and its black semblance," a discourse might emerge to explain mimicry leading to ambivalence.[36]

27. Bhabha, "Of Mimicry and Man," 125–33.
28. Bhabha, "Of Mimicry and Man," 125–33.
29. Ashcroft et al., "Cultural Diversity/Cultural Difference," 53–54.
30. Ashcroft et al., "Ambivalence," 10–11.
31. Ashcroft et al., "Ambivalence," 10–11.
32. Bhabha, "Of Mimicry and Man," 126.
33. Bhabha, "Of Mimicry and Man," 126.
34. Ashcroft et al., "Ambivalence," 11.
35. Bhabha, "Of Mimicry and Man," 132.
36. Bhabha, "Of Mimicry and Man," 131.

These conclusions suggest that African Americans committed to black respectability politics emphasizing literacy had not fully grasped complexities embedded in their existential dilemma. The first misunderstanding is based on their Cartesian commitments on the mind-body problem: What is the relationship between the mind and body? An understanding that distinguishes mind from body in a manner that privileges thought and values. The second point is related to the first one. The failure to recognize that racism is at the core of the social contract, which is in fact a racial contract intended to further establish, maintain, and reproduce white supremacy.[37] Bhabha explains,

> In the ambivalent world of the "not quite/not white," on the metropolitan desire, the *founding objects* of the Western world become erratic, eccentric, accidental *objets trouves* of the colonial discourse of presence. It is then that the body and the book lose their representational authority. Black skin splits under the racist gaze, displaced into signs of bestiality, genitalia, grotesquerie, which reveal the phobic myth of the undifferentiated whole white body.[38]

Later, we will discuss tensions between black elites and the black folk based on the prerequisite to demonstrating bourgeois values—good hygiene, moral behavior, and hard-earned literacy—as a tactic to appropriate citizenship and equality. Both the promoters and their adherents of the gospel of literacy misunderstood the fact that mimicry was not intended to reproduce cultural and intellectual capabilities (or whiteness) among blacks. Instead, one finds their operating within a "Third Space of Enunciation"[39] that contains ambivalence and contradiction leading to a hybridity in cultural identity, which demonstrates unbreachable difference and forecloses the function of literacy as the path towards freedom and racial transcendence.

Scholars interested in literacy's significance among African Americans have discovered themes in the historical linkage between autobiography, citizenship, and reading in the black experience. According to Henry Louis Gates, "There is an inextricable link in the Afro-American tradition between literacy and freedom."[40] One can identify within slave narratives and black memoirs a naïve commitment to literacy on the surface. Robert B. Stepto affirms the idea that "one does not have to read very far into the corpus of Afro-American letters to find countless examples of the exaltation

37. Mills, *Racial Contract*, 122.
38. Bhabha, "Of Mimicry and Man," 131.
39. Ashcroft et al., "Hybridity," 108–11.
40. Gates, *Classic Slave Narratives*, 1.

of literacy and the written word."[41] Moreover, the deeply held belief that an effect of literacy is "true freedom" persists in our shared cultural sensibilities. Although the imagined black community is far from monolithic, the literacy-as-freedom ideology has informed African-American literacy narratives since slavery.[42] Gates explains:

> [Literacy] and the production of literature was taken to be the central arena in which persons of African descent could, or could not, establish and redefine their status within the human community. Black people, the evidence suggests, had to represent themselves as "speaking subjects" before they could even begin to destroy their status as [nonpersons], as commodities, within Western culture. In addition to all of the myriad reasons for which human beings [read] and write books, this particular reason seems to have been paramount for the black slave.[43]

Scholars interested in probing these narratives to gain more in-depth insight into the black psyche have unveiled skepticism regarding African Americans' literacy myth. The authors who wrote for freedom and social acceptance experienced inner turmoil due to the perceived contingencies related to their social position. Katherine Clay Bassard's research on nineteenth-century African-American women's biographies unveils the fact that the authors who penned their slave and spiritual narratives "were keenly aware of the limits of the literacy-as-freedom ideology, due to their [multifaceted] marginalized position in the social order, and they express everything from mild tension to outright suspicion of the power of [literacy] to provide freedom, economic security, and a restructuring of the social formations of power."[44] Consequently, Bassard's findings provide a warrant for interrogating literacy ambivalence among African-American men in the past and our contemporary historical moment under the shadow of the hip-hop regime. "Nineteenth-century Afro-American writers 'bought into' the ideology of literacy, freedom, and economic advancement to varying degrees, and the extent to which they absorbed it into their values (and their texts) is directly related to a given writer's own social position," she argues.[45] This thesis implies a challenge to the belief that African Americans, as a monolithic group, have been gullible enough to believe that "literacy in and of itself is a liberating force" with an inherent ability to promote political friendship

41. Stepto, *From behind the Veil*, 195.
42. Bassard, "Gender and Genre," 120.
43. Gates, *Signifying Monkey*, 141.
44. Bassard, "Gender and Genre," 120.
45. Bassard, "Gender and Genre," 120.

and drive economic advancement.[46] Yet, it's more. "Literacy is not chiefly about matching pronouns with the right antecedents or comprehending why Willie and Janet went up the hill. Literacy is first and foremost a racial performance."[47] It also suggests that literacy resistance has been intentional for some African Americans who refused to allow society to dupe and blame them for their oppression due to their inadequate literacy performances.

The intimation that literacy is insufficient to gain personal autonomy, cultural assimilation, and social mobility is based on African Americans' historical experiences within our racial caste system. According to Dan Nelson Salvino, "While blacks embraced and subverted the white ideology of literacy for the freedom it could provide from physical bondage, their hard-earned literacy skills did not mean especially much in terms of social and economic acceptance among whites."[48] Freedom from physical bondage did not remove the cultural, economic, and racial barriers that "kept them socially segregated once free."[49] Literacy as a path to citizenship and social inclusion, however, remained a powerful trope throughout the twentieth century until the assassinations of Martin Luther King Jr. and Malcolm X. Its persistence resurged during the ascendance of former President Barack Obama.

The generations of black urban youth who grew up under the shadow of neo-black nationalism would reject the belief in deracialization through literacy, bourgeois respectability, and social distancing from lower-class African Americans as the path to "good black citizenship."[50] These youth elaborated on Malcolm's respect for both the book and black folk culture. He embodied a more sensible approach to the politics of literacy. "My Alma mater was books, a good library," he declared. "I could spend the rest of my life reading, just satisfying my [own] curiosity."[51] The library is a theme in numerous black male literacy narratives, including Richard Wright's *Black Boy (American Hunger)*, and initiates Vernon E. Jordan Jr.'s "Horatio Alger" evoking narrative, *Vernon Can Read!: A Memoir*. Malcolm did not, however, acquire literacy to become a renowned author or bleach his blackness and distance himself from the poor black masses on the path to social mobility. When giving his eulogy, Ossie Davis immortalized him as "our shining

46. Salvino, "Word in Black and White," 150.

47. Young, *Your Average Nigga*, 142.

48. Salvino, "Word in Black and White," 150.

49. Salvino, "Word in Black and White," 142.

50. Hohle, *Black Citizenship*, 9.

51. Malcolm X, *Autobiography*, 207.

black prince."[52] Davis's homage lays bare the link between Malcolm's authenticity politics, indomitable spirit, and literacy.

The prison-educated Malcolm's remarkable literacy performance(s) conveyed his passion for learning on his own terms. On debating and reading, he writes, "Right there, in the prison, debating, speaking to a crowd was as exhilarating to me as the discovery of knowledge through reading."[53] Malcolm seemed to maintain a profound commitment to black autonomy by performing a hybrid literacy that resonated with African-American males residing on society's furthest margins. Thus, Davis's eulogy concludes: "And we will see him then for what he was and is—a Prince—our own black shining prince."[54] This black masculinity icon "best articulated and represented authenticity among [black nationalists in the sixties]."[55] Even so, his cultural resistance through articulacy and knowledge acquisition reveals the limitations of literacy in the struggle to advance racial equality.

The inheritors of his legacy "broke from the liberal project and began to use discourses of black authenticity to [expose] the limitations of organizing urban blacks around good black citizenship."[56] In the decades following his death, Malcolm's picture hovered above black barbers' heads in barbershops throughout the United States. bell hooks describes Malcolm's cultural and ideological impact when she writes,

> More than any other black male who come to power in our nation, Malcolm X embodied black male refusal to allow his identity to be defined by a system of race, gender, and class domination. His was the example that young black folks in the sixties followed as we struggled to educate ourselves for critical consciousness. We studied Malcolm's words, accepting that he gave us permission to *liberate ourselves*, to liberate the black male by *any means necessary*.[57]

Ossie Davis was right: the literate and loquacious martyr was our shining black prince. Malcolm's literacy, oratory ability, and self-narration began to exert a hidden influence on the black male literary imagination while his resistance to white supremacy, assassination, and "do for self" ideology in response to economic deprivation, police brutality, and social marginalization

52. Davis, "Our Shining Black Prince," xi–xii.
53. Malcolm X, *Autobiography*, 212.
54. Davis, "Our Shining Black Prince," xi–xii.
55. Hohle, *Black Citizenship*, 9.
56. Hohle, *Black Citizenship*, 9.
57. hooks, *We Real Cool*, xiii; emphasis mine.

were reinterpreted (or remixed) to create a legacy informing the subsequent generation's approach to black masculinity.

The once illiterate Huey P. Newton exemplified a new approach to the book and knowledge in *Revolutionary Suicide*. He embodied the reality that "young black power advocates were avid readers. They were well-educated critical thinkers. Some of them were organic intellectuals. There is no anti-intellectualism in their writing and no equation of education with being white."[58] Newton developed an ambivalence about education as a grade-school child, however. He explains, "I knew only that I constantly felt uncomfortable and ashamed of being black. This feeling followed me everywhere, without let up. It was a result of the implicit understanding in the system that whites were 'smart' and black were 'stupid.'"[59] Hence, he began to look beyond the classroom for self-knowledge. "Throughout my life all real learning has taken place outside the classroom. My family, friends, neighbors, and the streets educated me. Later, I learned to love books, and I read a lot, but that had nothing to do with school. Long before, I was getting educated in unorthodox ways," he wrote.[60] Newton's quest for self-knowledge in writing compelled him to develop his own canon. *Revolutionary Suicide* referenced *Muhammad Speaks* and Malcolm's ideas and program as foundational to the Black Panthers' ten-point program. These ideas permeated the air in California.

As a chubby kid growing up in Los Angeles and San Diego, I'd buy my fair share of bean pie from brothers in the Nation of Islam selling *Muhammad Speaks*. The neighborhood households seemed to fall into four categories: church folk, black Muslims, and black nationalists, as well as those casually embracing black consciousness, soul music, and the streets. Southeast San Diego had a black-owned bank and other black-owned businesses on Logan Avenue. Our first apartment sat across the street from the black-owned bank where black news journals sat on the counters. In this countercultural environment, I would encounter community members who performed their literacy in a manner that implied the rejection of white superiority in their refusal to "act white" or emulate the black elite community members who sought cultural and social integration. Before hip-hop and gangster rap culture emerged, I had not experienced anti-intellectualism regarding literacy. However, when we began to catch the school bus to the suburbs in middle school, my black schoolmates started to invoke the term "acting white."

58. hooks, *We Real Cool*, 43.
59. Newton, *Revolutionary Suicide*, 17.
60. Newton, *Revolutionary Suicide*, 21.

While attending San Diego State University, I'd hang out with a young black Muslim activist who encouraged us to listen to Malcolm's speeches on audiocassettes. Ta-Nehisi Coates captures my attitude towards gaining "the knowledge" in his book *The Beautiful Struggle*. "I became a plague upon my father's books. He treasured them as much for what they said as for what they were. But I cared for only for what was inside. I devoured the books, then flung them aside like emptied husks."[61] Although I shunned 5 percenters, my zeal for neo-black nationalism shone out in my red, gold, and green regalia and conversations filled with references to black nationalist male heroes. As a hip-hop entrepreneur in my mid-twenties, I started Strong Black Images: a retail business focused on neo-black nationalist clothing and jewelry. I'd stand on the pre-gentrified corner of 23rd and Union in Seattle, Washington, as a dreadlocked hustler selling t-shirts to the black men and women who drove and walked through the intersection. One shirt, in particular, stands out in my mind. It had the image of a paranoid Malcolm X holding a machine gun as he peered out a window searching for potential assassins from the Nation of Islam. Below Malcolm X on the t-shirt was the slogan, "By Any Means Necessary." Boogie Down Productions had reproduced Malcolm's pose on the cover to their second album *By All Means Necessary* (1988). At the time, I thought that I transcended double-consciousness to embrace a self-defined black authenticity. As I contemplate the trajectory of my life, however, it's apparent that I was unremarkable. In a significantly new way, the cultural and social forces shaped many young black men coming of age at the end of the twentieth century.

These forces had shaped my literacy ambivalence. Growing up in Southern California, the funky, secular testifying soul music was the soundtrack to our lives. We danced and played in the streets, we sang along to songs that testified black pride like James Brown's "Say it Loud—I'm Black, and I'm Proud." Consequently, before entering the schoolyard as a kindergartner, I had already absorbed resistance to assimilation-based education and black respectability politics. Yet, my young mother, who'd embraced the hippy culture and rock music, had raised me to embrace different cultural aesthetics. The whole while, I had unwittingly internalized a cultural belief based on the ubiquitous "black is, black ain't" ideology.[62] Beginning my racial formation in an urban setting amidst cultural bricolage, I would develop what by the end of this book may be a clichéd black male reaction to academic literacy expectations: literacy ambivalence. This inner turmoil reveals that "skin color alone is simultaneously an inadequate yet sometimes

61. Coates, *Beautiful Struggle*, 157.
62. Ellison, *Invisible Man*, 9–10.

a socially, culturally, and politically necessary signifier of blackness."[63] Even as an innocent child growing up in the ghetto, I recognized that identity and group memberships were contingent and fluid.

In middle school, disco and funk music began to usher in a new era. The black Muslims and other black nationalists seemed less visible in the ghetto's landscape. Many of these community-activist-oriented neighbors became stylish buppies and moved into more mainstream roles as they began to embrace conspicuous consumption and cocaine-drenched decadence. Yet, a few community organizations remained bastions of black consciousness. The local mosque started a Boy Scout troop at the community center in our projects. Of course, I joined the endeavor. Leo Triplet, our scoutmaster, was a military guy from Philadelphia, Pennsylvania. He'd show up at every meeting in starched uniform and shiny patent-leather shoes. With a smile and swagger that revealed Denzel Washington, Leo would brag that his troop in Philly had more than two hundred young studs. He had been a gymnast, the first brother I met to admit as much. Black men in Southern California weren't into gymnastics. Back in the day, the old-heads and grandmothers referred to gymnasts as "sissies." At the time, I believed that adults used this pejorative term to intimidate boys who might consider transgressing their heteronormative expectations for boys and men. Without warning, Leo would take off his shirt to show off his cut physique and then deploy his body in never-ending cartwheels. The feat convinced me that he wasn't "soft." Leo and the Muslim brothers who mentored us were more righteous than radical. He taught us to march with a unified cadence and flair. After my girlfriend, a thick red bone, showed up to support me at an award ceremony, he gave me the most giant box of condoms that I'd ever seen, with a warning not to ride bareback to avoid illegitimate babies and socially-transmitted diseases. My conversations with Leo were more around our burgeoning manhood than social activism. Eventually, I'd wander away from the scouts as girls began to capture my attention, and I could hear the streets calling. I didn't encounter too many real brothers out in the woods.

During our middle-school years, my more street-identified homeboys would mock my attempts to code-switch from the Standard English Vernacular to the Black English Vernacular. I can still remember practicing the phrase "What's happenin'?" in the mirror to impress my girlfriend, Kim Earl, and her family. Kim had a real ghetto family. Her mother didn't listen to gospel music in the morning. Instead, she'd put on Richard Pryor. It's not without a bit of embarrassment that I remember her original gangster brother, Duane, falling on the floor with a reefer joint in his hand when I

63. Johnson, *Appropriating Blackness*, 18.

strolled into their apartment and uttered, "What's happening?" It'd been an excellent skit for the Richard Pryor show. Over time, I'd begin to master a more credible street-based swagger. I'd, however, never fully relinquish my love of the book and culture beyond the 'hood. As I began to gain the means to move beyond Bay Vista Methodist apartments in Southeast San Diego, I'd approach that world as a classroom. Those experiences established a trajectory that caused my literacy narrative to intersect with personal experiences with the War on Drugs and the Ivy League. As one might expect, my life-long participation in diverging communities has led to a bit of inner turmoil.

As a young man, the inability to resolve this cognitive dissonance culminated in my pursuing the path of a preppy hustler. One admiring street don bemusedly described me as a "button-downed Cosby kid." He smirked at the idea that I hung out with reputed criminals and drug dealers as well as sold powder cocaine to upper-middle-class African-American students at HBCUs, fastidious black gay men, and conspicuous-consuming buppies in San Diego and Washington, DC. It turns out that I'd move beyond the pathological outlook, or obliviousness, that defines the average self-pitying Oreo to embrace both my inner hustler and inner nerd. Peer ridicule had little impact on my unorthodox identity performances. I was as agile at altering my persona as Natasha Kinski was at shapeshifting in *Cat People*. My construction of identities suitable to diverse environments—incognegro, metrosexual buppie, and street—granted me access to the social worlds needed to earn and learn while avoiding incarceration. And still, I was indecisive about it all, including my nomadism.

On some level, my masculinity was as illegible as the notorious drug dealer Russell "Stringer" Bell on HBO's acclaimed crime drama *The Wire*. Bell is the second in charge of Avon Barksdale crime enterprise. During Barkdale's incarceration, Bell steps into the leadership vacuum, and the audience learns about his life due to his being under the surveillance of Detective Jimmy McNulty. Because Bell takes an academic, calculating, modest, and street-informed approach to his aspirations to transcend gaining respect as defined in the hyper-masculine and violent drug culture, he emerges as someone "illegible" to those with presumptions about what it means about authentic black-street masculinity.[64]

"Illegible masculinity" is a concept Mark Anthony Neal has written about and published on, contemporary to my use of the term and my own research on ambivalence, black masculinity, and literacy under the hyper-masculine regime in hip-hop culture. Ironically, I trafficked and sold dope

---

64. Neal, "Man without a Country," 400.

in the same region as *The Wire*'s drug peddling transpires. Bell and I had similar motivations.

> Bell's corporate demeanor provides some clue into his motiva-
> tion for being in the drug game in the first place; despite his
> evident skill set, intelligence, and discipline, the glass ceilings
> and doublespeak around issues of diversity in the workforce and
> on elite college campuses . . . would have likely made it more dif-
> ficult for Bell to function in those institutions at the high level he
> does within the Barkdale's operation. Bell's embrace of the drug
> trade enables him to make his way on his one terms, enabling
> his literal ownership of the game, if you will, mirroring the rise
> of the so-called hip-hop mogul.[65]

Paradoxically, I used my own illegibility to avoid detection and incarceration, yet I only gained academic notice once I disclosed my background. As
a more mature black man with a broader spectrum of experiences, I find
myself concurring with a judgment that Barksdale divulged to Bell, who
persists in his appeals to reason in advising Barksdale to resist his respect-
based motivation to invoke war to gain corners and reverence. Bell wants
the drug kingpin to realize what's personally at stake for their partnership.
Barksdale states his long-held concerns in condemning terms. "I look at you
these days, and you know what I see? A man without a country. Not hard
enough for this right here and maybe not smart enough for that out there.
No offense, I don't think you ever were [street enough]."[66] Mark Anthony
Neal argues that Barksdale reads Bell as ambivalent, vacillating, or soft. This
harsh judgment is based on his calculated approach to wealth accumulation and personal transformation. Still, his naivete and inexperience with
the street dynamics is, so to speak, hidden in academia and the political
and professional white world with their underbelly and Malthusian moral
calculus.[67] This failure was less about his academic ambitions, entrepreneur-
ial naivety, literacy aspirations, or masculinity performance(s), as a mature
corner boy or real nigga, and more about a dichotomous mindset committed to false distinctions that frame the streets as immoral and the world of
civilians as law-abiding and respectable.

Stringer Bell's mindset, however, is committed to the streets, according
to Neal. Yet, I find ambivalence in the dialogue Neal deploys to support his
argument that Bell failed due to his inability to translate his cosmopolitan
worldview and social mobility into the street vernacular. Neal explains,

---

65. Neal, "Man without a Country," 400.
66. Quoted in Neal, "Man without a Country," 408.
67. Neal, "Man without a Country," 409.

"Central to that worldview are the conflicts and contradictions that animate his efforts to move beyond the block, yet remain wedded to it, because it is where his black masculinity is so firmly inscribed and vital. Bell may no longer be of the block, but the block clearly still matters to him, else he would be content with just being another black businessman."[68] From my perspective, Barksdale was unwavering, but not Bell. Where Neal sees an expansive commitment to code-switch between the streets and the legal world, I find an unarticulated ambivalence. Their dialogue reveals as much when Bell responds to Avon on their implied shared vision: "Was it for rep? Was it so our names could ring out on some fuckin' ghetto street corners? There are games beyond the fuckin' game!"[69] Neal interprets Bell's statement as leading to coherence and legibility. However, I'd argue otherwise. A scholar on *The Wire*, Jason Read interprets the crime partner's dispute in a manner that echoes a Du Boisian's double-consciousness. He writes, "They have come to represent two sides of an uneasy duality—the [street] soldier and the [respectable] CEO—that has been torn asunder. While this particular duality reflects the drug trade [or underworld], it is not without its resonances with the culture at large."[70] My response is more aligned with Bell's conclusion on his or their motives for running a criminal empire. Bell was pursuing the American Dream with a vengeance and even more: black authenticity and transcendence on his terms. This vision leaves him a man without a country—a sure-fire trigger for ambivalence.

Bell represents the Gramscian organic intellectual who defies legibility. Following Bell's death, Detective McNulty and his colleague get a warrant to search Bell's tidy condominium decorated in minimalist elegance. Read shares his observation on the scene and its significance. "When McNulty searches the apartment of the recently deceased Stringer, it is no accident that he stumbles upon a copy of Adam Smith's *The Wealth of Nations* alongside a pair of Samurai swords: this represents the idea of the CEO as 'knight of industry,' as one who conducts business while consulting Sun Tzu for strategy." More importantly, the conflict between Barksdale and Bell "is a conflict between two ways of establishing a reputation, violence, and money, which come into such bloody conflict because they are so intertwined."[71] Ernest L. Gibson III provides a more illuminating explanation based on a Gramscian analysis. He describes Bell as a "Black Cartesian" or "thinking thing," *a la* Rene Descartes, who adds intellectual heft to the Barksdale

68. Neal, "Man without a Country," 409.
69. Quoted in Neal, "Man without a Country," 409.
70. Read, "String Bell's Lament," 132.
71. Read, "String Bell's Lament," 132.

crime enterprise. So, "Barksdale's success is partly due to his ability to re-cruit a traditional intellectual into his crime family. He, a master of manipu-lation himself, understood the power of having a black Cartesian."[72] Yet, he struggles in a manner that suggests that the ambivalence has structural foundations. Gibson writes,

> In the end, he is neither a traditional [mainstream] nor an organic ['hood] intellectual. He is denied entrance into a white-capitalist world because of his race and denounced by a black-crime world because of his thought. Undoubtedly, Russell Bell emerges as a quintessential model of the black intellectual's Promethean struggle.[73]

Bernard Bergonzi best defined the black Cartesian's dilemma as "mind and body are regarded as totally separate, the former [mind] being reluc-tantly imprisoned inside the absurd and inefficient mechanism of the latter [body]."[74] In black males and Stringer Bell, race renders as brutally tragic the body and mind dichotomy. Based on his Gramscian analysis, Gibson predicts misfortune for black males with intellectual or literacy aspirations. He writes,

> The historical white world, one defined by white-male patri-archy, racial slavery, social and economic oppression, allows no space for a black Cartesian subject. And the black world, submitting to the stereotypes of an oppressive structure, only embraces the black masculine figure when he is outwardly antagonistic to the powers that be, radical in his orientation or proud in his racialization. There simply is no room for the black thinking thing, not a male one at least.[75]

As the episode closes, McNulty holds Adam Smith's tome on capitalism; the detective ponders what he has uncovered in Bell's condominium. He asks, "Who in fuck was I chasing?"[76] The question suggests recognition of hubris on his part, which includes an implied racial bias in his assessment of Bell's literacy aspirations. "There is honesty here, bleak candor which illuminates the tragic fate of black Cartesian subjectivity. Given this thought, Stringer Bell's death was inevitable, preordained by the racial dynamics surrounding him and the body that embodied him. The tragedy rests, not in his death,

---

72. Gibson, "For Whom the BELL Tolls," para. 20.
73. Gibson, "For Whom the BELL Tolls," para. 21.
74. Bergonzi, "Black Cartesian," 509.
75. Gibson, "For Whom the BELL Tolls," para. 19.
76. Gibson, "For Whom the BELL Tolls," para. 20.

but in his birth," explains Gibson.[77] In the end, we might learn a lesson from the detective. Let us not presume to know much about the subjects represented in *Speech Is My Hammer*. As detectives, we might investigate their writings to uncover as much as possible to determine their agendas and their own words. We might also develop humility alongside Gibson, "who understands the existential reality with the American city [for black males], as an African-American male intellectual."[78]

African-American male writers have filled their canon with literacy narratives that often detail similar ambivalence about black authenticity and bookishness. These stories resolve cognitive dissonance through personal achievement and the transcendence of the author's perceived social constraints. By studying my narrative of socialization, I have come to recognize literacy anxiety as an essential tension for the middle class and upwardly mobile black males. These men have gained nourishment from their roots in marginalized African-American communities. Nevertheless, they remain committed to literacy aspirations that require them to travel across cultural boundaries into academic and professional white society. According to Janet Eldred and Peter Mortensen, "What we call literacy narratives are those stories, like Bernard Shaw's *Pygmalion*, that foreground issues of language acquisition and literacy."[79] These narratives "sometimes include explicit images of schooling and teaching; they include texts that both challenge and affirm culturally scripted ideas about literacy."[80] In black male literacy narratives, I discovered these "explicit images of [the] school and teaching" shaping acquiescence and resistance to the black male portrayal.

Based on personal experience, observation, and research, I am arguing for a Foucauldian analysis grounded in his power-knowledge (*le savoir-pouvoir*) thesis to excavate the fact that, among African-American males, in particular, language instruction might implicate discipline and domination, on the one hand, while on the other, one might observe that language acquisition(s) and the subsequent literacy performance(s) become paths towards resistance and liberation. Foucault's understanding is that power is established through forms of knowledge (literacy) leading to constructions of the truth (regarding adequate and inadequate literacy performances). Hence, language education might function as a form (or mechanism) of discipline in inculcating literacy truths to achieve power over its subject (i.e., upon black male students). Educational techniques are designed to

77. Gibson, "For Whom the BELL Tolls," para. 19.
78. Gibson, "For Whom the BELL Tolls," para. 21.
79. Eldred and Mortensen, "Reading Literacy Narratives," 513.
80. Eldred and Mortensen, "Reading Literacy Narratives," 513.

maintain power through a subtle mechanism of control. This power includes the authority to define adequate literacy performances. However, Foucault's analysis and interests do not consider "the streets" as an institution, mode, or structure.

On the other hand, I observed "the streets" function as a countering institution that forms its own knowledge and exerts power to counteract the knowledge-power inherent in the white gaze. The Black English Vernacular, hip-hop culture, street literacy performances, and the underground economy are opposing mechanisms. "Where there is power, there is resistance," Foucault concurs. We find one form of resistance in street-informed black literacy performances.

MacArthur award-winning photographer Dawoud Bey's reflections on his burgeoning 'hood masculinity lay bare the role of class aspirations, literacy, and race on his own muted-street identity and suspect academic swagger. He inadvertently unearths its countering characteristics that enable black males to resist complete acquiescence in their literacy performances. Bey's parents critiqued "the kinds of behavior likely to keep a Black boy from successfully moving through the world and toward a productive adulthood put little emphasis on outward expression while privileging the life of the mind and an outer life of decorum."[81]

The firmly middle-class Bey attended predominately white schools to gain the cultural skills and knowledge essential to social mobility. He was among the first African-American children bussed to all-white schools to get a presumably better education. Bey discovered that educators were skeptical about academic performance. He explains:

> To survive in that world, especially in higher quarters, we had to become adept at what you might call a kind of behavioral code-switching, the use of more than one language in speech. It soon became apparent that Black intellectual swagger was also suspect in such an environment, as I was constantly asked where I copied my homework from, especially those assignments that required original thinking, such as writing a poem.[82]

In this brief discussion on black male (intellectual) swagger, Bey describes his literacy narrative involving code-switching and his literacy performance challenges. Swagger is "a way to both reclaim and celebrate viscerally an aspect of the self that [racism has] historically eroded."[83] Swagger, however, might elicit contempt and attract danger. When describing a friend's older

81. Bey, "Swagger," 152.
82. Bey, "Swagger," 152.
83. Bey, "Swagger," 152.

brother, Michael, a young man who "walked down the street with an exaggerated dip in his step," Bey notes his mother's disdain for his arrogance and aggression.[84] The awestruck Bey, nevertheless, perceives a more profound meaning:

> Michael's brother sure looked dangerous to me, like he knew his way around a switchblade, but he also looked like he gave full rein to what might be called the expressivity of the individual Black body, moving himself through the world with a power, grace, and style calculated to bring the body into alignment with its own stylistic and expressive powers through sheer celebratory comportment.[85]

According to Bey's account, black adults in their community and non-blacks beyond their neighborhood perceived these swaggering black male youths as dangerous. Bey notes that black boys with too much swagger, such as Emmett Till, are at risk and every so often snuffed out. Unlike his friend's brother Michael and Till, Bey chose a less risky path to cultivate black intellectual swagger, which the faculty in his all-white school found suspect. Bey renders transparent the cultural challenges and power African-American males wield to confront power-knowledge and maintain an authentic and uncompromised sense of manhood and successfully move through a world in which literacy is a prerequisite to the American Dream.[86]

Moreover, I find his narrative conveys a certain ambivalence. I'll never forget meeting Bey at a friend's gallery on Newberry Street in Boston's Back Bay neighborhood. At the time, Bey was on his second round as artist-in-residence at Phillips Andover Academy. I felt the tension between his polaroid pictures depicting a nitty-gritty Harlem and his genuine connection with our well-heeled friends in Andover and Cambridge, Massachusetts. Bey was still code-switching.

Although I have been tutored on the proverb that "Fools give you reasons, [where] wise men [would never] try," I am seeking to understand the roots and perpetuation of this ambivalence not only in an abstract form but also in the concrete: my literacy narrative. This project proposes a new path for helping African-American males. My goal is to encourage other black men to examine and embrace their emotional and cognitive vacillation regarding their literacy performances. We must begin to address the schizophrenia that emerges due to our Cartesian tendencies to divorce emotion and reason, body, and mind. According to Michael J. Dumas, we

84. Bey, "Swagger," 151.
85. Bey, "Swagger," 150.
86. Bey, "Swagger," 153.

must embrace a black existential analysis that ask the questions "What are we?" and, "What shall we do?" This critical approach to black life embodies a more robust form of critical thinking. Dumas explains, "[It] is not a skill or method to bring meaning to Black existence; it is a crucial form of Black existence. In the act of thinking, Black people affirm their own humanity, assert their right to self-determination, and develop individual and collective purpose."[87] In *Speech Is My Hammer*, I hope to model Dr. Dumas's admonition to open (conceptual) spaces for inquiry and generate possibilities for transformative interventions.

87. Dumas, "Black Existence as Critical Thinking," 156.

I began to marvel at how smoothly the black boys acted out the roles that the white race had mapped out for them. Most of them were not conscious of living a special, separate, stunted way of life. Yet I knew that in some period of their growing up—a period that they had no doubt forgotten—there had been developed in them a delicate, sensitive controlling mechanism that shut off their minds and emotions from all that the white race had said was taboo. Although they lived in an America where in theory there existed equality of opportunity, they knew unerringly what to aspire to and what not to aspire to. Had a black boy announced that he aspired to be a writer, he would have been unhesitatingly called crazy by his pals.

—Richard Wright, *Black Boy* (1945)


God, how I ricochet between certainties and doubts.

—Sylvia Plath

Howard University (c. 1984)

# CHAPTER 1

# Straddling Two Worlds

## *Literacy and Double-Consciousness*

HAVING GROWN UP IN a poor single-parent household in Southern California, I have discovered within my biography a "literacy narrative"[1] that requires describing a nuanced racial reality that resonates with W. E. B. Du Bois's theses concerning the "color-line," "double-consciousness," and "the veil."[2] The scholarship suggests that the primary concern shaping literacy narratives are "a battle over language that is foregrounded in the text. Yet, it is important to see not only the center, but the margins. To do justice to [*Pygmalion*-esque African-American male literacy narratives], we must examine competing logics [of the relationship between identity and literacy]."[3]

Du Bois began his classic *The Souls of Black Folk* with a thought that continues to be found valuable by academics interested in describing the African-American experience. He writes, "Herein lie buried many things which if read with patience may show the strange meaning of being black here at the dawning of the twentieth century. This meaning is not without interest to you, Gentle Reader; for the problem of the twentieth century is the problem of the color-line."[4] One hundred years later, at the dawning of the twenty-first century, one found in the emerging scholarship in African-American studies the constant invocation of Du Bois's work on the color-line and double-consciousness. The English Professor Suzanne Jones's

1. Eldred and Mortensen, "Reading Literacy Narratives," 512–39.
2. Du Bois, *Souls of Black Folk*, 43–51.
3. Eldred and Mortensen, "Reading Literacy Narratives," 529.
4. Du Bois, *Souls of Black Folk*, 54.

introduction to *Crossing the Color Line* begins with a prescient illustration, which captures its relevance. She writes,

> At the turn of the last century, W. E. B. Du Bois predicated that "the problem of the twentieth century is the problem of the color line." Since the hopeful years of the civil rights movement, the United States has made uneven progress toward solving this problem. In 1968, at the end of a turbulent decade, the National Advisory Commission on Civil Disorders concluded, "Our nation is moving toward two societies, one black, one white, separate and unequal." Although we have since passed laws to foster racial equality, real economic, social, and emotional gulfs still exist. Strains between blacks and whites, which were hidden for a couple of decades, have become painfully evident in the last few years.[5]

A decade ago, when I began my research, I'd felt that black intellectuals might have turned this Du Bois's statement on the color-line into a cliché, rendered meaningless through overuse had it not continued to ring as true. As I read Jones's introduction to *Crossing the Color Line*, it became clear that she provides cover for its ubiquity. She writes, "Highly publicized and legally complex cases of Rodney King and O. J. Simpson and the divergent public reactions to their trials generated suggest just how vexing the problem of the color line remains."[6] Twenty-one years later, following Barack Obama's presidency and Donald Trump's disastrous tenure in the White House, the pendulum continued to swing away from fulfilling our democratic ideals. Still, concerns related to the color-line seemed to culminate in white unmasked supremacists moving beyond the shadows to storm the Capitol in an insurrection that altogether uncovered the awe-inspiring chasm between "the two societies, one black, one white."[7]

Based on the recent focus on police brutality and social violence against black males, it seems appropriate to read black male memoir and personal narrative. By intentionally reading on the color-line, my goal is to unveil and then describe the logic informing the cognitive dissonance that black males experience regarding literacy due to double-consciousness. My interest in literacy narrative reveals that black men continue to invoke a discourse that intersects with class and racial politics to create the context(s) for the ambivalence that some black males experience toward literacy and masculinity. More interestingly, ambivalence is prominent among elite and

5. Jones, *Crossing the Color Line*, xiii.
6. Jones, *Crossing the Color Line*, xiii.
7. Jones, *Crossing the Color Line*, xiii.

non-elite men attempting to either deconstruct the ideologies that justify barriers to social equality or to resist white social norms.

Du Bois's description of the phenomenon of "double-consciousness" and "the veil" permeates African-American literature and scholarship. In *The Souls of Black Folk*, he describes the black psyche as being "born with a veil, and gifted with a second-sight in this American world—a world which yields him no true self-consciousness, but only lets him see himself through the revelation of the other [white] world."[8] Du Bois posits that African Americans are hyper-aware of the white gaze. He writes, "It is a peculiar sensation, *this double-consciousness*, this sense of always looking at one's self through the eyes of others, of measuring one's soul by the tape of a world that looks on in amused contempt and pity."[9] Du Bois and the literature that references him suggest that this double-consciousness is pathological. It implies a cognitive dissonance because it leads to feelings of "—twoness,—an American, a Negro; two souls, two thoughts, two unreconciled strivings; two warring ideals in one dark body, whose dogged strength alone keeps it from being torn asunder."[10] The implication here is that Du Bois is actually describing his powers of meta-cognition in such a way that transcends the traditional understanding of self-consciousness.

In other words, Du Bois's burgeoning racial awareness led him to develop the ability not only to reflect upon his own thoughts and actions, but also to perceive "one's self through the eyes of others."[11] He describes double-consciousness as a psychological experience as a phenomenon that grants one a unique perceptual ability *and* burden. Du Bois perceived the world through the veil of race as cultural and political schizophrenia that needs healing: "The history of the American Negro is the history of this strife—this longing to attain self-conscious manhood, to merge his double self into a better true self."[12] This inner conflict leads to the ambivalence that their own reasoning based on social norms links to expectations about the relationship between literacy, racial identity, and black masculinity.

The literature on black masculinity and black manhood is directly relevant to black male literacy. Within the last decade, Martin A. Summers, Marlon B. Ross, Maurice O. Wallace, Ronald L. Jackson, Charise Cheney, bell hooks, Mark Anthony Neal, and other scholars have produced scholarship on the tensions that have emerged as African-American men have

8. Du Bois, *Souls of Black Folk*, 45.

9. Du Bois, *Souls of Black Folk*, 45; emphasis mine.

10. Du Bois, *Souls of Black Folk*, 45.

11. Du Bois, *Souls of Black Folk*, 45.

12. Du Bois, *Souls of Black Folk*, 45.

competed for manhood, citizenship, and a self-defined conception of humanity. In seeking to define and express their own assimilated, self-determined, and hybrid identities as a means of embodying counter-narratives to the demeaning stereotypes of black masculinity in the United States. In some instances, black male literacy narratives provide insight into how the persistent questions about black manhood intersect with discourses concerning blackness and literacy to produce ambivalence and anxiety among black males with erudite literary aspirations due to the ever-present white gaze.

I wanted to understand my conflicted feelings about being literate—a tension that I experience every day as I struggle to tolerate those thoughts. While I value my literacy, I haven't fully embraced the literacy myth. The literacy myth grows out of the easy and unfounded assumption that better literacy necessarily leads to economic development, cultural progress, and individual improvement. Mark Twain had implied as much when sharing Pap Finn's observations about literate black men:

> There was a free nigger there from Ohio—a mulatter, most as white as a white man. He had the whitest shirt on you ever see, too. . . . They said he was a p'fessor in a college, and could talk all kinds of languages, and knowed everything. And that ain't the wust. They said he could VOTE when he was at home. Well, that let me out. Thinks I, what is the country a-coming to? It was 'lection day, and I was just about to go and vote myself if I warn't too drunk to get there; but when they told me there was a State in this country where they'd let that nigger vote, I drawed out. I says I'll never vote agin. . . . And to see the cool way of that nigger—why, he wouldn't a give me the road if I hadn't shoved him out o' the way. I says to the people, why ain't this nigger put up at auction and sold?—that's what I want to know. And what do you reckon they said? Why, they said he couldn't be sold till he'd been in the State six months.[13]

Even as a child living in government projects, I understood Malcolm's mocking question. When he asked, "What do you call a black man with a PhD?" and answered "Nigger,"[14] he was pointing out that literacy alone wasn't enough to deconstruct the racial logic informing white supremacist ideas and our social inequalities. In my young mind, Malcolm X, one of the most intelligent and literate black men in the African-American literary canon, had gained literacy on his own terms. Yet, Malcolm X wasn't

13. Twain, *Adventures of Huckleberry Finn*, 20.
14. Norris, *Street Lit*, 61.

confused by the idea that acquiring academic literacy inherently enhances one's liberty or social status.

Over time, I grew to dislike the barriers that academic literacy threatens to set-up between many African-American males who strongly identify with either hip-hop or street culture and me. Malcolm presaged our dilemma. "I was to be confronted by handpicked scholars," he writes, "both whites and some of those PhD 'house' and 'yard' Negroes who had been attacking us [Black Muslims]."[15] The self-taught Malcolm's experience in school, as a ward of the state, in the streets, as a hustler, in prison, and in academic forums set him up to embrace an ambivalence regarding enforced literacy.

Likewise, African-American men who strongly identify with hip-hop and street culture resist the designs of those seeking to school them in unquestioning conformity to mainstream literacy and encourage them to mimic dominant culture in their literacy performances. According to hip-hop scholar Murray Forman:

> [Hip hop] emerged from within particular geographies of oppression and opportunity combined, where interlocking forms of race and class . . . often tend to reproduce the most intense conditions of lack, but which also portend positive and optimistic perspectives [on the creativity, culture, literacy and social possibilities] among the inhabitants.[16]

This cultural discourse has been "crucial in the redefinition of the American urban environment and, more pointedly, the redefinition of the relationship between minority youth, [society], and the American metropolis."[17] And it has implications for both black male literacy and masculinity.

Hip-hop culture has created discursive spaces interested in generating "counter-discourses, representing an attempt to circumvent constraining and outdated programs for social empowerment."[18] However, the hip-hop politics of authenticity tend to mirror other black ideologies in the production of exclusionary authenticity narratives designed to police the boundaries of blackness. The demand for an individual to adhere to their subgroup's cultural standards creates ambivalence. Forman explains, "The disjuncture produced by rap's alternative or progressive [counter-discourses] . . . illustrates the problems with identifying the black 'voice' as homogeneous or the black public sphere as a unified concept when they display several

15. Malcolm X, *Autobiography*, 266.

16. Forman, *'Hood Comes First*, 41.

17. Forman, *'Hood Comes First*, 41–42.

18. Forman, *'Hood Comes First*, 13.

overlapping points of antagonism."[19] Literacy is central to participation in this discursive space because an individual's knowledge and speech signify identity and ideological commitments. Consequently, we can see that black males and others constantly interrogate the black male literacy performance.

Before my exposure to hip-hop music, I grew up with an expansive, fluid, and liberatory black masculinity conception. I find it represented in African-American musicians who reject normative genre and gender construction based on an implicit racial categorization. It first appeared in 1979. During my sophomore year in high school, I experienced a growth spurt into manhood. Suddenly, my older cousin began to invite me to hang out with his older friends. According to Moms, my cousin and his friends used me as his babe magnet. Most days, I had no idea where we might be headed when he took me out partying. Most of the time, my cousin had plans to hit up the skating rink, or we'd go over to his gay homeboy's house, Jay Fletcher, who had three fine-ass sisters. Jay's father was a professional, and he was the youngest child and only son. With so many gorgeous sisters and a well-known fair-skinned "pretty boy" himself, he got invited to every party worth attending. We'd go over to his house to get the party invitations he wasn't going to use.

Early spring, my cousin invited me to a Prince and The Time show at a small downtown concert venue. No big deal, I thought. In 1979, Prince had gone on tour with Rick James. Following the tour, he'd drawn on James's androgynous look when he set out to produce his *Dirty Mind* album. We had front row seats at the aisle's center in the modest concert hall. The concert began with a foppish performance:by Morris Day and The Time. Morris Day and his crew performed their show as retro-seventies pretty boys with an edge reminiscent of the pimps in Martin Scorsese's *Taxi Driver*. Prince's performance, however, merged Little Richard's persona with Dr. Frank N. Furter from *The Rocky Horror Picture Show*. I'll never forget when Prince entered the stage in a London Fog trench coat, black high heeled boots, black bikini underwear, and leggings. By the end of his first song, Prince had contorted and fused genres and genders in a manner that shattered my somewhat taken-for-granted ideas of the boundaries of black masculinity.

On some level, I'd experienced it before in entertainment with David Bowie, and more personally with Moms's gay friends and men in the sporting life. Back in the day, she'd perm her clients' heads in the kitchen of our Bay Vista apartments. Moms was a cosmetology student, a big word for hairdresser, at City College, so she didn't have a license to open a salon. She was bootlegging. We regularly had same-gender-loving people in our home.

19. Forman, *'Hood Comes First*, 13.

On occasion, pimps would come through to get their hair permed. They'd shout, "I have curls for the girls and rolls for the hoes." I, however, detected that something other than their interest in "hoes" informed the attention these peacocks gave to their fastidious appearance and narcissistic focus on their beauty and on their women. One evening, I'd hovered near the periphery as two pretty boys prepared to leave our apartment. Once they'd gone, Moms shared a juicy bit of gossip. "Those two are lovers," she divulged with the corners of her mouth curling.

I was a silent child. The old mothers would look at me and say, "still waters run deep," or "every closed eye ain't sleep." Quiet as it's kept, I was always peeping game. I mean, I'd been working at my grandfather's shoe-shine stand downtown on First Avenue. What did folks think? I'd witnessed street life, and sometimes the streets got in the backseat of Grandpa's Cadillac and rode home with us. As a younger child, I'd spent countless hours cruising in my Uncle Billy's rebuilt Chevy Chevelle. On random occasions, he'd "unexpectedly" run into a *gentlefellow* whom he'd known from prison. It always seemed to happen around the corner of 47th and Market in the notorious N-Hood (aka neighborhood) Crips territory around Samuel Gompers Middle School. He'd pull over to give him a ride. Of course, everyone knew my uncle was a ladies' man, a thoroughbred, who hardly ever held down a job. But somehow, he kept gas in his car, cigarettes in the glovebox, and dry-cleaned clothes hanging in his closet. While riding both shotgun and peeping game from the backseat while listening to his 8-track tape, I discovered that macho behavior might veil grown-up realities that black men didn't dare openly discuss in the seventies and black children didn't dare question. Of course, I didn't know the term "heteronormative," but Grandma used the word "homosexual" as a pejorative term all the time. She went further using a nastier disparaging turn of phrase if she saw two men riding in a car.

In retrospect, I wondered what about gay men triggered Grandma. Did she know about the man with extra-long fingernails that Uncle Billy picked up? Men who looked like they'd just removed their drag queen apparel, makeup, and nail polish. Based on more primitive standards, my uncle was a "man's man." Our version of Ike Turner. I'd seen him beat one beautiful chocolate-covered girlfriend in front of her precious daughter Tiffany and raise his hand at Moms when she came to defend her. Of course, I'd heard the stories about him beating up six street punks on Bay Vista's basketball court—where he reigned as a don. However, the unspoken lesson that I learned from Uncle Billy went beyond domestic violence, drinking, pot, and bad-assed masculinity, which sure as the hell seemed toxic to me. I learned that anger, dominance, and lust were unpredictable for certain men without boundaries. Cruising in his ride prepared me for my early discoveries in the the kitchen "beauty salon" and Grandpa's shoeshine stand. Considering the childhood and adolescent epiphanies that emerged from my peering through the veil shrouding the streets, or simply getting in grown folks' business, as Moms might say, I still find it challenging to explain the shift in my perception that occurred in the wake of Prince's live performance.

On an intuitive level, I understood that Prince's illegible masculinity had implications for gender and racial identity beyond his apparent challenge to heteronormativity. "Don't hate me because I'm Fabulous," once declared the sassy Prince. Madison Moore's book, *Fabulous: The Rise of the Beautiful Eccentric*, describes individuals embracing a particularly peculiar aesthetic that leads to personal transformation. Moore is "interested in queer and other people [as beautiful eccentrics] forced to the margins who create themselves for themselves."[20] Cultural theorist Andrew Ross confirms Moore's theory. In his commentary in *Black Male: Representations of Masculinity in Contemporary American Art*, Ross's view on the relationship between "The Gangsta and the Diva" bridges the gulf between two seemingly disparate forms of masculinity. Ross compares gangsta rapper Treach's street-informed swagger and RuPaul's sashay appropriated from the runway to create diverging presentations of fabulousness.

> In the ghetto street or in the nightclub version, being fierce is a theatrical response to the phenomenal social pressure exerted upon black males in the waning years of the twentieth century. This is why the rise to prominence of the black drag queen ought to be linked (one could say, dialectally) with the much more widely debated emergence of the gangsta rapper as a dual symptom of the conditions that have made it commonplace to speak of young black men as an endangered species.[21]

Moore's book excludes celebrities and gangsters. However, both Moore and Ross make a genealogy for black men who resist conforming to heteronormative masculinity performances. Prince's fierceness presented an archetypical beautiful eccentric in the early eighties. Fabulousness is "a form of protest, a revolution against the norms and systems that oppress and torture us all every day, things like white supremacy, misogyny, transmisogyny, patriarchy, toxic masculinity, gender policing, and racism."[22] When a marginalized (black male) person, whom society might deem a social outcast, decides to refuse to acquiesce to gender norms, embracing fabulousness initiates a "turning point, a shedding of a past way of living for oneself in

20. Moore, *Fabulous*, 7.

21. Ross, "Gangsta and the Diva," 159.

22. Moore, *Fabulous*, 8.

another dimension in the here and now . . . [and implies]a story of struggle, survival, and resistance," I suspect that Prince's performance might have contributed to a shift in my thinking about my identity performance (i.e., literacy, masculinity, and racial presentation).[23]

To further explain blackness beyond the bounds, the late great trumpeter Miles Davis comes to mind. A close friend of Prince, Davis rejected musical straitjackets based on genre. These days, I hear it when listening to The Robert Glasper's Experiment *Black Radio*. The eclectic album includes covers from Bilal covering David Bowie's "Letter to Hermione," Nirvana's "Smells Like Teen Spirit," and Lalah Hathaway covering Sade's "Cherish the Day"; alongside Yasiin Bey's featured on Glasper's *Black Radio*. Interestingly, as I listen to Glasper, it dredges up the reality that I'd somehow figured out that blackness and masculinity are both fluid and malleable as a young child. Both reside equally inside and outside the box. I mean, what was blacker than Little Richard, Miles Davis, or Rick James? Nothing.

But blackness and black masculinity aren't relevant in a vacuum.

In the months following Prince's concert, my young mind determined that one's individual choices and preferences were the critical factors informing (existential) black authenticity. Bowie State University philosophy professor Robert Birt's reflection on the matter challenged anticipated conceptions of black authenticity (and inauthenticity). Birt begins with the obvious question regarding the legitimacy of pursuing authenticity: "Is not the quest for authenticity a quest [to fulfill one's most important life mission] to become more [fully] human?"[24] Birt answers the question by characterizing blackness as "the identity and consciousness of an oppressed [black] people desirous of liberation, and expressive of their striving for the emancipation of their denied or *thwarted transcendence*, [however] it can coincide with existential authenticity."[25] While Birt does not equate blackness with authenticity, he does believe "it is at least possible to live the experience of blackness in authentic ways. It is possible (if not essential) to choose authenticity precisely through the creation and affirmation of radical black *subjectivity* and *peoplehood*."[26] This quest necessitates resisting the urge to define, conform, and limit one's racial identity based on limiting biological fictions, cultural dogmas, and political philosophies.

As I read black male literacy narratives, I've discovered that efforts to conform to other-defined forms of literacy (and masculinity) on

23. Moore, *Fabulous*, 4.
24. Birt, "Blackness," 269.
25. Birt, "Blackness," 266.
26. Birt, "Blackness," 267; emphasis mine.

occasion create ambivalence (or cognitive dissonance). Consequently, I am interested in the personal and psychological crises emerging among black males who embrace the idea that mainstream literacy is the fundamental path towards egalitarianism, personal autonomy, and racial transcendence. As Prince powerfully stated, "A strong spirit transcends rules [and social constraints]."[27] Birt's argument, however, implies that black males' need to clarify the relationship between anti-black racism and literacy indoctrination as normative cultural and educational requirements for inclusion into dominant (or white) society, a deceptive ruse.

Ann Arnett Ferguson clarifies the issue in her book *Bad Boys: Public Schools in the Making of Black Masculinity*. In fact, she describes elements of racial identity that presage an experience of ambivalence or cognitive dissonance leading to double-consciousness because, when an individual chooses to embrace an ascribed black identity, that identity connotes agency, resistance, and political struggle and racial subordination. She writes,

> Identification with and through "Blackness" is itself split through the work of representations. Blackness is doubly constituted: as systematically demeaning, derogatory, and dehumanizing through the representational system of the dominant social order; as well as resourceful, creative, diverse through the cultural production of black communities. This splitting means that on the one hand, black identity is always refracted through the norm—whiteness—and inscribed with distorting, disfiguring images the internalization of which results in self-hatred that often manifests itself in an uneasy, ambivalent embrace of whiteness [and sometimes blackness].[28]

Favor concurs when he writes, "Race consciousness, particularly, when employed by members of the African-American elite, also expresses certain ambivalences toward class, gender, and geography."[29] Ferguson concludes that "schoolboys" and "troublemakers" manifest this odd duality that performs both embrace and denunciation. Nevertheless, this critique reveals that a subordinate identity becomes the standpoint from which one critiques and resists the dominant or dominating culture. Since the Harlem Renaissance, the inclination to embrace a folk, ghetto, or "ratchet" black identity have laid the groundwork for black activists, artists, and common folk to generate and sustain counter-discourses and counternarratives intended to subvert the illogical authority endowed in both whiteness and

27. Pareles, "Prince," para. 9.

28. Ferguson, *Bad Boys*, 209–10.

29. Favor, *Authentic Blackness*, 30.

black respectability politics that only serves to further marginalize those residing on society's periphery.

Lissa Skitolsky's *Hip-Hop as Philosophical Text and Testimony* sheds light on literacy-as-freedom strategy as a disingenuous snare, as racial identity is overdetermined for African Americans. According to Skitolsky, "Anti-black racism is not a problem of individuals who are 'ignorant' or 'irrational,' in need of more knowledge, but instead a problem of white sensibility as the framework in which people appear as white or black, who can only be 'read' in terms of the racist categories that allow the term to be visible at all."[30] Birt reminds us, however, that black authenticity is not solely a response to anti-black racism.

We must return to Birt to understand the implied agenda in the hip-hop "keep it real" approach to black authenticity, which Skitolsky illuminates as discourse intended to resist white supremacy. Birt explains,

> The quest for authenticity is a quest to become more authentically human. And the quest for *black authenticity* can certainly be no less. For in [Aimé] Césaire's words, 'as blacks . . . we are dealing with the only race which is even denied humanity.' But blacks cannot affirm their denied humanity without affirming themselves.[31]

In this context, black men interested in pursuing black authenticity and transcendence feel the need to address anti-black racism through their literacy performances. Denzel Mychal Smith addresses these concerns in his book *Invisible Man Got the Whole World Watching*. He writes, "[Our] invisibility is established through white people's refusal to see black men as fully human. In one sense, ceding this much power to the white gaze makes sense, as the world we inhabit is dominated by the economy, government, and culture that imbues whiteness with every conceivable benefit."[32] Stated differently, anti-blackness and the white gaze (or sensibilities) inform black men's (cultural and political) consciousness and identity formation.

Yet, Skitolsky suggests self-creation should forsake the failed project to legitimate one's humanity and obtain whites' validation through academic and cultural performances, which create existential crises due to internalized and structural racism. Drawing on a critical analysis of Franz Fanon's *Black Skin, White Masks*, Skitolsky quotes Lewis R. Gordon when he explains,

30. Skitolsky, *Hip-Hop as Philosophical Text*, 41.

31. Birt, "Blackness," 270; emphasis mine.

32. Smith, *Invisible Man*, 126.

Here is Fanon's argument: Blacks have attempted to escape [or transcend] the historic reality of blackness through language, which offers semiotic resources for self-deluding performances of emancipation. If blacks can speak the European language well enough and even use it against the European with the ferocity of Shakespeare's Caliban, perhaps they will "become" European and consequently "become" white. Value-neutral semiotic resources do not exist, however, in an antiblack world. Signifiers that overtly deny color are governed by a colonized life-world . . . from the perspective of many blacks, a black who speaks the national language well is someone who "speaks like a white person." . . . In other words, the semiotic turn only leads to phony whiteness and pitiful blackness. . . . The black discovers, however, that he or she is always already negatively signified by the system of signs that constitute antiblack racism.[33]

In his most recent book, cultural critic and *New York Times* contributor Thomas Chatterton Williams provides a confirming response while attempting to dismantle normative racial ideologies. He writes, "My life has shown me repeatedly that racism at once persists and is also capable of being transcended—especially on an interpersonal level."[34] Skitolsky goes further in her examination to argue that one cannot transcend racial oppression by shifting toward a neutral approach to communication and knowledge acquisition, which mirrors the critiques of the color-blind political imagination.[35] She helps us to see that black males, gifted with Du Boisian second sight, intuitively recognize that literacy-as-freedom is a ruse because "he is trapped by the way he necessarily *appears* to citizens racialized as 'white,' who see him as someone who is not-white, and thus trap him within the confines of' 'blackness' from which he cannot escape as he cannot appeal to a false idea they have of him, or appeal to their reason to recognize their error."[36] While the cultural critic Williams wants to reject the "legitimacy of the entire racial construct in which blackness functions as one orienting pole,"[37] he confesses that as a teenager, he adhered to a blackness reduced to athleticism and rhythm, a blackness he describes as apophatic, as it is defined in lack or opposition to whiteness or vice versa.

Nevertheless, most black males emerging from hip-hop culture continue to choose to speak in the black vernacular to avoid being ensnared by

33. Skitolsky, *Hip-Hop as Philosophical Text*, 41.

34. Williams, *Self-Portrait in Black and White*, 127.

35. Skitolsky, *Hip-Hop as Philosophical Text*, 47.

36. Skitolsky, *Hip-Hop as Philosophical Text*, 42.

37. Williams, *Self-Portrait in Black and White*, 33.

the idea that language is colorless or impartial, according to Skitolsky. Although whites might assess blacks based on their literacy performance, the primary consideration is not an individual's literacy performance. Skitolsky points to Fanon, again, who explains that "I am given no chance. . . . I am a slave not of the 'idea' that others have of me but my own appearance."[38] This assertion implies that African Americans, who reside beneath the pervasive (and internalized) white gaze, might sense that their identity is assumed because blackness is "overdetermined" based on physical appearance. Based on Skitolsky's perspective, one can imagine blackness as a prison or a "trap."[39] The literature on black masculinity substantiates her argument, pointing to the "polyvalent mobility" of racism and its implications for black masculinity and literacy.

Based on Foucault's theory, anthropology professor Ann Stoler describes a genealogy of gender, racial identity, and sexual arrangements in which she argues "the most striking feature of racism [and racial tropes is] that racism [and performances of race] always appear renewed and new at the same time."[40] Stoler's thesis informs how I read Ross's claim about the common social origins of the "gangsta" rapper and the black male diva. Both scholars indicate black men's opportunity to recognize how seemingly contestatory and disparate ideas, regarding gender, literacy, and race, co-produce to inform their literacy and masculinity performances and create ambivalence. Ross explains:

> Whether underplayed or overplayed, these theatrical versions of black masculinity are as much methods of deflecting or neutralizing white disapproval as modes of expressing *black traditions*. Of course, white culture has always compelled black males to be performative. . . . Performance was the obverse of black invisibility. . . . But todays normative social environment is not invisibility, it's disappearance.[41]

Ross indicates that rupture and recuperation through "black traditions" to avoid the "white disapproval" leads to black invisibility and disappearance. Although these ideas emerge in different social environments that one might imagine as distinctive and oppositional, these supposed new forms (identity and ideology) reveal "a fundamental paradox of racial discourse."[42] Stoler explains, "Namely that such discourse invariably draws on a cultural

38. Skitolsky, *Hip-Hop as Philosophical Text*, 42.
39. Skitolsky, *Hip-Hop as Philosophical Text*, 41.
40. Stoler, *Race and the Education of Desire*, 89.
41. Ross, "Gangsta and The Diva," 161–62.
42. Stoler, *Race and the Education of Desire*, 90.

density of prior representations that are recast in a new form; that racism appears at once as a return to the past as it harnesses itself to progressive projects."[43] It is the promiscuous nature of racist ideas that enable them to transmit sedimented and subjugated forms of knowledge to create black "discursive bricolage."[44] The reader is encouraged to move forward into the text to discover the relationship between rupture and recuperation in the discourse(s) on black male literacy.

Because racist narratives are "polyvalent" and "promiscuous," our discussion on contemporary and historical black male literacy narratives will demonstrate that evolving narratives regarding black male literacy and masculinity are partially older ones that are modified or recovered conventions from earlier discourses—both racist discourse and discourses intended to resist racist ones—on blackness in general, and black manhood in particular. In bell hooks's book, *We Real Cool: Black Men and Masculinity*, she states without equivocation that black men, in general, have made few interventions on these stereotypes and tropes, which is not without consequences.[45] She explains,

> As a consequence, they are victimized by stereotypes that were first articulated in the nineteenth century but hold sway over the minds and imaginations of citizens of this nation in the present day. Black males who refuse categorization are rare for the price of visibility in the contemporary world of white supremacy is that black male identity be defined in relation to the stereotype whether by embodying it or seeking to be other than it. At the center of the way black male selfhood is constructed in white-supremacist capitalist patriarchy is the image of the brute, untamed, uncivilized, unthinking, and unfeeling.[46]

Based on the rhetoric used in the War on Drugs, mainstream media, and hip-hop culture, I might add criminal, clown, crack addict, deadbeat dad, drug dealer, gangster, rapist, street hustler, and unemployed. African-American sociologist George A. Yancy describes his own experience with this existential predicament when revealing that being black in "America is to be always already known, and white people assume that they know everything about me [based on historical racial tropes and their reconfigurations]."[47] In this context, language is a futile or ineffective strategy for transcending negative

43. Stoler, *Race and the Education of Desire*, 90.
44. Stoler, *Race and the Education of Desire*, 61.
45. hooks, *We Real Cool*, xii.
46. hooks, *We Real Cool*, xii.
47. Yancy, *Backlash*, 11.

stereotypes involving language and other considerations used to articulate, reinforce, and justify anti-blackness. Because "negative stereotypes about the nature of black masculinity continue to overdetermine [or constrain] the identities black males are allowed to fashion for themselves."[48]

Language and literacy have been used as concealed and unconcealed codes for whiteness and the grounds for denying blacks their basic humanity, freedom, and enfranchisement. In that case, socially conscious black males, who choose not to accept the literacy-as-freedom myth, might be considered reasonable in their choosing to adhere to a more informal and organic literacy performance grounded in black folk culture. Moreover, I'd argue that ambivalence occurs due to individual black men's inability to disaggregate English language usage from the worldview that underwrites anti-black racism in fictitious biological, intellectual, political, and social terms. In the end, Skitolsky argues that participants in hip-hop culture adopt and remix language to aesthetically resist the strategies constructed to deny the humanity of African Americans through "epistemic overdetermination."[49]

Yet, one must consider whether hip-hop's resistance is up to the task. Because as one former hip-hop devotee acknowledges, "I confused racial authenticity with behavior and taste and flattered myself to think that I was somehow purer than [upper-middle-class blacks]."[50]

Charis L. Cheney's *Brothers Gonna Work It Out* considers rap nationalism in a manner that reveals both acquiescence and resistance (i.e., ambivalence) embedded within hip-hop musical genres. She writes,

> As a form of creative expression, gangsta rap spotlighted the socio-economic conditions facing many young black men in urban America—black-on-black crime, drug trafficking, police harassment, and brutality—at the same time that it tapped into fantasies that resonated with many young heterosexual men regardless of race: rebelliousness, irreverence, fierce aggression, and the sexual exploitation of women.[51]

Hip-hop artists and others participating in the culture claim a "keeping-it-real" authenticity—based on "ghettocentrism" (a term coined by cultural critic Nelson George) and street credentials—to insulate themselves against music reviews and cultural critiques on the content in their music. The ghetto, as an imagined community, is inhabited by the unsullied black urban

48. hooks, *We Real Cool*, xii.
49. Skitolsky, *Hip-Hop as Philosophical Text*, 42.
50. Williams, *Self-Portrait in Black and White*, 56.
51. Cheney, *Brothers Gonna Work It Out*, 6.

poor and their "lawless, violent, and hypersexual" counterparts.[52] African Americans who remain in the ghetto experience economic and political exploitation, while their elite counterparts abandon the 'hood in figurative and literal terms. These "ghettocentrists" (i.e., real niggas) define their identity "not only against white Americans but against middle-class (and middle-aged) blacks as well."[53] According to this discourse, "Rap music's ghettocentrists,' or self-proclaimed 'niggas,' claim they bear witness to the struggles of the black urban poor. . . ."[54] These prophetic narratives fail to consider the narrators' social embeddedness and co-production between the (bourgeoisie and white) society and the streets.

Interestingly, Cheney locates a form of ambivalence (an inconsistency) within ghettocentrism. She writes, "Ghettocentrism is not only decidedly [committed to the black] vernacular [and ghetto styles and sensibilities], but it is also purposefully masculine; and in spite of itself, it is strangely bourgeois, a trait that is most evident in the race/gender politicking of rap [black] nationalists."[55] Hence, one discovers the hip-hop trio Migos, a Southern rap group, generating a confusing slang term for nouveau rich ghetto women when describing them as "bad and boujee" (both street and bougie or bourgeois). On its face, this paradoxical hip-hop phrase is *black bricolage*. Bricolage is the creative and ingenious use of whatever materials are at hand (regardless of their original purpose) to create something new.

This definition illuminates the paradox in hip-hop-based ghettocentrism. As a counter-discourse or counter-narrative in hip-hop culture, black authenticity constitutes a hybrid identity incorporating contradictory narratives regarding black pathology (see Moynihan Report), class-based estrangement among African Americans, and cultural nationalist Afrocentric concepts in contemporary black culture to signify power in authenticity.[56] Darnell L. Moore's coming-of-age memoir captures these tensions and provides material for subsequent consideration. He writes,

> All of my life I had identified as black even if I sometimes, with or without awareness, distanced myself from black people I deemed too hood and poor even as others distanced themselves from me for the same reason. A world away from Camden, with little less than a year in the belly of a predominately white campus, I had begun the process of a new becoming. I was

52. Cheney, *Brothers Gonna Work It Out*, 11–12.`
53. Cheney, *Brothers Gonna Work It Out*, 11–12.
54. Cheney, *Brothers Gonna Work It Out*, 12.
55. Cheney, *Brothers Gonna Work It Out*, 12.
56. Cheney, *Brothers Gonna Work It Out*, 8–13.

becoming politically black: aware, awake, in love with my people, and enraged by racial injustice. I cared less about perfecting
appearances I had been taught to perform most of my life. I lost
interest in those negotiations: displaying intelligence, knowing
and staying in my place, quieting my voice, and downplaying
my street smarts so white people would not interpret me as a
threat. I changed—for better or worse.[57]

Cheney's observations and Moore's confession suggest that inherent within
hip-hop and street culture is a counter-discourse on black authenticity in
which participants are incapable of fully disaggregating the contradictory
foundations incorporated in the construction of their ghettocentric identity
(and worldview)—a racial identity based on their invoking a narrative involving class divide among blacks and structural racism, which ignores the
bourgeois aspirations informing their ambitions, behaviors, and conspicuous consumption.

This brings me to one last question before moving on to further explore
black male literacy narratives: Can "keeping-it-real blackness," as defined in
hip-hop culture, facilitate authenticity and transcendence? Based on Birt's
definition, 'hood-based authenticity cannot facilitate the quest to resist being foreknown, which requires their reclaiming our denied humanity and
transcendence on the path to becoming authentically human through self-
creation, as an expression of existential freedom.

On some level, Birt is referencing the idea that black authenticity has
been created in a bricolage manner. Its black bricoleurs draw on both dominant narratives and counter-discourse narratives on African Americans'
existential realities in the United States. He argues, "An insurgent affirmation of black transcendence implies no insistence on 'natural' or essential
properties as definitive of the being of the black. What is implied is the common praxis of [an entire] people's self-discovery and community."[58] Birt's
argument points us towards a radical black subjectivity based on individual
subjects participating in communal dialogue to develop a liberating inter-
subjective perspective. I will attempt to initiate this dialogue through reading black male literacy narratives to uncover the source of ambivalence that
inhibits both black authenticity and black transcendence.

As a black male coming of age in the hip-hop era, my story serves to
function as an introductory exploration of the tensions emerging for black
males who over-emphasize an individual focus on gaining the appropriate

57. Moore, No Ashes in the Fire, 135.
58. Birt, "Blackness," 269.

academic literacy in self-creation and a "transcendent existence in black."[59] I use the word "literacy" throughout this book as an expansive notion that includes a broad spectrum of skills, abilities, attainments, and performances, from that of a young boy as he proudly writes his own name for the first time to the jazz poet Langston Hughes's appropriating the African-American vernacular to write about the cultural, physical, and spiritual exquisiteness of the black folk. The meaning of literacy can range from a path to freedom [or self-creation or freedom] to a form of acquiescence that feels like a violation of oneself. The story of the acquisition of literacy and the meanings ascribed to that acquisition constitute a *literacy narrative*. In my exploration, I will consider hip-hop for its cultural and lyrical influence on the generations from its birth in the seventies. "Music deepened my thinking. And the music was always hip-hop back then," R. Dwayne Betts reminds us in his memoir on coming-of-age in prison.[60] He found places to hide or blend into the environment while listening to hip-hop because "there was no place for me in prison [or the world], but there was nothing else to lose—and they say freedom is born when there is nothing left to lose."[61] At the twenty-first century's dawning, hip-hop culture and music content began to suggest the path towards authenticity, freedom, and realization for black males in the United States.

I limit my consideration here to black males only and only some black males. In doing so, I intend not to claim a universal African-American experience. Instead, I tell my story contextualized with help from philosopher Jane Roland Martin. In *Educational Metamorphoses*, Martin has deeply pondered the tensions created when an individual crosses cultural borders into new social spaces and thought worlds to acquire academic knowledge. This outside perspective will enable me to reflect on my literacy narrative to clarify my ambivalence regarding mainstream literacy. Martin describes the turning points, culture crossings, and personal transformations that constitute a life's story as contributing to whole-person changes.[62] These "educational metamorphoses" are comprised not only of shifts in understanding but also of deep emotional currents. These pivotal moments in personal development are the meaningful events that find their way into autobiographies, including literacy or educational narratives, such as the one I share.[63]

59. Birt, "Blackness," 270.
60. Betts, *Question of Freedom*, 189.
61. Betts, *Question of Freedom*, 189.
62. Martin, *Educational Metamorphoses*, 50–55, 140–42.
63. Martin, *Educational Metamorphoses*, 50–55, 140–42.

I have become aware of my own ambivalences, as if insight and love were at war, generated by splintered parts of myself that reflect the "literacy wars" among black males—with President Barack Obama and Bill Cosby on one side, and Michael Eric Dyson and Vershawn Ashanti Young on the other. Even Michelle Obama has jumped into the fray. In a commencement speech at Bowie State University, Maryland's oldest historically black university, the First Lady invoked her literacy politics. She states:

> But today, more than 150 years after the Emancipation Proclamation, more than fifty years after the end of "separate but equal," when it comes to getting an education, too many of our young people just cannot be bothered. Today, instead of walking miles every day to school, they're sitting on couches for hours playing video games, watching TV. Instead of dreaming of being a teacher or a lawyer or a business leader, they're fantasizing about being a baller or a rapper.[64]

The First Lady goes further in linking career aspirations to literacy ambivalence. She concludes, "And as my husband has said often, please stand up and reject the slander that says a black child with a book is trying to act white. Reject that."[65] Many African Americans embraced her remarks, and others took offense at her "targeted scorn."[66] If I may push the earlier stated warfare metaphor, I believe former Secretary of Defense Robert McNamara can elucidate the limited effectiveness of such conflict. He says, "There's a wonderful phrase: 'the fog of war.' What 'the fog of war' means is: war is so complex it's beyond the ability of the human mind to comprehend all the variables. Our judgments, our understanding, are not adequate."[67]

Warfare among African Americans against black illiteracy leads to reason-obscuring intolerance on both sides. It is challenging to live alone with the pain of feeling that, in many ways, my literacy separates me from other black men. This very literacy has brought me the power of insight into literacy ambivalence. It is difficult to feel as though others might cast me in the same light as those in the literate's priesthood who mock and disregard "less" literate or illiterate black males as social inferiors and vice versa. Yet, I hope to find a way to help myself and others resolve, or come to terms with, the tensions between being literate and loving, without losing either.

64. Coates, "How the Obama Administration Talks to Black America," para. 1.

65. Coates, "How the Obama Administration Talks to Black America," para. 1.

66. Coates, "How the Obama Administration Talks to Black America," para. 12.

67. Morris, *Fog of War*.

From the time that I can remember having any thoughts about anything, I recall that I had an intense longing to learn to read. I determined, when quite a small child, that, if I accomplished nothing else in life, I would in some way get enough education to enable me to read common books and newspapers.

—Booker T. Washington, *Up from Slavery*

Throughout my life all real learning has taken place outside the classroom. I was educated by my family, friends, and the street. Later, I learned to love books and I read a lot, but that had nothing to do with school. Long before, I was getting educated in unorthodox ways.

—Huey P. Newton, *Revolutionary Suicide*

Although I wrote letters every week, I didn't tell anyone all the books I read, the nights I spent writing in a journal to make sense of the books and the cell I was in.

—R. Dwayne Betts, *Question of Freedom*

Who do we think we are?

We think we are people who risked not existing at all. People who might have had a mother and father killed, either by a government or by nature or even before we were born. Some of us think we are accidents of literacy.

I do.

—Edwidge Danticat, *Create Dangerously*

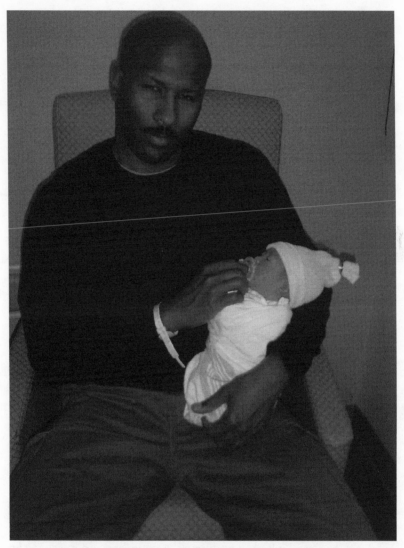

Brigham and Women's Hospital, Boston, Massachusetts (c. 1986)

# CHAPTER 2

# Young, Ambivalent, and Black

I WATCHED EAGERLY AS the nurses took the vitals of my newborn son, cleaned him, and finally handed him over to me. I held the tiny Buddha in my arms and sat next to his mother, just as I had held his two older sisters. But this time, I began to weep. I wept for several reasons, the most prominent being that my father had abandoned me before birth. Arashi had entered our lives in mannish splendor. His triumphant entry involved kicking and flailing. I bounced from one foot to the other as I watched the nurses warm him under their enormous lamp and tend to his vitals. The postpartum ritual ended with them wrapping Arashi into a gigantic burrito and then placing him in my arms. As the powder-colored baby settled into my arms, the unexpected epiphany began to creep into the moment, coloring my reproductive triumph in a melancholy tone and giving it new meaning.

I began to realize that I hadn't had a man to welcome me into the world at my most vulnerable moment. I was overwhelmed both with the love I felt toward my son and by my yearning for my own father's love. A self-taught man, he had a heart attack jogging around the track at the University of California Los Angeles. During my senior year in high school, he'd call to quiz me on imaginary numbers. Eventually, he'd push me to enter the military, which I refused. My father struggled with schizophrenia since young adulthood. Yet, he carved a life out for himself. A national guard member who worked for the city of Los Angeles, Big Bob was a bodybuilding runner who capitulated to the good life in his forties and died of heart disease, as did his father in his fifties. Bob wanted me to be an educated and independent man. After I hired my half-sister to work for me at our family's business, we fought in the early eighties, and his paranoia kicked in. We were estranged when he passed away.

When Arashi entered the world, I was a Harvard graduate student struggling to survive in a conservative academic culture that worshipped the life of the mind; inclusion required the highest literacy levels. Lacking the best academic preparation and money, I had spent many a sleepless night, often after doing odd jobs and menial labor, trying to manage my studies. My daughters were already reading and writing in two languages, and my wife and I would make sure that my son became literate. Yet, I also felt torn and grief-stricken in so clearly wanting him to become literate. How might I explain my grief?

Without understanding the particulars, I felt in that moment that I was grieving over my Sisyphean struggle to become a literate African-American male in a world that often placed black authenticity—grounded in black cultural nationalism with its fist held high fused with black street culture swaggering in defiance to middle-class norms—in conflict with the academic literacy our nation held out as the path towards patriarchal masculinity and the American Dream. Hip-hop scholar Murray Forman captured my twenty-first century double-consciousness when explaining,

> The discourse of ghetto authenticity and the evolution of a "real nigga" mentality in the late 1980s and 1990s emerge as prominent and complicated features [under the ascending regime of hip-hop]. These expressions are actually continuations of prior discourses of difference within black cultural spaces and in relation to white society, as can be found in the words and writings of Malcolm X and others who have noted contestatory attitudes relating to the inherently different social-class positions occupied by the "house nigger" and the "field nigger" in the antebellum South.[1]

I had grown up a "field nigger" among "field niggers" with both field and house nigger aspirations. As an uneducated child living between Southeast San Diego and South Central Los Angeles, I thought being literate meant being educated, intelligent, and spending evenings reading and writing books. My older cousin, Sandee, had begun elementary school a year before me. I recall her heading off to school in the morning, and accompanying her on the trip home after school. Sandee's face shone with Vaseline with fresh white ribbons in her hair and knee socks on "lotioned" legs. Booker T. Washington describes a similar vision in his book *Up from Slavery*. He writes, "The picture of several dozen boys and girls in a schoolroom engaged

1. Forman, *'Hood Comes First*, 54.

in study made a deep impression upon me, and I had the feeling that to get into a schoolhouse and study in this way would be about the same as getting into paradise."[2] However, I began to develop anxieties about manhood at Manchester Avenue Elementary School. The 'hood would start to become my frame of reference for black authenticity.

On the way to school, I'd walk past winos waiting for the liquor store to open with frightening questions on my mind and in my gut: Who would keep me from this fate? Who would make sure that I became an educated, strong, law-abiding, and respectable black man? Everything in my family life and neighborhood pointed in the opposite direction. The corner liquor store seemed to have a black man magnet.

On the first day of school in Los Angeles, my kindergarten classmates and I plopped down on the cool floor around our new teacher when a bigger girl behind me commented on my blocking her way and sassily told me to move. Having heard someone use the term "punk" in a demeaning manner, I retorted, "Oh, you're a little punk." She responded with a hard, painful blow to my back. The sound of her punch's impact, and my involuntary yowl, echoed through the room. It felt like the attack of a five-hundred-pound gorilla. I didn't know how to respond. If I hit back, I was in trouble. If I didn't, *I was the punk*. Grandma had taught me never to hit a girl. In reality, I had never faced the need to fight. She even killed flies on my behalf. What did I know about violence? I suddenly felt as if I were falling through a trap door. Having a bully punch me at the beginning of the first day of school marked my initiation into the world of schooling.

Manchester Avenue Elementary School did not provide the kind of cultural edification that I'd anticipated in my romantic childhood dreams from the outset. I cannot tell you where the ridiculous images came from, but I'd imagined ivy-covered brick buildings with colorful and light-filled classrooms before going to school. I expected my teachers to be attentive and kind. My days at school, I thought, would include learning the alphabet, reading books, finger painting, fresh lunches, and schoolyard pranks. But after being socked in the back on my first day of kindergarten, a dark shadow overtook me. Once my teacher ignored the punch to my back, her presence diminished to the "wha-wha-wha" trombone effect representing the teacher in a Charlie Brown cartoon. The educational benefit of going to school was no longer apparent.

That blow to my back was nothing unusual, however. I was regularly beaten at home, always for some reason. My mother feared that we would lose respect for her and turn out like her brothers, who had all been to prison.

2. Washington, *Up from Slavery*, 32.

In retrospect, I suppose that she was also overwhelmed by the responsibility of raising two boys in a challenging environment. Although Mom's motives for smacking us around and beating us with a belt were understandable and perhaps part of the culture, her reasons did not make it any better. As a tender young child, the beatings drove me into a perpetual dark cloud. In the end, I did not learn to read, write, or do arithmetic until we returned to San Diego during the spring of 1971, toward the end of second grade. I can still recall the teacher's look of bewilderment when she discovered that I could spell only my first name and the word "September." That year, I was enrolled in summer school to catch up.

In San Diego, I met Ida Azucena, a cute Filipino girl with a *Leave-It-to-Beaver* family. Mrs. Azucena and Ida's sister Inez began to help me learn to read. It felt good to have these girls and their mother give me that sort of attention. In contrast, Moms seemed too preoccupied or uninterested in helping me learn, though she required that I behave myself in class.

A native of San Diego, Moms seemed more upper class than our neighbors in Bay Vista, many of whom were from the South. She'd vacillate between snooty airs when discussing her interest in architecture and interior design to ghetto minimalism in identity performance. Grandma had invested in Catholic school until the eighth grade in her effort to immerse my mother in black elite respectability politics and encourage her upper-crust aspirations. Grandma's employer had arranged play dates for Moms with their daughters. Consequently, I thought that she could code-switch with the best. Yet, she had bought into the "keep it real" mentality of the late sixties and seventies. Amidst the challenges of raising her sons in the projects on a welfare budget, she became depressed and short-tempered. And after one of my uncles and his wife went to prison, two of our cousins ended up on our doorstep as well. During this period, a heavy funk permeated our apartment with such a dense presence that I felt as though I were walking in a swimming pool at times. One evening, I brought flashcards home and asked her for help. Our session ended with Moms, as I had begun to call her instead of Mommy, yelling, "Sound it out phonetically! Shit, sound it out!"

Things didn't get much better during the next school year. My third-grade teacher was Mrs. Malveaux, a well-dressed, light-skinned, middle-class African-American woman—Pam Grier with a frosty demeanor. I had not been as acutely aware of class distinctions among black people until I became her student. In my 'hood, we would have called a person with her bearing "bougie," as in bourgeoisie. Mrs. Malveaux could send an arctic chill through the air with a single comment: "I got mines, you gotta get yours." Although this comment did not sound like something one would expect from a bougie person, when we'd get on this black queen's nerves, she would let us know, in subtle and not-so-subtle ways, that she had ascended to get her college degree; now we poor ghetto negroes must get ours. But she didn't seem much interested in helping us along by managing our chaotic classroom and teaching us the subject matters that she'd been hired to teach.

Unaware of my interior life, Mrs. Malveaux and I developed a bond—an illicit bond of sorts. Despite the invisible wall she created between herself and her ghetto charges, Mrs. Malveaux and I found rapport. On occasion, she'd send me with a note to the local grocery store to buy her a pack of cigarettes. I was allowed to buy a snack as a payoff for running the errand and returning with her contraband. A young hustler, I'd secure the smuggled goods and keep my mouth shut. I usually bought Hostess fruit pies—the apple or lemon ones. However, the graft didn't remove the sting of her condescension or academic challenge.

Though only a young eight-year-old, on the one hand, I felt conflicted about accepting Mrs. Malveaux's "bribes" to run errands while learning very little of the subjects she was supposed to be teaching us. I found myself not only feeling that Mrs. Malveaux was ripping me off as a student but, on an intuitive level, I understood that she had underestimated all of us. Because I, too, lived with my classmates in the notorious Logan Heights, and in the projects on 49th and Logan Avenue, I knew that many of the other children were gifted athletes, actors, comedians, dancers, musicians, singers, and storytellers. But Mrs. Malvueax could not tap into our collective genius. My third-grade experience in a noisy bungalow classroom left me with a yearning for real schooling, a longing that had less to do with the love of learning and more to do with proving something to the hypocritical, bougie, black snobs who looked down their noses at us kids from the projects. But there was one big problem: I didn't know anyone who could appreciate or support my nebulous literacy aspirations. My unschooled grandmother encouraged me to do well in school ("Just keep going to school, baby," she'd say). I wanted to fulfill her noble ambition for me. However, I had no consistent adult presence to help me translate her ill-defined plan of action intended to culminate in a college degree, prosperity, and social capital.

At the end of the school year, I went to summer school again and began to hang out with a group of tough boys who were slightly older and more "street." I learned about shoplifting, drugs, and "grown folks' business." These miniature outlaws were the young brothers of the ghetto luminaries who taught me how to make go-carts and never encouraged me to do wrong, except for stealing the wood and the shopping carts for our home-made racing machines. Afterward, they'd break into the local Granny Goose potato chip warehouse for snacks. I looked up to these "real" black dudes who talked about blackness and greeted each other in Arabic (As-Salam-u-Alaikum) or Swahili (Habari gani).

Although Moms made dashikis at home to sell at a local record store, and she was down for the cause and all, she warned me to stay away from the little heathens in Bay Vista. Who else were we going to play with, I'd think? A thought I kept to myself because I didn't want my teeth knocked out of my mouth. If I'm honest, though, *I was wary* of the older dudes' drug use, unpredictable violence, and attitudes and behavior toward girls and women. Early one evening, I had watched from the periphery when the fellas began to take advantage of a young woman with a mental disability sitting on a mauve concrete bench at 4–5 Park overlooking the main freeway. As the copper evening sun began to set, I became uncomfortable with her smiling but nervous countenance.

As I recount the memory, the remembrance points me to an observation in R. Dwayne's memoir on coming-of-age in prison, *Question of Freedom*. He recounts,

> Some of the boys I grew up with were now the boys my mom always told me to avoid. But I couldn't avoid them because we'd had birthday parties together, the pizza parties, and they weren't just thugs who [I could simply dismiss]. . . . Now here I was, twelve years old, and I was starting to see the complicated space that I lived in, where people you thought you knew could be out there doing things you'd never imagine.[3]

As I reflect on Betts's insight, I think he'd say he didn't realize that he was one illicit act away from the homies. He'd be right about that—one carjacking catapulted him into prison and real nigga status. We were, in fact, the same heathens. Like the HBO special *The Wire* that features corner boys and schoolchildren dealing with incomprehensible existential dilemmas for school-aged children, Betts points to the detrimental and unimagined corruption of innocence.

I do, however, see another possible point of view on the matter. In my Bible study, Tim Dearborn (who his wife Kerry reminded me was a Dearborn Street Dearborn) will bring up children and innocence. We both attend a weekly men's study. An ex-pimp, Marvin Charles, began to gather men who have a history with criminality, child support, domestic violence, drug addiction, making-ends-meet, or parenting (or all the above). Marvin's non-profit for fathers is in a rapidly gentrifying neighborhood. It began focusing on black men until high-status white men began to attend as a form of Christian slumming. Well, Tim Dearborn seems to feel it's important to

3. Betts, *Question of Freedom*, 102.

remind us, on occasion, that no one is innocent because he sees something other than innocence in his grandchildren. As I've raised my own children, I always counter Tim's perspective about small children based on the Christian theology of Adam's fall and original sin. I concede that children might be cheeky or naughty. Yet, my own childhood experiences led me to invoke a 'hood-based theology when imagining an innocent black child's face. When I read Bett's vignette about corrupted children, I imagine him and myself as fat-faced middle-schoolers coming of age in the 'hood. And I'm fully aware that our existence tempts some adults to judge children as adults, as they did when they sent the too-young Betts to prison. Yet, these same adults might find unfathomable the happenings a blameless black cherub might experience, hear, witness, or get ensnared in while growing up in the ghetto. Bearing witness not only alters their moral imagination but also impacts their ideas about the relationship between gender and literacy.

At the end of summer, my school experience began to change for the better. During the fourth grade, I had a highly focused teacher named Miss Jackson who, for some reason, reminded me of the stern Reverend Mother Plaseato on the television program *The Flying Nun*. She had short hair, wore long skirts, and took a structured approach to education. I needed her discipline to gain lost educational ground. Besides, I could handle it. I had begun to work with my grandmother's janitorial crew at night. When Grandma wasn't around, I led the squad without her. I knew every key on the two colossal key rings to the office buildings we cleaned. I'd bring them to school to show off. I knew the variations in the weekly schedule. And I could run the vacuum to make perfect patterns in the carpet while emptying garbage cans and cleaning the ashtrays along the way. In other words, in my own way, I was a worldly little guy up for any challenge life might offer.

Based on Miss Jackson's initial assessments, she placed me in reading and math groups on opposite ends of the performance continuum. She called on me to read daily—or, if she didn't, I'd volunteer. By the fourth grade, I had gained confidence in my reading abilities and loved the sound of my voice. In the early seventies, black fourth-graders weren't embarrassed or self-conscious about having solid reading skills or speaking Standard English in the classroom. I can vaguely recall looks of envy when I read aloud. I rarely had the opportunity to hear my own voice at home unless we had guests interested in children. Moms talked *at* me, not *with* me, even when she occasionally had too much to drink and became incredibly talkative. Regardless of my weaknesses, I could lead in the fourth grade because Miss Jackson played to my strengths. In the safety of her classroom, nothing could make me feel dismissed or out of place.

We all knew which groups to arrange ourselves into and what needed to be done during different periods of the day. We knew her expectations for us, and she kept us on task. During the school day, an ordered calm would fall on the class in which I could work in silence and observe myself as a student. I felt an inner disorder and became aware of my shortcomings. Although I could read, I was doing poorly in math and my studies overall. This unfortunate fact gnawed at me. I was in the blue math group with an obese and snot-nosed kid named Desmond, a magnet for bullies. During our math sessions, I began to see myself reflected in him, as if in a mirror. I could not bear the image I saw. I couldn't stand how this situation tainted how I was beginning to view myself and how others (I imagined) viewed me. In the world between our apartment on Logan Avenue—the boulevard our ghetto was named after—and the classroom, I had been getting respect or felt included. I didn't want to be perceived as a loser in class any longer.

Miss Jackson made sure that I sat near her desk, on the other side of Lynn Brown. She was a chocolate brown cherub who had been "lotioned" every day since her birth into the world. Lynn was quiet and did everything with a working-class two-parent household precision and tact. She was my first crush and nemesis. When we played math bingo on Fridays, I would spread my bingo cards out on the floor beneath Miss Jackson's massive desk. Even though I was terrible at math, when I played bingo, it was like I was born to win. One auspicious day, I hit bingo time and time again. I sat beneath Miss Jackson's desk with three cards arrayed in front of me, keyed up, almost hyperventilating while I waited for the next equation. I was one number away from hitting bingo again. For some reason, Miss Jackson took longer than usual to call out a problem. I looked up to see what was going on—and caught her checking out my cards and shuffling the math problems in her hand. In a flash, I realized that Miss Jackson had been the deity behind my good fortune all this time. Here was a teacher who seemed to care about my school performance and, for the first time in my life, about my well-being. I felt like the old mothers in the church would say, "My change had come." At the time, I enjoyed having the rules bent for me, not as a form of entitlement or privilege, but as evidence that my square teacher was as slick as a street hustler and committed to her students' success. More importantly, Miss Jackson looked past my deficits, my single-parent household, my free lunch pass, my lopsided Afro, and my acting out to perceive my need for a non-traditional approach to schooling.

By the middle of spring term, my "scholarly" abilities had improved to the point that I was a leader at the top of my class in all subjects, alongside Lynn Brown. A number of things motivated me. I wanted to show Miss Jackson that I appreciated her kindness and compassion. But I also wanted to replace Lynn Brown as the top student. I imagined her as Mrs. Malveaux's daughter. I wanted Miss Jackson to like me more. One bright spring afternoon, I was on a roll, working through math set after math set. Thirty minutes before the end of class, Miss Jackson handed me a note for my mother and sent me home.

Entering our apartment, I found Moms smoking pensively on the couch. I quietly handed her the envelope. She took the note, silently got up, set the message down on the kitchen counter without reading it, went to get her wallet, and sent me to the store to buy her a pack of Salem 100's. When I returned home, she was in her bedroom, so I picked up the note and read it. Miss Jackson had written to tell my mother about my progress and how proud she should be. Moms never mentioned the message to me, nor I to her, though I can still recall that moment like it happened two minutes ago. Saying nothing, we both quietly went about our business. After fourth grade with Miss Jackson, things changed again. The school district divided the students at Knox Elementary: those who lived on the north side of Logan Avenue, in Bay Vista, would attend Kennedy Elementary School, an arrangement that concentrated fewer welfare families at Knox. My mother and grandmother decided to send my brother Dinky and me to Catholic school.

Around the same time, I noticed that Grandma had beautifully bound books around the house, yet I had never seen her reading these artifacts of respectability. I knew that she'd bring home cast-off furniture and household items from her generous bosses. They'd send me gifts as well. When I asked Grandma about the books that she'd smuggled from her wealthy employers' homes, she explained in storytelling that, as a young girl, she had had to leave the schoolhouse to work in the cotton fields and in the homes of Christian ladies, one of whom had led her to the Lord right on the front porch. Under these white women's supervision, Grandma became a "make-you-wanna-slap-somebody" cook and a hard worker with deep faith. The cotton fields left her with permanently scarred shins and functionally illiterate. After telling me her story, she remembered something that caused her to pause and look up.

Grandma climbed on a ladder in the garage's area above her beloved Ford Mustang. She brought down a nondescript cardboard box. Getting on my knees, I opened the box to discover clothe-bound books with titles like *Aesop's Fables*, *Alice in Wonderland*, and *The Adventures of Huckleberry Finn*. My puzzled facial expression drew a response from Grandma. According to her, she had ordered these for me during my mother's unexpected pregnancy. Even as a young boy, I grasped that the gift of books she gave me that day embodied her trauma, loss, and unspoken hopes for the world-opening possibilities of literacy.

Later I'd learn that my intuition resonated with Booker T. Washington's reflection on his unschooled mother's literacy dreams for her children. She secured Washington an old copy of Webster's "blue-back spelling book."[4] Washington didn't know "how and where she got it."[5] Yet, he was sure about his mother's intentions. He explained, "Though she was totally ignorant, so far as mere book knowledge was concerned, she had high ambitions for her children, and a large fund of good, hard common sense which seemed to enable her to meet and master every situation."[6] Our close relationship led to my intuiting Grandma's "high ambitions." She wanted me to pursue the formal education that Jim Crow and poverty had denied her and that my mother and uncles had neglected. I wanted to please her, but I felt that she was suggesting something more.

My sage grandmother took a subtle approach to our conversations that connoted her deep reservoir of wisdom. She'd tell me, "You have to have the understanding to get at what's underneath a thing." Her stories seemed to carry with them the weight of a historical burden or obligation. Whereas fate had forced my grandmother, a black child who lived under a racial caste system, to pick cotton and serve white families, whereas bad fortune had spoiled her children's futures, she sought an entirely different narrative for her favored grandchild. So it was out of love for Grandma and with a sense of being part of a larger story that I set out for Catholic school, determined to get the education she wanted for me. But it didn't work out as I had hoped.

It was 1975, and my fifth-grade teacher, Sister Jeanne, had little knowledge—book-wise or experiential—regarding black people and other minorities. We treated the young nun like a substitute teacher. The male students had an unspoken pact. Our unsaid aim for each day was to make her leave the classroom in tears by the afternoon. I found myself abandoning our bond once Sister Jeanne began preparing me for our first communion— after the first disappointing parent-teacher conference and a "debriefing" with my mother at home—I decided to stop cutting up at school and began to back out of the fifth-grade boys' social contract.

Every Wednesday, Sister Jeanne kept me after school to study the Bible. Sometimes we met her at the convent or the place of worship to talk about church history and Scripture. We discussed the Parable of the Sower about a million times. In the process, we formed a bond. She had become a real

---

4. Washington, *Up from Slavery*, 19.

5. Washington, *Up from Slavery*, 19.

6. Washington, *Up from Slavery*, 19.

person to me, someone who had a family and who had given up everything to become a bride of Christ—a sacrifice too great for a ten-year-old from the projects to get his afro-covered head around. One might say that Sister Jeanne became a human subject with emotions, thoughts, and a distinctive perspective. Her transparency and vulnerability granted me a new point of view into the meaning of the relationship between teachers and students.

Our growing camaraderie began to change my attitude toward the guys who got their day-to-day jollies by giving Sister Jeanne a hard time. These Catholic school wannabe punks thought their behavior made them hip and street on some level. At first, I thought it was cool, too. But I gradually saw things from a more human and mature perspective. This point of view caused me to take my studies more seriously. My mother had given birth to my youngest brother, Jason, and helping her with his care made me feel more mature. I had even started writing books for him before he was born. And reading Scripture with Sister Jeanne nurtured these changes of heart, especially one passage following the Parable of the Sower:

> And he said unto them, "Unto you it is given to know the mystery of the kingdom of God: but unto them that are without, all these things are done in parables: That seeing they may see, and not perceive, and hearing they may hear, and not understand; lest at any time they should be converted, and their sins should be forgiven them." (Mark 4:11–12)

In studying and spending weeks reflecting on these words, I began to feel my classmates were missing the point of what school at St. Rita's was all about. One Latino classmate's Cheech and Chong impersonations began to wear on me. One day, I moved my seat across the classroom to sit among the studious girls, feeling conflicted as I watched the guys go through their daily drill, which regularly culminated in Sister Jeanne walking out the door into the afternoon sun in tears.

The next year in sixth grade, I found myself going to the local library with my younger brother Dinky after school. I'd check out armloads of books on male historical figures in history, wars, and mythology. In the sixth grade, I was eleven but felt as if I were older. I had started to leave my peers behind the previous year in many ways. To begin with, I had walked alongside my mother during another pregnancy without the support of her partner. His behavior seemed aimed at causing her grief. After my youngest brother, Jason, was born, I began to take on more home responsibilities. When Jason turned two, my older cousin, Porsche, got into trouble and moved down from Los Angeles to live with us. These changes forced me to grow up.

Moms was an authoritarian well-known for her ability to discipline children and to throw "those hands" in the streets. My Uncle Billy's ex-wife decided to exile her rebellious daughter to San Diego to help her settle down. Porsche was a cute, tough, and well-built ninth-grader. Within a week, the local gang members and players began to visit our apartment after school. At the time, I was a dominant "pencil break" player at St. Rita's with an arsenal of stolen pencils. I earned the respect of these well-known gang bangers with my uncanny ability to break their pencils with a single karate chop from one of my green and yellow Saratoga pencils. Reggie Bo Bo, a genuine original gangster, dissolved to the ground in laughter the first time round. He couldn't believe a chunky-chocolate-bar eating parochial schoolboy like me could break his pencil with a single snap. These guys began to initiate me into the world of street gangsters. I'd go with them to 7-Eleven to buy sunflower seeds, fruit pies, dill pickles, pig skins, and other ghetto snacks during the weekend. We'd return to Bay Vista to smoke pot, listen to music, dance, and drink alcohol.

All the same, my educational horizons continued to expand when Grandma had two heart attacks, lost her house, and moved from her working-class neighborhood in Emerald Hills into the government-funded Bay Vista apartments. Most evenings, I'd go over for dinner to keep her company; read books; listen to Stanley Turrentine, Earth, Wind and Fire, and the Ohio Players; and watch art-house and foreign films on Channel 100 on cable television. On occasion, my Grandpa Jack would visit for a meal, and we'd drive him to downtown La Jolla to buy shoes and suits. On Sundays, we'd go to the children's pool at La Jolla Coves. We'd dine on food many of my friends in the 'hood knew nothing about, including shrimp and lobster, as well as hum bow, bagels, and chopped liver. Our culinary excursions didn't cause me to look down on anyone. It seemed to me that my life was bricolage, random. It didn't make sense. Moms would save up her money to take us to the Jewish delicatessen on El Cajon Boulevard or posh restaurants on the waterfront or in the artsy Hillcrest. Our short trips beyond Southeast San Diego led me to become more curious about the world beyond the 'hood. Consequently, I could feel myself maturing beyond the fellas who lived in Bay Vista or other sixth-graders who went to school at St. Rita's. Although I was too chubby and insecure to feel superior to them, I did perceive their narrowness, immaturity, and closed-mindedness.

When I was in seventh grade, the school district decided to follow the national trend to integrate schools by transporting the kids who lived in my neighborhood to a predominately white school near La Jolla. My grandmother's health was a factor in our decision. Grandma developed issues with her heart. Her physicians required her to stop working. Because we could no longer afford St. Rita's, the choice was apparent. I sensed Providence's advocacy in this turn of events. It did not upset me a bit. It was not uncommon for Grandma to take us to La Jolla on Sundays. Uncle Gene and Aunt Mona lived in the suburbs. During summers, he'd rent an apartment on Mission or Pacific Beach. Dinky and I would spend a few days with him. As an eleven-year-old seventh-grader, I did not feel bound to Southeast San Diego in the least bit. I craved the opportunity to move beyond Logan Heights. Because I had been at St. Rita's and had mixed-race cousins, I had no real hang-ups about going to school in the suburbs, nor did I think that certain extracurricular activities were only for white students. However, my ghetto colleagues informed me that student government, the ski club, and long-distance running weren't for black kids on our rides to school.

Even as an afro-wearing middle-school kid, I knew that their "black is, black ain't" racial logic conflicted with both democracy and Martin Luther King's *raison d'être*. It sounded kind of nuts to me. Straight out. In the end, I developed a well-deserved reputation for being an "Oreo." On one level, I was guilty as charged. Our suburban colleague's upper-middle-class lifestyles looked good to me. On another level, I can't deny that being called an Oreo hurt me as an accidental black nationalist. I attributed these comments to junior high school nonsense. I'd grown up with a deep love of black people and paid attention when local activists indoctrinated me into the knowledge of our strong black history. Although I began to wear surf brands to school and imitated what became known as Valleyspeak, I knew I was still the same little chubby dude with an orange-tinged afro. In my young and practical mind, the only thing that had changed was our school's location and the opportunities to experience new things it afforded.

But my attitude shifted as I began to face disappointments connected to either race or racism. Although I believed that I was popular, I lost two bids for student government leadership. It seemed as though many of the black students were apathetic about voting due to race-based perceptions about what black kids should and should not do. I can't recall one of the students bussed from my neighborhood getting involved in student government, though many of them loved physical education, band, and music class. My suburban friends supported the popular white students. I tried to keep my faith in Grandma's dream of literacy, racial harmony, and social mobility while focusing on my studies. After *Roots*, the miniseries, aired on television, it became impossible to ignore the ubiquitous "black is, black ain't" talk in the cafeteria and on the school bus.[7] Several fights broke out on campus, and white students targeted our school bus. The racist attacks

7. Ellison, *Invisible Man*, 9–10.

on black students caused me to ponder whether or not I had been naïve—whether on some level my black friends may have been trying to protect me from the white world's inevitable betrayal.

Moreover, Grandma might have expected me to ride the educational escalator to the top, but she never minced words about racial animosity. As in all things, she'd advise a wise estimation of our racial state. I had to wear that mask and veil material progress or pay the price. My image of what it meant for me to gain an education and learn polysyllabic words to comport myself with eloquence and grace was becoming increasingly complicated. I wanted to be more intentional in educational aspirations and what I thought of as street knowledge. As I moved toward graduating from junior high, I realized that teachers and textbooks provided specific kinds of information. Still, even in classes intended to prepare me for life, such as sex education, teachers could not answer my emerging questions about manhood and masculinity. In short, they could not tell me how to become a black man. Although my friends were going to house parties, slow dancing, and having sex, after my cousin returned home to Los Angeles, I'd abandon the gang bangers who Porsche had introduced me to during her parent-imposed exile from the City of Angels.

In the ninth-grade, I hooked up with Sandrine Fournier. Sandrine epitomized the muse who inspired the Commodores' song, "Brick House." We were together most nights. Our decision to hook up was unexpected. She was one of the gorgeous ones in our middle school, and our families were close. In short, I had great family networks. Still, like most ninth-grade boys, I was for the most part as innocent and naughty as a puppy—feeling the rumblings of manhood. On the verge of entering manhood, I wanted to avoid becoming a father and a negative parenting statistic. Most of the children in our apartment complex lived with their single mothers. They experienced many of the Moynihan Report's prescient concerns about the "tangle of pathology" in African-American households. These aren't conservative ideological observations. Even as a child, I felt that something wasn't right in Bay Vista. Without the consistent presence of healthy men, the young males in our projects were dying in stupid accidents, getting locked up, or being idle without a plan or guidance. None of us had the same father in our own home, and extended family members moved in and out of the house due to family crisis and parenting challenges. My colleagues in the 'hood had similar household configurations and household dynamics (i.e., abuse, domestic violence, drug addiction, neglect, and, on occasion, homicide). When it came to theories on African recidivisms shaping black family life, I was ambivalent. I didn't want to repeat what the teenage me perceived as other people's mistakes. Other people being Moms "and dem."

Moms always said that I was selfish. I thought one mistake was enough. She could have stopped with me, I thought. Yet, Moms was a free spirit not to be reined in by mainstream norms or conventional wisdom. Although I felt awed by the creative family networks around me and the more consciously "ghetto" or "ratchet" cultural sensibilities were beginning to emerge in the government housing projects in Southeast San Diego, I had never aspired to be a gangster nor have children out of wedlock. The burden of my illegitimacy seemed enough.

Moreover, Grandma's sacrifices kept me from getting Sandrine pregnant. She didn't seem to have many aspirations beyond going to the next house party or church. A rebel with a burgeoning bourgeois cause, I wanted to have elite class experiences before settling into a more traditional American family. I had not heard the term buppie, but their acquisitive avaricious and hedonistic sensibilities aligned with my vision for myself as a young adult. For that, I needed to seek teachers beyond the schoolhouse.

My transition to high school could not have come at a better moment. Unexpectedly, I went to three different schools. The first year was a blur at Clairemont High School. Clairemont is known as the school that inspired *Fast Times at Ridgemont High*. I began the same year that Cameron Crowe went undercover on campus. Fatigue set in sophomore year when I took long bus rides to another suburban school. The obligation to catch the bus meant that I didn't get enough sleep when I was growing into manhood. And more, we spent too much time on the bus. Transferring to the neighborhood high school seemed the best solution. By attending the infamous Lincoln High School—known as "Ghetto High" in San Diego—I had the good fortune to hang out with friends who were black Muslims, gang members, geeks, jocks, partiers, black preppies, and an aspiring pimp named Ricky. I absorbed what these guys taught me about fashion, pop culture, and how to "mack on" or court women. Because Moms was always working, our apartment became the after-school hub. But when we needed a car on weekends, we'd hang out with Mark's mom, Geraldine, and his stepfather, Crosby, who were schoolteachers by trade.

Our families were sort of related. I considered Mark a "cousin" because our mothers had a history. We were a "fictive family." Mark had returned from Buffalo, New York, where his mom had been in a black-centered graduate program in education. Geri had an unspoken commitment to the black community and racial uplift. Once returning to Southeast San Diego, she began to teach in an adult education program and spent days with the elderly in a community center. The ebony-toned Geri had a subdued self-dignity and quick-witted humor. A down-to-earth mentor, she took a personal interest in me and helped me begin to think about college.

We all bonded over chips and unlimited bowls of guacamole and Geri's chocolate-chip cookies at the Williams's house while listening to Bob Marley records. The Williams' had avocado trees in the backyard. Crosby seemed like a big teddy bear but was quite worldly. He'd been involved in community work. We were his captive audience. Before turning over the car keys, he would lecture us about community politics and how to survive the streets. But, of course, our teenage, Southern Californian world with its sun-kissed aspirations seemed much less political than Crosby's description of New York streets.

Nevertheless, I liked Crosby and paid attention. His street wisdom later kept me out of prison when I found myself in a sticky situation south of the border. Together, they created a safe space to have conversations about school, about what New York was like, and whether or not Prince was a "fag": a word Geri threw around to convey disdain, back in the day. As a sophomore, I sensed something else: fear. Most black mothers feared raising boys who might be into boys as much as they feared drugs or gangs.

On the other hand, one needed "understanding" to fully grasp Crosby's urban sermons. Often, we'd have heated debates about something trivial before taking the car out to find the party. The pre-party mental jousting reminded our gang to maintain a black consciousness and stay out of trouble. Moreover, the Williams prized our social gatherings. As an adult, imagining Crosby's condescending smirk as he leaned back against the refrigerator as Geri washed dishes in a sink filled with empty bowls, I can sense their love.

In our spare time, the fellas would go to Coronado and La Jolla to see how the other (better) half lived. Because we moved through different neighborhoods and communities, we had to learn to negotiate the geographic and social spaces between the Crips and the Bloods. Soon, we were explorers venturing outside the gang-ridden Southeast San Diego into Del Mar, La Jolla, Solana Beach, Hillcrest, and as far as the international border. During my high school years, I learned new things about the world but studied little in the classroom. Unlike me, my best friends were not into books. In the age of affirmative action, they did what they needed to do to get into college. It wasn't that my friends weren't smart. Instead, they used their bandwidth to learn about the alternative scene, youth culture, and pursuing the opposite sex. Without a doubt, my clique studied coolness. As buppiedom and yuppiedom became *très chic* in the 'hood, we'd school ourselves on our icons. Nile Rodgers and Bernard Edwards of the band Chic defined black elegance. Fashion magazines offered Larry Nash, Jason Olive, Rashid Dilworth Silvera, Mario Van Peebles Jr., and Charles Williamson.

While studying men's *Gentlemen's Quarterly* (*GQ*) was acceptable among us, Mark gave me crap for reading for pleasure. His father's people were educated, and he had a cosmopolitan uncle who belonged to a black ski club to coach him through things. Mark noticed my mispronunciation of words that I had only read but never heard. He'd give me crap about it. My high school reading interest consisted of pop psychology, fiction, and fashion magazines, both men's and women's, that I found captivating and glamorous. However, it might have seemed strange that a straight teenage boy would devour fashion magazines—during a period when I was, for some still strange reason, yearning for the perfect woman. In retrospect, the couples splashed across GQ's magazine covers embodied the beauty, refinement, and worldliness a young 'hood aspired to imitate.

Though I never talked to my friends about the women's magazines, I think Moms knew and thought it was peculiar. I wasn't the only one who longed for the perfect world found in architecture and fashion magazines, though. It was her magazines that I was perusing. She'd given me my first GQ magazine. One of my high school friends was a new dude from San Francisco, California. He brought a more cosmopolitan swag with him from the Bay. He carried the magazine around all the time. Norm's presence in our community suggested that heterosexual young men might be interested in fashion. The magazine communicated Moms's approval, I thought. She liked reading and enjoyed seeing the finer things in life, but it seemed that "life"—involving an abbreviated youth and young adulthood due to teenage pregnancy and an early divorce—had crushed her dreams. When Moms discussed life, she mirrored my great grandmother's approach to discussing soap opera characters as actual people. She conveyed the sense that Life was a person. Life personified was somewhat cold-hearted, sadistic, and transcendent. Her favorite well-worn saying was "Life is a tough teacher," implying that I'd learn this too and feel beaten down. As usual, I was ambivalent.

During my sophomore year, my other best friend Norman talked me into going to the movies to watch *American Gigolo*. The film starred Richard Gere as the protagonist and Julian Kay, an Armani-suit-wearing male escort, who drove a convertible Mercedes-Benz. Julian embodied the burgeoning hedonistic response to seventies decadence, the veneration of the finer things in life (i.e., status symbols) that defined the eighties. This sexual chameleon was our saint of all things cool. We hadn't noticed his sexual ambidexterity, however. At least, I had not.

In the evenings, I'd study GQ magazine while listening to the R&B group Chic, who represented an elegant black urbanity and worldliness. In my bedroom, I'd imagine myself a well-read and cosmopolitan black dandy who crossed class and cultural boundaries with ease. Norm and I would visit vintage clothing stores near the beach and on the edges of the gay community near Balboa Park. We knew that our outings might suggest risqué behavior—these adventures underwritten by curiosity, escapism, and an innocent hedonism. We had an attitude akin to fashion-worshipping rapper ASAP Rocky, who has been mislabeled gay. In our neighborhood, folks seemed suspicious of black youth who admired fashion. We were kind of odd, but some people liked our GQ swagger. All the same, we had other respected homeboys who were athletes, players, and formidable scholars. Leonard Blevins, Chris Jackson, Darren Lee, James Primus, and Edgar Sharp were notorious for their debonair style and prowess as womanizers. Our local icon was a Heisman trophy-winning convertible-Mercedes-Benz-driving running back. He, too, ended up on GQ's cover. Marcus Allen had come out of our 'hood and he was considered a straight player. My emerging ideas on self-reinvention flirted with an androgynous cultural refinement and subtle brawn. Consequently, I pushed past homophobic reactions to my interest in fashion and foppishness.

One evening during my senior year, Moms took me to a downtown bookstore by the seaside. A routine trip away from Southeast San Diego, this Sunday excursion wasn't a real anomaly. Our weekly Sabbath involved escaping our community to enjoy the beach, food, or window shopping. Something different was going on, however. I was down in the mouth about breaking up with a Naomi Campbell-esque cheerleader named Moe, who I had been "kicking it" with since the end of my junior year. Moe was a "to-die-for" feline beauty with creamy chocolate skin and a husky voice who was down for almost whatever. I thought we'd be the perfect partners in crime. She was a Skyline girl who embraced a wannabe-bougie attitude. Skyline was the mecca for bougie Negroes in Southeast San Diego.

Moe's family was a nomadic tribe of women moving together up and down the West Coast. We'd pet right in front of her mother and stepfather. We broke up two weeks before her tribe moved to Arizona. Moe's mother, however, convinced Moms to let Moe live with us. A complete disaster. The whole situation was straight out of a ghetto art film.

Moms probably thought that if I listened to "Gotta Broken Heart Again" on Prince's Dirty Mind cassette one more time, I'd slit my wrists. That night, she bought me Toni Morrison's Tar Baby. I chose the book based on the title and its cover art, which pointed to a tropical locale. It had a real eighties aesthetic. Yet, the name pointed to African-American folklore. I was intrigued. However, my young mind hadn't expected what I discovered between the covers. Morrison's writing was as different, subversive, and attractive as Prince's music. Reading Tar Baby was the first time I ever encountered someone who viewed the world as I did, someone with the heart to write on unspeakable acts. Morrison's prose floored me when I read:

He used to slip into her room and wait hours, hardly breathing himself, for the predawn light to bring her face out of the shadows and show him her sleeping mouth, and he had thought hard during those times in order to manipulate her dreams, to insert his own dreams into her so she would not wake or stir or turn over on her stomach but would lie still and dream steadily the dreams he wanted her to have about yellow houses with white doors. . . .[8]

I wondered how someone could write about things that I'd actually done, thought, and believed were crazy—things like describing eyes as being of the color "mink"—a vision I see and texture I feel whenever I think about a former girlfriend's eyes—and knowing what it's like to want to slip into someone else's dreams and to make your dream their dream. Morrison's other books would affect me as well. *The Bluest Eye* captured the sense of inferiority I had observed among bougie, 'hood, and suburban blacks. Because I'd also grown up under the narrative of white superiority and black inferiority, I got it.

*Song of Solomon* spoke to my unforgettable dreams of flight that I experienced from time to time. In these dreams, black folks sat around on small hills covered with glistening emerald green blades of grass. These folks sat waiting around patiently. My ancestors were dutifully waiting for me to learn to fly. It seemed like I could feel their patience and tolerance. I felt slow. It was painful. On occasion, a gust of wind would catch me, and I'd begin to set sail until the breeze gently sat me down. One night, it happened. I didn't have to wait on the wind, I just began to ascend of my own volition. I got it. Transcendence. Still, I digress.

*Sula* described boundless freedom and dangerous promiscuity that threatened the patriarchal notions of manhood that I had learned from Grandma. But it was *Tar Baby* that first gave utterance to my ideas about the black mind, spirituality, and the African-American literary voice. In retrospect, Morrison helped me find the strength to live with an unimaginable and unspoken existential pain. Her characters endured tough lives with audacity, ingenuity, and moxie. She wrote women like Grandma and Moms. Women with agency, laughter, stoicism, and strength. Morrison became my intellectual and spiritual mother. Without her, there ain't no me. But I am digressing.

In 1982, I entered San Diego State University, where I immersed myself in campus life and sexual trysts but found little substance or sustenance outside of my obsession with art, music, and words. I could never find these

8. Morrison, *Tar Baby*, 119.

interests all together in a single person. No one seemed able to immerse themselves into books, food, culture, *and* sex in the way that I did. It was always one side of things or the other. I tried to settle into a pre-medical program that wouldn't work out not only because no one encouraged me, but also because my white classmates insulted and mocked me. I had graduated from substandard high schools as a somewhat young and immature seventeen year old. I was gasping for air like the proverbial fish out of the water at a massive Southern California state college defined by football, Greek Row, and Mexican food. *Playboy* magazine ranked San Diego State University among the top ten party schools in the nation during this era. It appeared in the top three regularly. I'd begun partying at State in the tenth grade, however. As a college freshman, I was ready for books and culture—the life of the mind. Without a dorm room on campus, every day, I'd return to the suffocating environment of the 'hood, where no one seemed to be studying botany or chemistry. Moms watched me negotiate books, family businesses, parties, and street races. My head was spinning. Moms decided to give me a disheartening reality check. "You won't make it," she said. If she meant a college degree at the end of four years, Moms was right.

Eventually, I decided to take whatever courses seemed interesting to me, black studies, the liberal arts, the humanities. Where Moms saw futility, I saw civilizing possibilities. As winter term ended, I poured over the most interesting courses as I stood in the long snake-like registration line. When I turned in my registration card to the bougie-acting black girl who helped out in the registration office, her lips sadistically curled up around the sides of her face. She said mockingly, "Are you sure that you're pre-med?" It sounds pathetic to admit, but her rhetorical question stung. I suffered her crushing comment, along with others, in silence. Black masculinity, it seemed to me, required a modicum of stoicism.

During this period, I took courses with Maulana Karenga in African-American studies, Andrew Feenberg in philosophy, Robert L. Jones in creative writing, and Daniel Scarborough on the Harlem Renaissance and dance. I gave myself entirely to learning, working, exercising, and partying. It was a brief period of discovering who I was as a scholar and a human being. South African apartheid seemed like a metaphor for our lives in the United States as we discussed black identity and some students organized rallies. In Black Uhuru's song, "Solidarity," the reggae group distilled an awareness of unity based on shared human interests and captured the most nagging questions that I had about our moral obligation to other humans. Their simple songs evoked imaginations about our shared human wishes and grounds for solidarity among a shared human family. Theses lyrics led to questions that continue to haunt me.

My professors helped me change the way I saw myself and the world. While I received only a mediocre grade in Karenga's course, I became enamored with him as an authentic and self-defined black man (with a past)—his mind, passion, and organizational skills. Moreover, he and his wife, Tiamoya, paid attention to me. She'd comment on my ever-present smile without knowing that it was their humor and intelligence that made me beam. I felt their sense of mission and their efforts to impart their genius and commitment to the black liberation struggle to reappropriate an understanding of human dignity based on self-dignity and self-love. One day, Professor Jones surprised me by reading a Morrison-esque piece that I had written. My older colleagues were deadly quiet. Afterward, Jones told the class that my writing was worth stealing. The same year, Professor Scarborough, whom we called Danny, challenged me to surpass my limits. He'd dote on me and comment on my genius in our Harlem Renaissance course. I studied Langston Hughes until I became him. In dance and our literature class, Scarborough embodied freedom and self-love I'd never seen in my life. It was something I wanted badly for myself.

Even with this undeniable growth, intellectual and as a human being, I became disillusioned by my studies after realizing that I simply didn't have the resources to abandon myself to the life of the mind. That's an acceptable version of my thoughts. I was pissed. What was I thinking? Black kids from the 'hood seemed particularly vulnerable in our nation. Society expected us to be autonomous and accomplished adults too soon. We had to work to pay our bills, participate in our home life, and smash all our courses. Life was feeding me with a long handled spoon. I had other revelations as well. As I got involved in student organizations, worked on campus, and began partying with the other black, white, and Asian students, it became apparent to me that many of their families were committed to their success and had put financial resources behind their commitments. My colleagues could give their studies and college life their highest priority. In the pre-medical students' seminar, I didn't get the jokes or even know the novels the other geeks read for entertainment. On all fronts, my life was different. I had to work to eat grits, oatmeal, and rolled tacos.

The pre-medical students already possessed knowledge about the professional world. I, however, was just beginning to take it all in. In my young, to some extent entitled mind, these harsh realities seemed like more wrongs piled on a heaven's high heap of historical injustices. It began to feel like the odds were just stacked too high against me. Finally, I gave in. My mother was right: life was a severe teacher. I couldn't take it. Hanging out with some of the guys in Bay Vista apartments and Southeast San Diego, I eventually dropped out of school to sell cocaine. A long story that I hope to take up in a memoir.

When I became a drug dealer, I took an academic approach to the enterprise. I read books about cocaine—Freud's cocaine papers and other more scientific texts—and studied religion on the side of basketball courts while my homies talked trash to each other on the courts. Book reading led to a niggling existential angst I experienced due to my betraying an implied moral obligation to black people as defined by both respectability politics and a commitment to African-American people's well-being. I pushed past my conscience, however. Oddly enough, my redefinition of the old-school black nationalist "do for self" mantra informed my self-reinvention in pursuit of autonomy. I'd gone from Malcolm's "by any means necessary" to a mentality the rapper 50 Cent would capture in his movie *Get Rich or Die Tryin'*.

In no time, I had learned quite a bit about dealing drugs and, through my connections, began to move powder to the eastern seaboard. In DC, I hung out with the black elite and block boys from the go-go music scene. The local bougie college crowd, though smart, seemed mostly uninterested in the world of letters, black nationalism, or anything beyond conspicuous consumption—BMWs, $500 suits, fine dining, and their social lives. Everyone seemed into his or her own self-centered and anti-intellectual hedonism. Of course, there were exceptions and shades of gray. God seemed to send discerning individuals to tactfully prick my conscience into my life. I tooted powder with Pierre, a customer who had graduated from a name-brand college and a member of a black fraternity known for pledging pretty boys. He'd subtly insinuate that I'd given up on life, as though life still held out promise for me. Pierre was a sharp young brother, not your altruistic type by any stretch of the imagination. He got off on bedding his roommates' girlfriends. But his implied concern, in particular, made an impression. I didn't dare "go there" to reveal my doubts and vulnerability to guys "in the game" who hustled and dealt drugs. While I'd share my dreams and disenchantment with the dope game among associates after a couple of Long Island Ice Teas, I mostly kept my mouth shut.

The dope game had a way of removing the scales from one's eyes. During that era, I learned a lot from hanging out with veteran drug dealers, gang members, and pimps. Yet, while I wanted more out of life than money, pleasure, and the adrenaline rush from living on the edge, I still loved the curriculum one is schooled in when participating in street life. Here I'm reminded of the description of Satan in Genesis: "Now the serpent was more subtle than any beast of the field which the Lord God had made" (Gen 3:1). Like Adam, I learned that the tree of (street) knowledge was beneficial for intellectual development. My morbid fascination with the streets had temporarily distracted me from books. I'd mostly forgotten about the life of the mind, in the formal sense of the term.

A close friend came out to Washington, DC, for a visit. I met Mel and her friends when hanging out in the beer garden and missing chemistry at San Diego State University. I flirted with her clique while we sat people-watching and emptying cold pitchers of beer. Then, as the sun began to set, I decided to follow them to Dr. Scarborough's dance troupe. I had seen the troupe in the community. In San Diego, Mel had helped accelerate my career as a drug dealer by connecting me with Edward Abbot Martin, a fashionable inhabitant of Hillcrest. He, in turn, introduced me to a network of well-heeled gay men and women interested in acquiring quality cocaine. He was a curiosity. Eddie would explain that his father's wife introduced him to the finer things in life. More than anyone I'd met as a peer, he was into art, food, and music. He was built like a miniature African prince; Eddie was a quick study in Dr. Scarborough's dance troupe. When I'd visit for drinks and sales to his friends and lovers, he'd share his painting and furniture projects. He'd move from one gorgeous art deco apartment to the next. Eddie's core clique members were a real group of Neo-European Artist Funksters (NEAFs) with a few young gay cats from Southeast San Diego. This artsy and professional crowd fueled their endless partying with high-quality powder cocaine. In short, Eddie, a gay black man, was the coolest cat that I knew. Without a doubt, friends thought my business partnership in the Hillcrest gay community went beyond money. Eddie and a few other pretty boys had tried to move me in that direction. I was in control, however. It was the HIV/AIDS era. After dealing with light-weight STDs, I was deadly afraid of the risk that came with the mysterious disease. I'd, instead, choose the emotional path of Julian in *American Gigolo.*

Every week, Eddie tried to persuade me that he'd been celibate, which implied that I didn't need to worry about risks. He didn't know that I'd found notes on his door from his lovers. One night I arrived to deliver a package to find his art deco apartment dark except for a lamp set out in front of his couch. The artsy Hillcrest made the perfect setting for our film noir encounter. Eddie appeared as a svelte black panther behind the lamp, waiting to capture his prey. Flattered, I delivered the work and backed out of the scene. Early in life, I'd learned from an old head not to shit where I ate. I couldn't combine business with pleasure or even flirt with the possibility. My masculinity performance centered on a heterosexual-threatening foppishness based on a blend of gentleness, physicality, and warmth. I sought to convey the sense that you might not want to take my kindness for weakness. I was a vindictive soft dude with a quiet "I wish a nigga would" attitude.

Mel, a self-proclaimed "fag hag," had been the one to introduce me into the world portrayed in *American Gigolo.* She'd led me to Dr. Scarborough's dance troupe. I was four years younger than her. Mel tried to sell herself as the female homeboy. She is the first woman to give me the fist bump (or pound) and a bump of cocaine. She was the second to attempt to rape me. We moved beyond that, however. During Mel's visit to DC, she and I tooted Peruvian flake on stairs at the Smithsonian during twilight; she noted that I'd seemed less articulate. All that blow had dulled my wits, I guess. I told her about how her older gay homeboy Sir Marvin had laid some things out for me as he did my hair. Marvin had a "popping" or trendy beauty shop in Southeast San Diego. Although I had grown up with a hairstylist, it wasn't until I got "in the game" that I realized that beauty shops were like a vortex connecting the saints and sinners.

Car thieves, gangbangers, gospel singers, pimps, and street hustlers flowed in and out of doors at Sir Marvin's. Cocaine dealers as well. A few ballers (local drug dude and other "successful" outlaws) worked in the shop. While Marvin cut my flattop, we discussed my challenges in maintaining academic life at SDSU while clocking dollars in the streets. Marvin had been a lover of an underaged fashion icon in Diego, Jamie Nash. Jamie confessed that Marvin had introduced him to the fast life. Hence, I listened when Marvin advised, "You gotta piss or get off the pot, homeboy." I sat in silence. As an introvert, I didn't open up much in that space. Finally, he made it clear that I was at a critical juncture in my life.

Ironically, Mel had come to visit me when I lived in the shadows of American University, Catholic University, Georgetown University, and Howard University. At the time, I hadn't a clue about how I might pursue my growing hunger for the learning and literacy around me. As I traveled back and forth between DC and Los Angeles, the path toward becoming literate based on my self-defined path required being down with the streets and savvy enough to navigate the world of elites. The rapper Fabolous would capture it in his song about "the life" being so exciting; another irony being we used the turn of phrase to describe both the dope game and the gay world. Based on the conversation and space, "the life" was used as a double entendre. As a more synthetic thinker, I didn't see a compartmentalized world but a fluid and mutually constitutive one.

My friend Rock was still a student at San Diego State and a colleague "in the game" in California. Growing up as a bright and educated only child in Los Angeles, he had to learn to live by his wits. Something about him suggested that you might not want to let his baby face fool you. Rock was a sage street-corner philosopher who lived with two white Rastafarians on Mission Beach. He had a complicated life. Rock's dad had been a tennis hustler in Los Angeles. He'd fled the country after committing an act of violence against someone who owed him money. His father would show up on his doorstep at unexpected times for a visit. On the surface, Rock was a nerd. He wore round gold schoolboy glasses and could code-switch like no other. Yet, he'd seen a lot in traffic near Crenshaw in Leimert Park. Rock introduced me to some genuine gangsters. A few were considered family. In many ways, we were perfect accomplices. Going as "incognegro" as possible, I'd dress in the latest Giorgio Armani casual wear or Ralph Lauren tennis attire before we'd take my powder-white Renault Le Car on dope runs in the most dangerous areas in Los Angeles. No reasonable person would peg us as drug dealers.

In the beginning, I didn't do any drugs. Rock was the one who had been gung-ho about getting high. He admired that I didn't have the inclination to do drugs. I never suspected that we'd reverse roles one day. A master storyteller, one of his best stories involved young women passing out after inhaling crack from aluminum foil in their beachfront kitchen. He had looked at my sober lifestyle and decided to stop messing around with powder and crack. Now Rock was watching me plummet into addiction as a dealer. I could tell my addiction pissed him off. He'd held me in high regard. Based on first impressions, Rock believed in both my mind and humanity. It must have been my unwillingness to judge him. He witnessed my generosity in business when we went partying up and down the coast. I took care of everyone. Plus, he might have felt a tinge of guilt for ushering me into getting high on my own supply.

Rock knew that I loved him and our other homie, Maury Cole, as brothers. Cole was a street brother with an Oklahoman drawl that threw people off. By the time people found out he wasn't slow, it was too late. He'd introduced me to the game while watching baseball. I'd been broke, and he invited me to the apartment where he rented a room to watch a game that I hated. But I was broke, and the invitation included beer and roll tacos. He made $600 while pretending to watch the game, and I realized that he was either trying to make a customer or get me "in the game." He told me about being locked up in middle school. He'd met another kid who was Jamaican and Panamanian named Stuart. Stuart was his "connect" or "the plug." At the time, Cole was a part-time janitor whose daytime job was cleaning up the animal vivarium at Scripps and the Salk Institute for Biological Studies. Of course, no one imagined that Cole would end up working in a lab as a recognized scientist and contributing neuroscience engineer and eventually own the trademark of the term E-Vape. Cole taught me how to use the triple beam to weigh out and package the drugs. We started making tons of money and getting into lots of trouble. We were all "incognegro" in our code-switching identities and chameleon behavior.

Back in the day, I was known as a "pretty boy." When I approached Cole, I told him that I'd see a lot of women who snorted crystal methamphetamine. He talked to Stuart, who fronted me a package of meth, which I sold in less than a week, so he invited me to start selling "blow." We became a family. I'd sell blow to the gay men that I knew from the dance troupe at San Diego State and their friends. Once a week, Stuart would gather the fellas and snort mountains of powder. I didn't know it at the time, but these social gatherings turned me into a future addict. But at least it wasn't crack, I thought. Our situtation was like Tony Montana in the movie *Scarface* I got tired of Stuart overcharging us, so Rock and I began to find better prices in Los Angeles.

We pooled our money with Cole, and I'd drive my Renault LeCar up interstate 805. Then, one day, I ran into an old lover's brother who was a famous athlete. He'd told me about her new business endeavors in the game, so I decided to hang out in Los Angeles nightclubs until I found my petite friend, who was super sweet and notorious for "throwing them hands." We'd stayed cool because I had made a firm decision not to let her get me caught up, as she had so many brothers. The first time I connected with my ex-girlfriend turned kingpin, she was with her boyfriend in his old-school Datsun 280Z and holding a shotgun beneath an old blanket on her lap. I laughed. Gangsters were carrying semi-automatic firearms, and, as petite as she was, her gun of choice was a double-barreled shotgun. After that, I decided not to pay Stewart the money I owed him from Stuart "fronting me" cocaine. My old girlfriend and her new man had Peruvian flake at a better price. Maury and I had made him a ton of money anyway. But I had to avoid falling prey to Stuart's potential retaliation. So, I got two apartments to prevent his possible reprisals. I knew, however, he was too smart to shed blood over money. And we'd made him lots. Stuart went on to become a cop until an armored bank robber shot him in the infamous North Hollywood shootout at Bank of America. He then became an evangelist and moved back to Panama. But I digress again.

Whenever I'd fly into Southern California, I'd try to hang out with Rock. He'd invite me on road trips. In reality, Rock had a hidden agenda. He would hold me captive on these long drives to force me to listen to conscious reggae music. It was like throwing a glass of ice-cold water on a sleeping man. When I first began dealing drugs, Rock had drug connections in Watts and other 'hoods. We'd roll up to Los Angeles in my Le Car. At the time, he was into paper basing, that is, smoking marijuana and crack cocaine. I'd never been into drugs, but a friend from the local Kappa Sigma fraternity had introduced me to alcohol and then regular pot smoking.

As I entered the dope game, Rock encouraged me to avoid smoking crack cocaine. He'd fallen to its wiles and somehow gave it up. As I got deeper into the game, our roles were reversed. Rock watched me become a dope fiend. He hated it. Yet, I avoided smoking crack. I became a relatively brutish, ignorant, and depraved drug dealer. Ironically, he tried to help me with his self-styled Rastafarian approach. As he'd repeat the lyrics of the reggae artists' songs to me while I drank beer or cruised up the coast, he spoon-fed me life. Those prophetic words stimulated my conscience. I began to recall memories of my Grandma's stories about overcoming challenges in life. I thought about the delinquent homeboys in Bay Vista into black power and my teachers and schoolmates at San Diego State University. As the Rastafarians sang, that flood of memories created a hunger for more language of the same subversive nature to chant down Babylon.

Babylon signified the "complex of [Western] economic, political, religious, and educational institutions and values that evolved from the colonial project [leading to modern racism and structural violence against black people]."[9] My life was realigning with the African-American prophetic tradition's broader literacy narrative. Starving for self-knowledge, I'd visit a wealthy Jewish Rastafarian entrepreneur, Elliott Leib, who would spend afternoons reasoning with me on faith and spirituality—he had studied Rastafarianism at an Ivy League school. We discussed his research on the Nyabinghi. Then, I bought books from Elliott's shop to learn more about Rastafarianism. These books alluded to and quoted Scripture, so I found myself reading the Bible in earnest.

Encounters with the biblical narrative and the lives of dreadlocks changed me in person and in texts. This literature turned my challenges into an epic battle between spiritual forces, which required art, knowledge, music, and an ethics of love to overcome. The dreadlocks and their belief in "nommo"—the generative power of words—resonated with me based on my relatives' worldview. It was a cosmology Morrison wrote about in her books. In the process, I discovered that the brethren weren't simply pot-smoking outlaws, extras from a *Mad Max* movie set, social outcasts, or mere idlers. Rastafarians epitomized rebels with a cause. The new homies were intelligent and held to well-thought-out moral beliefs. These men valued family, deeply loved their children, and were street smart. I, too, wanted to become intellectually dreadful and terrible and a moral person. This process led to my developing my own brand of Christianity inflected with black

9. Edmonds, "Dread 'I' In-a Babylon," 24–25.

nationalism. I needed a clean break from my life "in the game," so I moved again. Leaving a new car at the airport, I removed my only bag from the trunk and flew to Seattle, Washington. While attending community college, trying and dropping out of university again, and traveling to Japan, I spent years reading black history, the Bible, and an expository dictionary filled with religious knowledge, listening to sermons on tape, and searching for biographies of great spiritual leaders. Without a doubt, I decided to do me. I began a process of embracing and integrating my many selves.

For reasons still unclear to me at the time, I moved from a strict black Pentecostal church to become involved in an all-white charismatic church under the shadow of another institution of higher education, the University of Washington. My new pastor, Ed, was a former businessman and wannabe hipster who liked jazz and gospel music. Within a year of my joining his church, we tentatively began a sort of surrogate father-son relationship. We'd eat great meals and finish them off with a raspberry cobbler and vanilla ice cream. Church leaders told me that I would emerge as a leader in the movement. But the unconscious racism and paternalism of the church members, including Ed, gradually became apparent to me. Even without the benefit of the scholarship on segregation in the American church, I perceived the racism informing our worship services.

Nevertheless, I hung in there. We had bonded, and the other options were dim. Ed was a stand-up guy, and my new faith community sustained me.

Ed would take me to a matinee movie along with his family on Christmas. One year, he providentially chose the movie *Good Will Hunting*. After watching the movie, it became clear that Ed, a film buff, had found the perfect picture to motivate us. Sean, his son, and I had dropped out of school one course shy of our undergraduate degrees. Although I didn't recognize it at the time, the film was prophetic. The protagonist is a twenty-something white guy who grew up in a foster home due to childhood abuse but is a self-taught prodigy drawn to higher education. Will Hunting works as a janitor at MIT, where a professor discovers his hidden talent for solving complex math problems and tries to point him towards the university. After getting into a fight, Will is forced into therapy by court order and placed under the math professor's supervision. Eventually, he leaves Boston's South End to pursue his girlfriend, who has just graduated from Harvard and is going to medical school at Stanford University.

Like Will, I, too, had been in court-ordered anger management. A detective in the gang unit claimed I was a sociopath because he had confirmed my past gang affiliation yet couldn't reconcile my middle-class attitude (or literacy performance) and polished answers with my upbringing in the projects and my criminal past. The evidence against his diagnosis was that I had spent five voluntary years in counseling for my childhood trauma. I worked in the financial aid office at a vibrant two-year institution in Seattle, Washington; everyone from the Seattle Central Community College president down to the janitors encouraged me to return to school. I had begun to recognize how I was becoming dull from hanging out with religious fanatics, which in many ways had stifled my humanity and curiosity. At the end of the movie, I knew that if I wanted to change my life, I'd have to follow Will Hunting's model and leave behind my hyper-religious and, alas, racist friends.

Unlike Will Hunting, I had learned in the streets that it's better to put a plate down slowly than to drop it suddenly. At age thirty-four, I held onto my community networks and enrolled at Bellevue Community College to run cross-country and study computer programming. Over a Christmas break, Pastor Ed confronted my doubts during a sermon out of the pulpit and said that I needed to run head-on into my undergraduate studies—this time at the University of Washington—with one aim in mind: graduation. He was persuasive. I vowed to give every course everything that I had in me. I thought that I owed it to God and myself to use the gifts and talents that the creator endowed me with at birth. From that point, I became single-minded about academics.

During my first term, I took a history of science course with a Tom Selleck-esque professor, Keith Benson. When I had attended San Diego State University, a professor alluded to the theological foundations of Isaac Newton's book on physics, *The Principia*. Benson encouraged me to pursue my interest. Within two years, he became a kind of Dutch uncle. I'd name my first son after him. Under his tutelage, I won several scholarships, and I gave a talk at the faculty club and a speech at a freshmen convocation. Our university president began to invite me to speak to benefactors on campus and attend social gatherings at the president's mansion, where I rubbed shoulders with industry captains. Benson supported my aspirations to pursue a doctorate. I graduated from the UW with a baccalaureate degree and then from Harvard University with two master's degrees. I returned to UW to enroll in and graduate from a doctoral program. Alan Brandt and Evelynn Hammonds, my advisors at Harvard, didn't think I could complete the doctoral degree.

Once back in Seattle, I returned to the art and music scenes and the church, and connected with my people in the street. The transition was difficult. I had crossed over into higher education, and both my academic and racial communities in Washington were skeptical. Former professors nagged me about my "Harvard gear." They assumed that I had pretensions to become a Northwest-fashioned Ivy League elitist. In my mind, my clothes did little more than signify the northeastern prep attire I dreamed about as a youth. Yet, at the same time, I might have judged my colleagues for wearing the ubiquitous bubble and fleece jackets and the REI outdoor wear one finds worn among the NPR-listening liberals and pseudo-socialist. The gear signals their granola-elite modesty and now techie-workforce membership in our region. Still, I was judged for moving to Queen Anne Hill—ten minutes from my job—where supposedly young girls named Bella and Sage played lacrosse and carried soccer bags with their names on them. Without a doubt, my well-off colleagues, who drove old Subarus and Volvos, were concerned that I'd join the ranks of the *nouveau riche*.

At the small private university where I work, administrators sometimes mockingly asked if I was wearing a "Harvard tie." Once the provost told me to hurry and take my tie off after introducing a national speaker in the chapel. These post-graduate school encounters define moments of ambivalence about literacy in the black male's experience. In brief, one plays the game in conforming to the myth of literacy to earn the social credibility and respect it promises. Grandpa Jack would say, "You're damned if you do, and damned if you don't." As contemporary black literacy narratives convey, there's a sense that one ends up catching flak for being a literate, credentialed, and earnest black man. At the same time, one is criticized for conforming to low expectations. More interestingly, my experiences reveal the lie in the literacy myth—the unfounded assumption that better literacy leads to progress regarding cultural, financial, and individual improvement. In brief, those committed to literacy as the panacea have not taken power into account.

I was straddling two worlds, speaking two different languages, a perceived outsider to both. At my private Christian institution, a set of liberal staff members gave me a nickname to describe my ability to attend graduate school, hold down a job, and support my family. A black colleague informed me that these coworkers spoke of my "black privilege," as though the academy had reserved for whites to attain academic and professional achievement in the Ivory Tower. Oh, the irony! They had no idea of the hidden tariff I had paid to work at a predominately white institution and similar graduate programs. These scoffers were dead set on undermining my love of learning and professional aspirations. They were unaware of the pot of beans and cornbread our family would eat week after week through the cold winters as we struggled to further my graduate studies and our children's educations.

On the other side, when I gave a talk at the University of Washington School of Medicine, an African-American student might challenge me. They'd ask, "Well, can you go back to the 'hood now?"—as though my

education had made me soft or weak and vulnerable, as though being literate had stamped me with an identity that those in the 'hood would reject out
of hand. "To speak of concerns beyond the block—something perhaps akin
to a cosmopolitan worldview in which one is seen as a citizen of the world—
is to risk censure from the tightly knit hood [mindset and] relations and to
raise suspicions about even more tight held convictions about what constitutes hood masculinities," according to Dr. Mark Anthony Neal.[10] Ironically,
when in the black community, I'm often made to feel that I need to come
off as a walking *Encyclopedia Britannica*. Friends and family members call
to ask me to define terms like "pandemic" and "virology." After answering
their questions, I suggest using a search engine in the future. I find myself
accosted by individuals who list off their own accomplishments and those of
people in their broad networks of family and friends. At times, I'm forced to
sit through boxes of pictures from week-long European vacations and other
events. At other times, I get seemingly random remarks: "You know, my
friend Tamara's son Jerome is working in Italy and learning the language?"
Or "Chanika's five-year-old son speaks fluent Spanish." When I go to community meetings, I try not to speak as if I'm in a graduate seminar; I choose
to use plain language. As a result, my intelligence might be questioned.
Blacks and whites might assume that I'm a product of affirmative action.
Of course, they need these accusations to cover up their own insecurities.
Even worse, on almost any occasion, a comment of mine can be interpreted
as condescending, leading to a silly fight that gets more volatile with my
increasing apologies. If others only understood that my education had been
more about a love of learning than the social competition. I mainly want to
be left alone with my books and bookish friends.

This existential reality (and mental space) is where I find myself
writing.

## Reading Literacy Narratives through Martin's Glasses

My study of black male literacy has led me to an unexpected question: Is
there something inherent in developing a personal canon of meaningful
texts and beginning to ascend the heights of literacy that, in and of itself,
creates ambivalence in everyone, but especially in black males? When I
stumbled upon *Educational Metamorphoses: Philosophical Reflections on
Identity and Culture*, Jane Roland Martin immediately brought me to consider ambivalence. Her thesis helped me to see it as an unavoidable part of
our stories as humans.

10. Neal, "Man without a Country," 399.

Martin makes three distinctions that can be used as tools for reading my literacy narrative. First, she distinguishes between education in a *narrow sense* and in a *broad sense*. In the narrow sense, education refers to what is learned incrementally through schooling; in the broad sense, it refers to the learning that happens in formal and informal settings, most of which has little to do with a planned curriculum. Second, she distinguishes between learning that adds incrementally to what we know (such as adding long division to one's arithmetic trove) and learning that amounts to recognizable "whole-person" transformations, the latter constituting a change so fundamental that it may leave one feeling in-between worlds, displaced, alienated. Third, she conceives any educational narrative (like a literacy narrative) as moving a person from being a "creature of nature" to becoming a "creature of culture," along a continuum that is limited only by time, opportunity, and choices. Using these three distinctions, she writes:

> Education [in the broad sense] has transformed almost every one of us from a creature of nature to a member of human culture. It discovers that a human life is a series of whole person or identity transformations brought about by education . . . because these great changes constitute crossings from one culture or cultural group to another, they tend to be fraught with alienation, inner conflict, accusations of betrayal, and anxieties about going home again.[11]

Martin stunningly captures what I believe I have discovered in my story and numerous black men's literacy narratives, both historical and contemporary. In the past, when I thought about my ambivalent feelings concerning being a black, literate male, I wondered if this might be an idiosyncratic problem, somehow reflecting my dysfunction or a deficit or even moral failing. Over the years, I have struggled to understand whether these tensions that have rendered me ambivalent are a function of my identity growing up as an underclass black male—an experience I wouldn't have had if I were white or affluent.

Martin helped me discover that feelings of inner conflict, alienation, and anxiety about "going home" are generally part and parcel of educational transformations. Her book provides a broader framework for rethinking the meaning behind the ambivalence in my literacy narrative. That is, if Martin is correct, then the tensions that constitute my ambivalence are not so much idiosyncratic as part of the unavoidable terrain of becoming educated or literate. Becoming literate consists of transformations that make "going home" impossible. It is inevitable that becoming highly, or even just academically,

11. Martin, *Educational Metamorphoses*, 8.

literate would put me at odds with those in the particular subculture of black men with whom I have had such deep connections. For me, Martin's conception of educational transformation is more than a professional academic fascination.

The following analysis is not constructed from theories and words that I have experienced with cool detachment. The tension between my literacy and my feelings of alienation from people I deeply care about sets me up for pain—a pain that feels personal. How could it be otherwise? The aching ambivalence that I experience is unavoidable so long as I hold onto both my literacy and my love for my brothers, who have chosen to reject mainstream (or "white") literacy. And so, under the regime of hip-hop, black males are encouraged to avoid literacy performances that might bring their manhood and sexuality under scrutiny informed by gangster or street masculinity.

Cultural theorists and educators have not grasped that a totalizing transformation in one's identity doesn't inherently mean a change in one's circumstances. Conceptualizing education as holding the potential to produce whole-person metamorphoses unveils something that the narrow sense of formal education measured by standardized tests can't address—namely, the "nodes" or "turning points" in our life stories. In these transformations, only emotion and cognition together can change lives. It is worth going back to underscore that Martin is *not* talking about schooling in which measurements focus on the incremental and cumulative learning of reading, writing, and arithmetic. Nor is Martin talking merely about gaining academic expertise in a way that reduces human beings to the cognitive. Instead, Martin sends us looking for the contexts, incidents, and situations to culminate in whole-person transformations.

The path to understanding these metamorphoses requires examining how the cognitive and emotional aspects of learning experience interact to either cause our students to reject learning or to catalyze shifts in their identities. I was working on writing my literacy narrative before I came upon Martin's theories. Since then, Martin has helped me understand why and how specific anecdotes have found their way into my story. She allows me to see that my sense that *I* mattered to Miss Jackson and that she wanted *me* to succeed has been crucial to my educational transformation, as was her organization of the fourth-grade curriculum. Martin helps me understand how my grandmother's loving attention could transform me into a boy who wanted to read and become a respectable man.

Let's think of life stories—here, literacy narratives—as consisting of educational metamorphoses precipitated by unforeseen events; then we are set up to discover unacknowledged tutors, concealed curriculums, and the power of emotion to promote or interfere with literacy aspirations and, more broadly, to transform lives. In reading my own literacy narrative in Martin's company, I can appreciate not just the role of Miss Jackson's caring and Grandma's love, but also the power of Crosby's "lessons" in the kitchen on Fridays and Saturdays and what it was that made them more potent and significant than geometry or history lessons in school. Martin helps me uncover the race and class conflicts that fuel the ambivalence I have felt about becoming academically literate, performing mainstream literacy, and living the middle-class lifestyle.

With these insights, Martin makes me want to return to the literacy narratives of black men that I've read before—men like M. K. Asante, R. Dwayne Betts, Paul Butler, Ta-Nehisi Coates, Frederick Douglass, Carl Hart, Randall Horton, Langston Hughes, Mitchell S. Jackson, Kiese Laymon, Nathan McCall, Darnell L. Moore, Wes Moore, Robert Peace, Bakari Sellers, Mychal Denzel Smith, Robert B. Stepto, Vershawn Ashanti Young, Thomas Chatterton Williams, and Richard Wright. These literacy narratives and memoirs connect me to other black males' literacy journeys. I want (no, *need*) to explore others' stories to dig myself out of my painful isolation. Moreover, Martin offers literacy aspirations as an important marker for educational transformation and ambivalence:

> Bringing into focus education's power to shape and transform our lives, it serves as a reminder that every single one of us undergoes whole person changes . . . some of them are educative and others miseducative, and that even the educative ones can be full of pain as well as joy.[12]

This statement encapsulates aspects of my story that I need to consider. My father's absence made me feel that he didn't care whether I even existed. When tears streamed down my face upon holding my newborn son, I felt simultaneous joy that he existed and pain in believing that my father had not felt that delight in me. Perhaps this is behind my perpetual struggle to be accepted and respected.

This same yearning for a father to accept me, respect me, guide me into a literate and authentic black manhood, also drove me into the classrooms of the street: to the homeboys, original gangsters, and older hustlers who "showed a brotha love" through their condescending inclusion. These guys gave me the experience and knowledge that allowed me to survive the emasculating abuse that I experienced in other settings. Thanks to their street education and formation, I was able to eat, become a man who

---

12. Martin, *Educational Metamorphoses*, 22.

developed courage and a self-defined sense of integrity, enabling me to endure the academy, the streets, and our racist society.

Moms, who hoarded fashion magazines and kept a cache of books on pop psychology in her closet, seemed to experience ambivalence regarding my aspirations to become a conscious, cultured, and erudite black man. Miss Jackson and Sister Jeanne took the time to teach the other students in our community and me. Their love was a catalyst for transformation. Of course, Grandma's traumatic experiences fueled my quest for knowledge. She grew up in the circumstances that interrupted her schooling, so Grandma hoped that I'd become a literate and distinguished man. Without a doubt, all these experiences have led to educational metamorphoses. At first, these educational metamorphoses felt exciting and positive. Yet, whatever direction I moved in, I also thought that I was becoming more removed from my friends. There was also a kind of painful "cultural crossing"—an agonizing departure, requiring choices between competing values. At the same time, these migrations weren't unidirectional. Because the literacy myth doesn't always culminate in permanent cultural and economic mobility, I had to code-switch across borders. More importantly, literacy was never about abandoning the black community.

Of course, in many ways, my story is the story of every human being reacting to circumstances and making choices. But as a literacy narrative, mine is that of a black male and, as such, needs to be placed in the context of black male literacy narratives.

The universe is transformation; our life is what our thoughts make it.

—Marcus Aurelius (AD 120–180)


Narrative is radical, creating us at the very moment it is being created.

—Toni Morrison, The Nobel Lecture in Literature (1993)

Los Angeles (c. 1970)

RSVP Nightclub, Washington, DC (c. 1986)

# CHAPTER 3

# Ambivalence in African-American Literacy Narratives

WHEN I THINK ABOUT ambivalence in literacy narratives in the black male experience or toward literacy more generally, I imagine an arc of uncertainty that begins its trajectory during the antebellum period with Frederick Douglass, an escaped slave and self-made scholar. As a child, he wanted to learn to read so badly that he broke the law, tricking his white playmates into teaching him to decipher the written word on the backstreets of Baltimore. Douglass recalls a period of severe inner turmoil in his narrative when, upon reading about the abolition movement, the literature opened his eyes to the horror of his position as a permanent slave in the racial caste system. His literacy-based awakening induced suicidal thoughts and a temporary yearning to return to a state of innocence, illiteracy, and ignorance.

Following the abolishment of slavery, the metaphorical arc continues to ascend through Reconstruction and into the Harlem Renaissance, where one finds ambivalence among both the black literati (such as Langston Hughes, Claude McKay, and Wallace Thurman) and the burgeoning black aristocracy (W. E. B. Du Bois and the black elites), all of whom attempted to redefine blackness. Hughes's struggle to publish poetry about underclass African Americans' lives in the Black English Vernacular is at the core of his first memoir, *The Big Sea*. This coming-of-age narrative describes Hughes growing up amidst poverty and privilege to enter the Harlem Renaissance as an acclaimed poet and student at Columbia University. Hughes experiences cognitive dissonance after receiving mixed messages from the respectable, middle-class and upper-crust members of the black literati.

Richard Wright's mid-twentieth-century *Black Boy* provides a striking representation of ambivalence. In his fictionalized narrative, Wright describes falling into depression due to his inability to identify with either the black underclass or the black elite throughout his myriad confrontations with those around him pertaining to literacy. For many black young men, the arc of ambivalence rises even higher following the civil rights era and the Black Power movements and then sweeps sharply upward again during the War on Drugs. The life narratives of Ta-Nehisi Coates, Wes Moore, R. Dwayne Betts, Thomas Chatterton Williams, Vershawn Ashanti Young, Mitchell S. Jackson, and Robert Peace reveal ambivalence regarding the implications of literacy for black manhood and their own identities. These writers came of age when respectable black social norms collided with the burgeoning criminalization of urban black youth and their culture. Before their births, a new generation of black nationalists emerged in the late sixties that rejected black respectability politics. The anti-assimilationist movement's leaders rejected arguments about black pathology as described in the Moynihan Report. Based on anthropologist Melville J. Herskovits's thesis on African cultural retentions continued existence in black culture, they drew on anthropological relativism to dispute ideas about "culture of poverty."[1] Although many activists in the movement embraced an implied aspirational black male patriarchy, many of these young black cultural activists and intellectuals promoted a countercultural black aesthetic, and, for them, African-American culture was adaptive, distinctive, and evolving.

During this period, the United States had initiated a War on Drugs based on re-inaugurating a "penitentiary rationality."[2] African Americans, once again, became the focus of a means of social control within the long genealogy of tactics used to incarcerate freedmen and force them into prison camps during the post-Reconstruction redemption of the South and the Jim Crow era.[3] Blackness intersected with a new epistemic regime using "crime as a metaphor for race."[4] William Faulkner argued as much in *The Sound and the Fury*, in which the neurotic Quentin Compson observes that he has "realized that a nigger is not [an actual] person so much as a form of behavior; a sort of obverse reflection of the white people he lives among."[5] Toni Morrison communicates the same understanding that what becomes explicit in this renewed social policy is the idea that "a nigger is

1. Gershenhorn, *Melville J. Herskovits,* 109.
2. Tucker, *Lockstep and Dance,* 7.
3. Tucker, *Lockstep and Dance,* 7.
4. Tucker, *Lockstep and Dance,* 7.
5. Faulkner, *Sound and the Fury,* 86.

not a person so much as a form of behavior."[6] Unfortunately, many urban African-American youths began to primarily choose as their inheritance the rebellious notion of blackness which they learned from the architects of black cultural nationalism. One can deduce from their masculinity performances the idea that resistance to domination informed the misguided belief that black authenticity meant embracing criminality, and gang life informed their wholesale rejection of conventional values.

In her book *Lockstep and Dance*, Linda Tucker argues, "The continuing problem of the color-line is perpetuated through representations that circulate within popular culture and map onto black men the image of criminal or the hybrid image of the criminal/clown."[7] On the one hand, in the broader culture "the white offender is considered the 'author of his act,' whereas the black male delinquent is seen as being connected to the criminal act by a series of innate traits and tendencies."[8] This mindset facilitates the "recoding of crime as blackness."[9] On the other hand, in the gangster rap culture, one finds the re-coding of blackness, using crime as a metaphor for race. The melding with the residues of cultural nationalism redefines authentic black masculinity. The distinguishing factors are anti-intellectualism, hyper-masculinity, violence, outlaw, and street status. According to Tucker, "This [definition of blackness] produces, teaches, and thrives on strategies that are necessary for survival within [penitentiary] institutions. The culture of violence then transfers to the streets, where the ethic of the street takes on the character of the rules by which one survives in a maximum-security correctional institution."[10] In the eighties and the nineties, gangster rap music embodied the internalization of the idea that *real niggas* embraced criminality and rejected dominant norms, including academic literacy and social mobility. "Understandably, young men of color often enter into hyper-masculine behaviors to combat the degrading effects of racism on their self-esteem. Since 'there is little diversity of images in the media culture,' there is great pressure to conform to the limited masculine ideals provided by the cultural media," according to Dr. Derek Iwamoto.[11] Thus, in the literacy narratives that emerged at the end of the twentieth century, we find the authors conflating criminality and black masculinity. We

6. Morrison, "Official Story," xi.
7. Tucker, *Lockstep and Dance*, 4.
8. Tucker, *Lockstep and Dance*, 8.
9. Tucker, *Lockstep and Dance*, 9.
10. Tucker, *Lockstep and Dance*, 4.
11. Iwamoto, "Tupac Shakur," 45.

also find that academic literacy became synonymous with being white, soft, and uncool.

Reading the literacy narratives of young activists, journalists, scholars, and ex-felons who grew up under the scourge of crack cocaine and after the golden era of hip-hop, I have discovered a different experience of ambivalence from my own. I find a group of young men who attempt to speak for their generation and describe growing up in a culture that rejected mainstream literacy as signifying deficient masculinity or blackness. I perceive the ambivalence about being black and literate intensifying for the children of hip-hop. Patricia Hill Collins hones in on the source in her book *From Black Power to Hip Hop: Racism, Nationalism, and Feminism*. She writes, "Coming to adulthood after the decline of the Civil Rights and Black Power movements of the 1950s and the 1960s, contemporary youth grew up during a period of initial promise, profound change, and for far too many, heart-wrenching disappointment."[12] This angst increases amongst this cohort of black men when upper-class members of the black community push for a greater emphasis on literacy, as seen in Bill Cosby's notorious "Pound Cake Speech" and Barack Obama's comments on black life made during numerous political campaigns.

## Frederick Douglass

By examining the ambivalence experienced by the erudite and prolific abolitionist Frederick Douglass (c. 1818–1895) one begins to perceive fundamental factors informing literacy ambivalence. Learning to read and write while still a slave, Douglass penned numerous autobiographies: *The Narrative of the Life of Frederick Douglass, An American Slave* (1845), *My Bondage and My Freedom* (1855), and *The Life and Times of Frederick Douglass* (1881). These narratives serve multiple functions. In one sense, they operate as extended abolitionist tracts that attest to Douglass's confidence in the written word's efficacy to battle slavery and racist thought. In a broader sense, as we will see, they testify to the transformative power of learning and acknowledge the role of human emotion in the educational process, including the connection between emotion, education, and ambivalence. Finally, Douglass's books reveal his inner turmoil and ambivalence about literacy in a much more subtle manner, particularly amid his transformation from a pre-literate and unaware child to a literate and conscious human. No one would have expected Douglass, born a slave, to write a memoir. The process of gaining the confidence needed to undertake this incredible feat

12. Collins, *From Black Power to Hip Hop*, 3.

began before he ever saw a book. Douglass spent time with loving grand-parents during his earliest years. The slave community esteemed the couple, according to Douglass. Until the age of eight, he was a "spirited, joyous, uproarious, and happy boy."[13] He believed that being a slave child had some advantages. The plantation system exempted black children from the challenges faced by both adult slaves and the white children who attended school as their initiation to society. Douglass described his life as "about as full of sweet content as those of the most favored and petted white children of the slaveholder"[14]—without the repression of strict social expectations or table manners.

Though he did have a certain amount of liberty, Douglass's childhood was not entirely peaceful as an unsupervised child on the plantation. Over time, he would learn the "sad fact" that everybody in his family belonged to "old master."[15] On occasion, this knowledge intruded into his tranquil childhood and left him with "something to brood over after the play and in moments of repose."[16] Yet, while "a chapter of horrors" portrays how little value white slave owners placed on black life, these torments did not keep Douglass from developing a sense of being cared for and loved.[17] Though his mother worked on a separate plantation, Douglass had a brief encounter with her that instilled in him a sense of human dignity and being loved, eventually giving him the confidence to learn to read.[18] One day, Douglass's caretaker, Aunt Katy, grew frustrated with him and threatened to starve him to death.[19] Coincidentally, that night his mother walked the twelve miles from her plantation to visit her son, arriving just as he was about to steal to satisfy his hunger. Handing him a piece of cake, she "read Aunt Katy a lecture which she never forgot."[20] Douglass reports, "That night I learned as I had never learned before, that I was not only a child but *somebody's* child."[21] The young boy's identity took pride in the fact the community esteemed his mother for her singular accomplishment: she was the only slave around who could read and *read* people. He writes, "I was victorious, and well off for the

13. Douglass, *My Bondage and My Freedom*, 145.

14. Douglass, *My Bondage and My Freedom*, 145.

15. Douglass, *My Bondage and My Freedom*, 143.

16. Douglass, *My Bondage and My Freedom*, 143.

17. Douglass, *My Bondage and My Freedom*, 199–205.

18. Douglass, *My Bondage and My Freedom*, 151.

19. Douglass, *My Bondage and My Freedom*, 154–55.

20. Douglass, *My Bondage and My Freedom*, 154.

21. Douglass, *My Bondage and My Freedom*, 155; emphasis mine.

moment; prouder, on my mother's knee, than a king upon a throne."[22] Although the origins of his mother's literacy are mysterious, Douglass credits her with providing a foundation for his "love of letters" and learning.[23]

The circumstances that enabled Douglass to become highly literate involved simultaneously receiving love, having the opportunity and leisure to learn to read and gaining a greater awareness of his position as a "nigger," a slave who was prohibited from reading. Around the age of nine, Douglass began serving the Auld family members in Baltimore. It's in Baltimore where he started to learn to read. Having not grown up in the South, the industrious Mrs. Sophia Auld had no inclination to treat Douglass like a slave but as a child "like any other child."[24] Young Tommy Auld offered Douglass companionship. And although Master Hugh Auld was indifferent to the boy's presence, he gave him an occasional smile. This new environment made a tremendous difference. Douglass explains, "I had been treated as a *pig* on the plantation; I was treated as a *child* now."[25] In other words, this care led to a further awakening of Douglass's humanity.

While Sophia Auld's tenderhearted gestures provided the emotional ground on which Douglass's literacy was built, Hugh Auld's interpretation of literacy's implications contributed to the young slave's ambivalence on the subject. Motivated by kindness, Sophia began to teach Douglass to read until Master Hugh walked in on them one day and ended their tutoring sessions with a cautionary lecture. He rebuked his wife, saying, "If you teach a nigger . . . how to read, there would be no keeping him. It would forever unfit him to be a slave."[26] Douglass recognized in this "philosophy of slavery" the naked truth about his unenviable condition, as well as a charge to resist this truth.[27] He explains, "[Master Hugh's] discourse was the first decidedly anti-slavery lecture to which it had been my lot to listen."[28] Hugh Auld clearly outlined the relationship between ignorance and enslavement, showing Douglass the pathway from slavery to freedom.[29] Auld's contextualization initiated "an entirely new train of thought" and set a process of change in motion. This immediate awareness was instinctual, writes Douglass. Shortly thereafter, he began to plan his path to educational freedom.

22. Douglass, *My Bondage and My Freedom*, 155.

23. Douglass, *My Bondage and My Freedom*, 155.

24. Douglass, *My Bondage and My Freedom*, 216.

25. Douglass, *My Bondage and My Freedom*, 216; emphasis mine.

26. Douglass, *Narrative of the Life*, 41.

27. Douglass, *My Bondage and My Freedom*, 222.

28. Douglass, *My Bondage and My Freedom*, 217.

29. Douglass, *Narrative of the Life*, 37–38.

Hugh Auld's "philosophy of slavery" affected the young slave boy in unobservable and unforeseen ways.[30] First, Auld unintentionally taught Douglass that enforced ignorance had created the context in which whites perpetuated slavery upon the blacks. According to Douglass, Auld had "underrated my comprehension, and had little idea of the use to which I was capable of putting the impressive lesson he was giving to his wife."[31] Reflecting on his impressions at the time, Douglass explains, "'Very well,' I thought. 'Knowledge unfits a child to be a slave.'"

As a consequence, the young boy developed an unquenchable desire to master the world of letters, stating, "That which [Auld] most loved I most hated; and the very determination which he expressed to keep me in ignorance only rendered me the more resolute to seek intelligence."[32] Prevented from learning at home, he developed a new plan—bribing his poor white playmates in the streets to be his teachers. He would carry a copy of a spelling book and bread while running errands. "This bread I used to bestow upon the hungry little urchins," he writes, "who, in return, would give me that more valuable bread of knowledge."[33] Douglass used similar strategies to learn to write. This knowledge would spur an understanding of literature that would dramatically alter his sense of himself.

Douglass developed a rapacious enthusiasm for abolitionist literature as he learned to read. Although his playmates had exposed him to apologetic anti-slavery tracts, the meaning of the term "abolition" seemed something his friends wanted to keep from him. He writes, "Here I was perplexed. I did not dare ask anyone about its meaning, for I was satisfied that it was something they wanted me to know very little about."[34] Naturally, this secrecy impelled Douglass to learn as much as possible about the topic. He began to study newspapers and eavesdrop on their conversations until he understood the terms "abolition" and "abolitionist."[35] Describing this political awakening, he writes, "The silver trump of freedom had roused my soul to eternal wakefulness. Freedom now appeared, to disappear no more forever. It was heard in every sound and seen in everything."[36] As one might anticipate, this burgeoning political consciousness began to torment him.

30. Douglass, *Life and Times*, 527.

31. Douglass, *Life and Times*, 527.

32. Douglass, *Life and Times*, 528.

33. Douglass, *Narrative of the Life*, 40.

34. Douglass, *Narrative of the Life*, 42–43.

35. Douglass, *Narrative of the Life*, 40.

36. Douglass, *Narrative of the Life*, 42.

In the beginning, Douglass mistakenly believed he would find relief in learning to read and in gaining more and more knowledge about abolition. The outcome, however, was more complicated. These educative agents promoted growth, self-discovery, *and* self-alienation. And the disparity between the concept and the reality of freedom had a distressing effect. In stunning prose, Douglass communicates the disruptive nature of literacy:

> As I read and contemplated the subject, behold! That very discontentment which Master Hugh had predicted would follow my learning to read had already come, to torment and sting my soul to unutterable anguish. As I writhed under it, I would at times feel that learning to read had been a curse rather than a blessing. It had given me a view of my wretched condition without remedy. It opened my eyes to the horrible pit, but to no ladder upon which to get out.[37]

Naturally, Douglass wished to relieve himself of this new knowledge and mental anguish—this deep ambivalence—but he found no means of escape. He writes, "I often found myself regretting my existence, and wishing myself dead; and but for the hope of being free, I have no doubt but that I should have killed myself, or done something for which I should have been killed."[38] Eventually, this despair would subside, though not the ambivalence, and Douglass would find ways to survive in slavery while bearing the knowledge of his condition.

## Martin on Douglass

While it is true that Frederick Douglass was committed to literacy from the time of his introduction to the world of letters, it is also true that the immediate impact of acquiring both literacy and a new understanding of the social order in the South caused him to question whether learning to read fit his station in life. These doubts emerged from whole-person transformations. Jane Roland Martin helps us to understand Frederick Douglass in two ways. Before his removal to Baltimore, Douglass had begun completing the transition from existing as a "creature of nature to an inhabitant of human culture."[39] Martin's framework on Douglass's experiences reveals that his ambivalence surrounding the subsequent educational metamorphosis resulted from a shift in identity without a corresponding change in

37. Douglass, *Narrative of the Life*, 42.
38. Douglass, *Narrative of the Life*, 43.
39. Martin, *Educational Metamorphoses*, 31.

his social status. With his introduction into the Auld home and his earliest engagement with the discourse of abolition at the age of thirteen, one finds two different metamorphoses at play in Douglass, culminating in ambivalence and anxiety.

As seen through Martin's lens, the familial care provided by Douglass's mother, grandmother, and Sophia Auld was the foundation upon which Douglass entered human culture and strove to solidify his place among evolved humans. As an adult reflecting upon his pre-literate state in childhood, Douglass describes his treatment as a creature of nature. He himself compares his earlier oblivious mentality and way of life to that of pigs or birds and animals of instinct. Yet, the love and tutoring of his grandparents and mother had clearly already led him beyond the awareness of mere animals. In Baltimore, further educational metamorphoses were to move him into a consciousness that set him exceedingly above the beasts. But it was the cumulative effect of the women's care in his family and Sophia Auld that was most transformative for Douglass. When he was a small child, his grandmother and mother began what Martin terms "the metamorphosis from nature to culture."[40] Douglass's slave status prevented him from entering the dominant culture like his white peers on the plantation. Still, Martin helps us recover evidence of the early stages of that transformation. His loving experiences with his mother and grandmother were seeds planted even before he describes being treated like a human child by his masters for the first time in Baltimore. After listening to and watching his mistress, Sophia Auld, read, he too longed to acquire that skill.[41] Her nurturing care and his maternal figures produced a transformation that ushered Douglass into white society.

Martin also renders visible the educational transformation leading to Douglass's momentary ambivalence regarding reading. One finds multiple educative "agents"—learning to read books, Hugh Auld's lecture, conversations with strangers, and abolitionist literature—intersecting to produce a profound whole-person change in Douglass. He explains:

> When I was about thirteen years old, and had succeeded in learning to read, every increase in knowledge, especially respecting the FREE STATES, added something to the almost intolerable burden of thought—"I AM A SLAVE FOR LIFE." To my bondage I saw no end. . . . I shall never be able to tell how sadly that thought *changed my young spirit*.[42]

---

40. Martin, *Educational Metamorphoses*, 28.
41. Douglass, *My Bondage and My Freedom*, 216.
42. Douglass, *My Bondage and My Freedom*, 224; emphasis mine.

Martin helps us recognize the acute identity crisis provoked by Douglass's experience with reading abolitionist literature that exposed his social condition. Whereas educational metamorphoses are generally assumed to be for the individual's betterment, Martin argues that "the idea of education applies to new states of being whether good or bad, beneficial or detrimental."[43] Douglass could not have predicted that decoding words and reading the Bible would lead to despair. Martin calls us to see that one cannot predict the outcome of such transformative educational experiences.

With Martin as an interpretive guide, Douglass can be said to have undergone two metamorphoses—from a creature of nature to a creature of the dominant culture; from a seeker of knowledge as an adolescent to a politically conscious young man. These educative agents and metamorphoses conspired to induct him into a whole new state of mind, leading to a crisis. The most apparent catalysts for these transformations involved his learning to read and gaining political knowledge—changes that made the world appear as an entirely new place. Martin compares educational transformations to shifts in perception, a movement from one way of being in the world to another. "Changes in a scientist's perceptions make the world look different," she explains. "Although [his] former world may look the same to everyone else, [his] new ways of thinking and acting and feeling make it an unknown territory for [him]."[44] Although Douglass did not experience social mobility, nor was he an immigrant being introduced to a new nation or culture, the pain of estrangement he describes resonates with descriptions of immigrants to the United States and African Americans in the twentieth century whom Martin describes in her book.

Martin helps us understand that while the popular conception of education is one of an acquisition that brings only good with it, learning to read and, through it, learning about the world beyond the Auld household and slave condition created pain for Douglass. She writes, "Despite the fact that many of the finest educational thinkers the West has known have stressed the ideas of growth and development and the fact that these notions tend to imply improvement, this is not so."[45] Martin is not arguing that our approach to education leads to trauma, but instead, she encourages educational thinkers to perceive the potential land mines. Education can lead to developing new skill sets and knowledge. But students may also experience miseducative people, settings, and institutions. Martin draws on "case studies . . . filled with reports of [the] pain and suffering" to uncover

43. Martin, *Educational Metamorphoses*, 20.
44. Martin, *Educational Metamorphoses*, 20.
45. Martin, *Educational Metamorphoses*, 19.

cultural nomads and of educational migrants, who describe feeling freakish in their educative settings.[46] During the Antebellum period in the United States, a literate slave boy was nothing less than an aberration. The cognitive dissonance of that revelation led to Douglass's bout with despair. Nevertheless, he eventually came to accept his ambivalence in such a way that it was no longer disabling.

## Langston Hughes

Langston Hughes (1902–1967) is the sole African-American author to capture the Harlem Renaissance's history in a firsthand account laid out in his memoir, *The Big Sea*. During this episode in African-American history, many Americans embraced black Southerners' culture. These late Exodusters rode the "chicken bone express" up North to escape the unpredictable racial violence occurring in the South. Hughes's modern approach to poetry was central to the younger generation of African-American artists, poets, and writers. To the chagrin of the black cultural elite, Hughes and other black moderns sought to recognize the Black English Vernacular's beauty and represent the lives of African Americans from different class backgrounds. The established black literati reveled in imitative literature. While the young Turks encountered resistance from respectable black leaders, both in the arts and in politics, in the end, Hughes and other writers like him prevailed. When the National Association for the Advancement of Colored People awarded him its highest honor, the Spingarn Award, the elite black community acknowledged Hughes as the poet laureate of the Negro. Although Hughes is praised today as America's first jazz poet, our collective historical amnesia impedes our recognition of the inner conflict and social turmoil he endured for daring to portray black folk's lived experience in the black vernacular.

Hughes wrote one of the most memorable poems in African-American history, "The Negro Speaks of Rivers,"[47] while traveling as an angst-ridden teenager on a train headed to the Mexican border shortly after graduating from high school. By birth, Hughes was a member of the African-American aristocracy. However, due to his parents' divorce, he often felt like a pawn whose life's circumstances moved between the two worlds of poverty and affluence. His mother wanted him to abandon his aspirations to attend college at Columbia. He writes, "She demanded to know how I would look

46. Martin, *Educational Metamorphoses*, 120.
47. Hughes, *Big Sea*, 53–56.

going off to college and she [was] there working like a dog!"[48] On the other hand, his father's effort to re-establish a relationship had brought with it the possibility that he would financially support the young Hughes throughout his college career. The decision to pursue his academic dreams left Hughes feeling anxious and ambivalent about leaving his mother behind to visit his father in Mexico.

In addition to the unease of being pulled between two worlds, Hughes experienced additional inner agitation during the trip—agitation related to his father's rejection of African Americans. According to Hughes, he wrote best when depressed, and his mother's guilt trip and father's internalized racism provoked him to write. He writes, "[The poem] came about in this way. All day on the train I had been thinking about my father and his strange dislike of his own people. I didn't understand it, because I was a Negro, and I liked Negroes very much."[49] Hughes admired the black soldiers who had fought in the Great War and the poor blacks he encountered in the city, escaping poverty, lynching, and disenfranchisement in the South. He thought they were "the gayest and the bravest people possible."[50] Under the shadow of divergent parental agendas and conflicting racial ideologies, Hughes penned a poem that traced the black experience by imagining the rivers that ran through Africa and the American South. Although he had grown up a black child in poverty, the poem marked him as a literary prodigy.

Growing up poor had not kept Hughes from experiencing the arts and culture. His ancestral, historical, and childhood connections to the arts and letters shaped his views on literacy. John Mercer Langston, his great uncle, was an author, congressman, and the first US ambassador to Haiti. While growing up, Hughes was aware that some of his more affluent Langston family members were still in "society."[51] In contrast, he and his mother lived a poor and solitary life in Topeka, Kansas.

Nevertheless, Hughes's mother arranged outings that exposed him to literary events. He explains, "My mother used to take me to see all the plays that came to Topeka like *Buster Brown*, *Under Two Flags*, and *Uncle Tom's Cabin*. We were very fond of plays and books. We once heard Faust."[52] His mother also got involved in the fine arts, giving dramatized readings at a literary society founded by her father.

48. Hughes, *Big Sea*, 53.
49. Hughes, *Big Sea*, 54.
50. Hughes, *Big Sea*, 54.
51. Hughes, *Big Sea*, 13.
52. Hughes, *Big Sea*, 15.

Lacking the resources to support her child, Hughes's mother sent him, when he was six years old, to live in Lawrence, Kansas, with his debt-burdened, underemployed grandmother. He spent a long, unhappy period with her. The grandmother sustained them with meals consisting of wild greens and salt pork and visits to the library. He writes, "Then it was that books began to happen to me, and I began to believe in nothing but books and the wonderful world in books—where if people suffered, they suffered in beautiful language, not in monosyllables, as we did in Kansas."[53] Books helped assuage the young boy's despair over his poverty. Hughes reveals, "The silence inside the library, the big chairs, and long tables, and the fact that the library was always there and didn't seem to have a mortgage on it, or any sort of insecurity about it—all of that made me love it. . . . After a while, there came a time when I believed in books more than in people—which, of course, was wrong."[54] Literacy and libraries offered Hughes a haven from the intolerable as a child. But as he matured, he found that books were insufficient buffers from reality.

While attending Columbia University in New York City, Hughes began to face pressures that made him lash out at his books. He found the cost of living in the city prohibitive and his studies uninteresting. When his mother left Cleveland to join him in New York, Hughes felt obligated to support her with his allowance and tuition money. He tried to escape into the arts and books, writing, "What an unpleasant winter! I didn't like Columbia, or the students, or anything I was studying. I went to shows, read books, [and] attended lectures."[55] The disappointing distance between Hughes's lived reality, and the world of books created a profound ambivalence in the young writer. Unable to reconcile himself to those realities, Hughes made the drastic choice to drop out of school and he eventually found work as a sailor.

Before launching out onto the high seas, Hughes returned to Harlem to collect his books for the voyage. But upon returning to the boat, he found himself disillusioned with his valued and valuable books. He writes, "They seemed too much like everything I had known in the past . . . like life isn't, as described in romantic prose."[56] Hughes's aversion was provoked by multiple associations related to personal autonomy:

> The memory of my father, the poverty and uncertainty of my mother's life, the stupidities of color-prejudice, black in a white

53. Hughes, *Big Sea*, 16.
54. Hughes, *Big Sea*, 16.
55. Hughes, *Big Sea*, 85.
56. Hughes, *Big Sea*, 98.

world, the fear of not finding a job, the bewilderment of no one
to talk to about things that trouble you, the feeling of always
being controlled by others—by parents, by employers, by some
outer necessity not your own. All those things I wanted to throw
away. To be free of. To escape from. I wanted to be a man on my
own, control my own life, and go my own way. I was twenty-one.
So I threw the books into the sea.[57]

The act was cathartic. "It was like throwing a million bricks out of my heart,"
he writes, "for it wasn't only the books that I wanted to throw away, but
everything unpleasant and miserable out of my past...."[58] Books could not
provide the insights into everyday life that he needed, nor the strength to
survive his adversities. Hughes sought a liberation that books couldn't offer
him. He would travel the world to become his own man. He'd also developed a discomfort with writing due to the black elites' critiques of his unvarnished portrayal of black folk language and life. For now, it's enough for
the reader to acknowledge that during the 1920s, a highly literate Langston
Hughes developed ambivalence toward reading.


## Martin on Hughes

Martin's conception of educational metamorphoses casts this sort of transformation as a product of a chronology of changes in a person's life. This
idea reveals intersections among multiple educational agencies and political
awakenings in his coming-of-age narrative. His earliest stirrings toward literacy came from hearing stories from his grandmother. He writes, "She sat
... in her rocker and read the Bible, or held me on her lap, and told me long,
beautiful stories about people who wanted to make the Negroes free."[59] We
should note here the political content of his grandmother's lessons. The message of black solidarity is a political one that he imbibed and never forgot.
With great care and a deliberate introduction to human culture, Hughes's
grandmother and mother conducted him through the gateway that divides
nature and human culture. Literacy clearly constituted a transformational
change in Hughes's life, one he refers to elsewhere as books "happening" to
him.

The Big Sea reveals how life experiences produce transformations not
as single events, but as a series of conversions. During his formative, childhood, and young adult years, Hughes underwent a political shift that would

57. Hughes, Big Sea, 16.
58. Hughes, Big Sea, 16.
59. Hughes, Big Sea, 17.

have remained invisible had it not been for his active reflection on the difference between his and his father's views on African Americans. Writing
"The Negro Speaks of Rivers," the young author drew on his connection to
the emancipation of slaves and his historical knowledge, linking the past
bondage of slavery and the irony of black soldiers fighting for democracy in
Europe during the Great War, only to return to Jim Crow conditions in the
South and segregation in the North. This burgeoning social awareness informed his developing political imagination. Meditating on the Mississippi
River and slavery in the Deep South, the Civil War, and black history prior
to the slave trade, Hughes wrote his most-recognized poem, manifesting his
anxiety over his father's stance on African Americans and black life in the
United States.

This literary artifact is a gem of the Harlem Renaissance and a representation of a political transformation taking place within Hughes and
the broader African-American culture. Historians have begun to examine
the military involvement of African-American men in search of the seeds
of political change, the kind of metamorphosis Martin describes in her exploration of the movements that emerged out of the identity politics of the
sixties and the seventies. She argues that while the political efficacy of those
movements is uncertain, "it is beyond dispute that many individuals who
came under their sway were radically transformed."[60] For Martin, change in
political identity is a form of educational transformation unrelated to party
politics or government action. Through this claim, she expands the definition of politics just as she does education. Emphasizing the relationship
between the personal and the political, Martin examines the transformation
of philosopher Sandra Bartky as a case in point, explaining, "the change of
identity that Bartky described involves understanding power relationships
at home and in the world, perceiving that what seem to be idiosyncratic
shortcomings might be systematically related to gender roles and stereotypes. . . ."[61] I have pointed out that Hughes began to receive a political
education on his grandmother's knee. But it was as a young adult coming
of age in the era of modern nationalism that Hughes experienced a political
transformation that altered his understanding of literature. In making the
connection between his father's racial ideas and the sociopolitical reality of
blacks in the United States, Hughes responded with a cultural intervention
just as political as involvement in social activism. He began to meld black
language and history together to reflect an educational transformation with
political repercussions. For the rest of his writing career, his work would

60. Martin, *Educational Metamorphoses*, 106.
61. Martin, *Educational Metamorphoses*, 107.

engage this ambivalence in mainstream American and African-American culture and politics.

Martin considers several other factors in her perception of what stimulates educational metamorphoses. One category involves the "events in the life cycle, personal traumas, professional training, political movements, migration from one country to another, changes in one's class position: representing occasions for [whole-person] transformations."[62] Hughes points toward adulthood and independence when he writes, "All those things [that restricted me] I wanted to throw away. . . . I wanted to be a man on my own, control my own life, and go my own way. I was twenty-one."[63] These feelings were incited by his setting out on his own. He tied his younger, less mature, less independent self to books. Hughes's response to narrow definitions of functional race performances stemmed from the conflict between his new emerging self and his long-held ideals about the meaning of literacy. Because his literacy was not creating a space of freedom, comfort, or eloquent suffering, he threw his books into the sea.[64] After living a life distinguished by focusing on books and words as companions, Hughes moves to attend Columbia University, an ideal reservoir of knowledge; his life-long literacy pursuit culminates in a shattering revelation. He realizes that he cannot find the knowledge and wisdom needed to transcend his circumstances in classrooms and libraries. Consequently, Hughes becomes a seaman and launches out onto the open sea to travel abroad and then make a his return to his literacy aspirations after gaining some independent life experiences.

## Ambivalence in the Age of Hip-Hop

In their respective times, Frederick Douglass and Langston Hughes dealt with ambivalence related to their aspirations to literacy and the educational metamorphoses that followed in the wake of their burgeoning erudition. These whole-person transformations had repercussions for each man's understanding of himself, his kinsmen, and society. The personal had political implications and vice versa. In our post-civil rights era, the notion that many young black men experience ambivalence regarding mainstream literacy permeates our cultural consciousness. Many of the current debates about literacy, cultural critics, educational theorists, and popular commentators would argue that rap music and hip-hop culture are the culprits. But when reading the literacy narratives of Vershawn Ashanti Young, who grew

62. Martin, *Educational Metamorphoses*, 66–67.

63. Hughes, *Big Sea*, 98.

64. Hughes, *Big Sea*, 98.

up in a poor urban setting, and Thomas Chatterton Williams, who grew up in a white suburban community, we must be willing to expand our understanding of literacy to validate the Black English Vernacular along with Standard English. Martin calls us to see that education must be understood in its broadest sense, including its unpredictable and miseducative aspects. Regardless of the language, to understand learning-based transformation, these men's stories about their struggles with literacy make it clear that growing up as a black male in a race-conscious society occasions culture crossing—intersections that inevitably provoke ambivalence. Such is the nature of transformation.

## Vershawn Ashanti Young

Vershawn Ashanti Young's "autocritography," *Your Average Nigga: Performing Race, Literacy, and Masculinity*, tells the story of a young English professor who experiences a high level of ambivalence and anxiety about speaking Standard English.[65] Young's personal story presents a picture of how gendered and racialized literacy binaries have led him and others to develop what he calls an "enforced educational schizophrenia."[66] He attributes his love of reading to his mother, who pursued her undergraduate and graduate degrees as a single parent. Even as a child who was interested in the world of books, Young experienced frustration dealing with teachers and administrators who, he reports, did not know how to support an underclass black male child who was trying to acquire academic literacy.

Growing up in the infamous Henry Horner Homes in Chicago, Illinois (where Alex Kotlowitz did the ethnographic work for his book, *There Are No Children Here*), Young describes himself as an anomaly in his community. He writes that his overprotective mother was afraid of violence, so "she locked the ghetto out. She told us not to get too close to it when it walked the streets or wanted to visit, reeking of alcohol or drugs."[67] Young continues, "My identity, however, was atypical, alienating me from my neighbors and 'hood and excluding me from representations of 'authentic' ghetto life. Thus, I didn't have to fight to get out of the ghetto. I was kicked out."[68] The strange behavior that led to Young's exclusion by his ghetto neighbors included reading books. The behavior in question resulted in inner confusion and betrayal, feelings on both sides of the equation based on his erudition

65. Young, *Your Average Nigga*.
66. Young, *Your Average Nigga*, 99.
67. Young, *Your Average Nigga*, 23.
68. Young, *Your Average Nigga*, xvi.

or his acting like a "faggot."[69] As a child, Young experienced an evident, palpable tension between his being black and being literate, a strain created by moving between the ghetto and his middle-class school.

On a trip back to the Horner projects as an adult and college professor, Young recalls the context of his unusual literacy. His Jehovah's Witness mother had gone to school to study sociology and become a registered nurse. Thus, he grew up in a house filled with medical, academic, and religious books. In the fourth grade, he read Franz Kafka's *Metamorphosis*. Too young to follow the story, his teacher and principal chastised Young for trying to convince his classmates and instructors that human beings could turn into insects.[70] Feeling alienated from everything outside his apartment—including his peers, teachers, and school administrators—Young, like Hughes, viewed books as his companions. Eventually, he moved beyond both the ghetto and public grade school to enter the world of academia. Yet, his ambivalence only increased in adulthood.

Young writes that he experienced anxiety as a college professor attempting to negotiate both the world of black males who were committed to the "cool pose" and ghetto blackness, on the one hand, and the world of the academe, on the other. For example, Young describes a trip to a barbershop on the black side of Cedar Rapids, Iowa.[71] He leaves his mostly white campus at the University of Iowa, where he is an English professor, on a mission to "get that fresh bald fade, one of the trendiest hallmarks of black masculinity."[72] Once inside the barbershop, Young finds himself intimidated by black men interacting according to street or hip-hop protocol standards. Their conversation, attire, and communication have an unsettling effect on him.

Although he lives in Cedar Rapids, Iowa, Young believes that the brothers in the barbershop carry themselves according to an unarticulated ethos defined as ghetto blackness. He has brought a book along but is concerned that reading it in front of the other men might create misperceptions about his blackness and masculinity. He explains, "Literacy habits . . . have always made me seem more queer, more white identified, and more middle class than I am."[73] Pondering his dilemma, he writes:

> I'm an English professor; that justifies my reading a novel in a barbershop. And what's this nonsense of trying to fit in, to avoid

69. Young, *Your Average Nigga*, 9.

70. Young, *Your Average Nigga*, 30.

71. Young, *Your Average Nigga*, xii.

72. Young, *Your Average Nigga*, xi.

73. Young, *Your Average Nigga*, xii.

alienation, to avoid name-calling: "Sissy!" "Faggot!" But I wonder: What does not fitting in cost me? This issue of trying to fit
in but never succeeding, of being perpetually on the margins of
various communities and never finding a way into any one of
them, is the trope of my life, making me something of a black
Sisyphus. Academic literacy is a heavy rock.[74]

Young experiences anxiety because of his need to connect with ghetto-
identified black men and to find a place to maintain expectations for black
male grooming, in Cedar Rapids, of all places, and to gain their respect, but
at the same time, he wishes to transcend his race:

To embrace my blackness, my heritage, my manliness, I identify
with men who represent the ghetto. I no longer want to deny
my class background or the racial experience associated with it.
I identify to belong. I disidentify to escape racism, to avoid the
structures that oppress black men—to punish them for what I
perceived as their efforts to disown me. This ambivalence pro-
vokes me to imitate and just as often to dissociate from the black
men I envy. Both efforts fail. Neither alleviates my racial anxiety.
Instead, they heighten the angst I experience. As a result, I am
hyperaware of how masculine I am (not) and how black I (don't)
act.[75]

In the end, Young wants to perform a black masculinity that tells the world
that he, too, is a "black male with balls."[76] Throughout *Your Average Nigga*,
he continues to share the varied contexts in which he experiences ambivalence and anxiety around his literacy performances (both black and white).
Most importantly, Young attempts to resolve this anxiety by advocating a
theory that allows students to "code-mesh" Black English Vernacular with
Standard English.

## Martin on the 'Hood, Hip-Hop, and Literacy

Martin argues that educational transformations make us all cultural "immigrants" and that such whole-person changes unavoidably, in some measure,
create anxiety and pain for the person so transformed. Thus, it's not surprising that, as a child who regarded books as companions, Young would read
Kafka's *Metamorphosis*, a tale of an isolating and painful transformation.

74. Young, *Your Average Nigga*, xv.
75. Young, *Your Average Nigga*, xii.
76. Young, *Your Average Nigga*, xii.

His misreading leads to in-school encounters that unmask Young's angst-driven educational metamorphosis with its unexpected ambivalence. He feels adrift as a perpetual cultural, geographic, and institutional wayfarer. Martin notes, "When educational metamorphoses are seen as culture cross-ings and culture is defined broadly, just about everyone who undergoes an educational metamorphosis can be said to be an [educational] immigrant."[77] While most actual immigrants seek to settle in a new land, Young is more like a ceaseless nomad without a home. The life of the perpetual migrant is one of alienation and calamity.

In this instance, Young enables us to postulate that, should one begin to understand that ambivalence is part and parcel of any educational trans-formation, then perhaps one could learn to expect, but not be overwhelmed by, alienation and calamity. In Young's case, Martin allows us to see how the life of the culture crosser is one of migration. The term "migration" implies movement that disrupts. Citing literature on American immigrants in the twentieth century, Martin writes, "The immigrants lived in crisis . . . because they were uprooted and because it was so difficult to adapt to the new condi-tions and challenges in the land they were entering."[78] Some have described this experience of immigration as being born again and developing a hyper-awareness of oneself. Martin relates the situation of an African-American professor from Harlem. His colleagues at a California university expect him to relinquish his personality and to take on a less threatening persona. According to Martin, this scholar exemplifies the culture crosser's anxiety about belonging, just like earlier immigrants to the United States.

Similarly, Young's narrative is replete with indicators of both am-bivalence and anxiety about fitting into both African-American and the dominant culture. When the courts struck down the barriers that excluded African Americans from the mainstream workforce, the cultural assimila-tion model defined the pathway to success for social-striving blacks facing laissez-faire racism, a new form of racial ideology, emerging in the fifties and sixties, to defend white privilege:

> Laissez-faire racism . . . blames blacks themselves for their poorer relative economic standing, seeing it as a function of perceived cultural inferiority. This analysis of the bases of laissez-faire racism underscores two central components: con-temporary stereotypes of blacks held by whites, and the denial

77. Martin, *Educational Metamorphoses*, 80.
78. Martin, *Educational Metamorphoses*, 80.

of societal (structural) responsibility for the conditions in black communities.[79]

According to Young, African Americans who assimilate or "act white" enact the new form of passing for white, a performance undertaken by earlier generations of fair-skinned blacks.[80] However, light-skinned blacks and whites have sought to pass for black. In *Life of William Grimes: The Runaway Slave*, the author claims that "he is about 40 years of age, that he is married to a black woman, and *passes for a negro*, though three parts white."[81] The act of migrating across the color-line isn't always voluntary. "Racial Passing is an exile sometimes chosen, sometimes not," according to Stanford historian Allyson Vanessa Hobbs.[82] Autobiographies and stories detailing racial concealment reveal profound psychological distress.

Following the civil rights era, one finds "acting white" as an innovation in racial passing. "That is," Young writes, "if [one wants] to achieve success in America's mainstream and elevate [one's] class status. This, of course, includes . . . me."[83] He looks to Signitha Fordham to explain that "behaving in ways and displaying the skills, abilities, and credentials that were traditionally associated with White Americans'"—is what matters once civil rights activists succeeded in dismantling racial barriers to social mobility.[84]

Young's academic experience exposes the coercive nature of structural racism. Before the passage of civil rights legislation in the sixties, one's fair-skinned appearance provided an opportunity to "pass for white" as a strategy for improving one's social condition. This strategy came with a cost. "Between the late eighteenth and mid-twentieth centuries, countless [fair-skinned] African Americans passed as white, leaving behind families, friends, and communities without any available avenue for return," according to Hobbs.[85] In the wake of the civil rights legislation and subsequent social disorder, white Americans began to view "the race problem as flowing from the freely chosen cultural behaviors of blacks themselves."[86] During the Jim Crow regime, scientific racism justified legal and social policy. With

79. Bobo and Kluegel, "Status, Ideology, and Dimensions," 97.
80. Young, *Your Average Nigga*, 43.
81. Grimes, *Life of William Grimes*, iii; emphasis mine.
82. Hobbs, *Chosen Exile*, 4.
83. Young, *Your Average Nigga*, 43.
84. Young, *Your Average Nigga*, 43.
85. Hobbs, *Chosen Exile*, 4.
86. Bobo and Kluegel, "Status, Ideology, and Dimensions," 97.

the expansion of civil rights at the end of the twentieth century, the perception of cultural inferiority informs laissez-faire racism.[87]

Young's literacy narrative describes "acting white" as a metaphor for racial passing in his generation as a costly individual response to structural barriers to social mobility.[88] Although the ideas of "acting white" and authentic blackness are contested, the social requirement to conceal one's race through conforming to dominant social norms leads to the reemergence of a crisis of authenticity. Those who chastise underclass African Americans for their non-conforming identity performances shed light on the implications of literacy in the struggle for political significance.[89]

The problem with emphasizing racial performance to ease racial anxiety, as Young unintentionally does, is that such attempts to pass do not render the individual's race invisible or transform the individual's membership in a marginalized group. It's all done for socioeconomic achievement, but these cultural travelers cannot bleach their skin enough. During the American slavery and Jim Crow eras, passing was made possible by the right phenotype and racial performance. Escaping from the community was a permanent act, however. But things are different today, Young explains:

> Because we participate in both sites, we suffer from the conflict that exists between them. So in order to get along on the (white) campus and in the barbershop, we must alter not the color of our skin but the ways we perform race in each location. These racial performances are most often carried out through language, the way we communicate.[90]

According to Martin, these attempts to change one's class identity and racial background and inhabit two worlds create problems for the sojourners, those seeking to pass. The black male culture crosser often feels inauthentic and incompetent in his native tongue. Martin contends that "marginality and loss are two sides of the same coin—assimilation."[91] This educational metamorphosis creates another problem. Pain emerges from feeling like a betrayer and being accused of feigning whiteness. Martin writes, "The pain and suffering . . . are not intrinsic to the act or process of learning."[92] They follow from the assumptions that inform the strategy of assimilation and that these personal transformations coincide with cultural crossings.

87. Bobo and Kluegel, "Status, Ideology, and Dimensions," 97.

88. Young, *Your Average Nigga*, 43.

89. Favor, *Authentic Blackness*, 29–30, 35–36, 41–42.

90. Young, *Your Average Nigga*, xiii.

91. Martin, *Educational Metamorphoses*, 121.

92. Martin, *Educational Metamorphoses*, 39.

## Thomas Chatterton Williams

Thomas Chatterton Williams's memoir, *Losing My Cool: How a Father's Love and 15,000 Books Beat Hip-Hop Culture*, explores how he felt compelled to hide his literacy abilities by code-switching into hip-hop culture.[93] Describing that culture in an opinion piece published in the *Washington Post*, he writes, "People might say that hip-hop is more than just a genre of music—it's a certain bounce in your stride, it's the way you shake hands, it's the ideas that circulate in your head. It's the ideas that don't circulate in your head. A philosopher might say it's a way of being in the world." The former hip-hop devotee describes hip-hop as black street culture, a departure "for blacks, who traditionally saw cultivation [of middle-class cultural norms] as a key to equality."[94] Ironically, Williams grew up among affluent and middle-class white families in Fanwood, New Jersey, raised by his white mother and his black father, who had a doctorate in sociology and a huge collection of books. His father, a native Texan, grew up under the harsh racial logic of the Jim Crow South. The system was so frightening that his own family tried to keep him from reading. As a child, his mother chided him, "You have no idea how hard he had to work, what he had to go through, just to get his hands on [books]. What kind of hell he caught—his own family told him an educated nigger in the South was a dead nigger. Do you realize he hid himself in the closet with a flashlight in order to read?"[95] As the son of an uber-literate black man, Williams read *The Autobiography of Malcolm X* at the age of seven. The results were predictable. Without a doubt, Williams experienced racial trauma when reading Malcolm's memory of his father's assassination at white supremacists' hands. As a young boy, these images haunted the young Williams. Then, as an unexpected consequence, as a seven-year-old boy, Williams decided he no longer wanted to identify with his whites.[96]

Other motivations were driving his racial assessment and identity resolution. Like Young, Williams, along with many other black men, has a barbershop story. Leaving the suburb of Plainfield, New Jersey, to get a stylish haircut at a black barbershop, Williams heard a black woman holler derogatory racial epithets at his family as his white mother drove them through the projects. He writes, "She [the shouting woman] had somehow stripped me of myself, taken something from me. I felt I had to protect myself from

93. Williams, *Losing My Cool*, 63.
94. Williams, "Black Culture," A17.
95. Williams, *Losing My Cool*, 126.
96. Williams, *Losing My Cool*, 6.

ever feeling that kind of loss again."[97] Entering the black barbershop, Williams decided that the best response to emasculation was racial redemption. He would attempt to reinvent himself through hip-hop hyper-masculine performances and domination on the basketball court, a sanctioned site of black masculinity. He realizes that "it was not enough, simply to know and to accept that you were black—you had to look that way, too. You were going to be judged by how convincingly you could pull off the pose."[98] Part of this poser status involved neglecting his books and feigning anti-scholarly attitudes among his peers and avoiding using Standard English outside his home life.

As Williams moved away from his parents' protective gaze, at school and on basketball courts, he encountered and spent time with black youth from the ghetto. These kids didn't care about books or school, according to Williams. Moreover, to them, middle-class life was dull. He confesses, "I hadn't had the courage or the imagination to go against the grain, to be that kid who says: Screw it. I'm different."[99] Instead, he spent his grade-school years reverse code-switching to the Black English Vernacular and performing the hyper-masculinity gleaned from hip-hop videos and violent basketball courts. He chose Union Catholic over better schools because "hip-hop style governed everything at Union Catholic, same as it did on the playground and in the barbershop."[100] At school, Williams acted tough and pursued the black women who were ghetto fabulous, with ample derrieres and connections in the streets. Of his high school sweetheart, whom his father despised, he writes, "What he found so troubling I found intoxicating—Stacey was street and that was what was hot. She was 'hood, she was hip hop, she was black, and she was real."[101] Being real included not reading, but Williams was ambivalent about this, as revealed at an impromptu vigil for the murdered rapper Biggie. He writes, "I was torn between allegiance to the fallen drug dealer and something else—something deeper coming from deep in the back of my head or in my conscience. I knew for an irrefutable fact that none of the other kids had ever managed to crease a spine of *The Autobiography of Malcolm X* or *The Souls of Black Folk*."[102] Ironically, many African Americans will not read these weighty tomes until enrolling in African-American studies courses at the university. Williams had

97. Williams, *Losing My Cool*, 9.
98. Williams, *Losing My Cool*, 8.
99. Williams, *Losing My Cool*, 9.
100. Williams, *Losing My Cool*, 39.
101. Williams, *Losing My Cool*, 79.
102. Williams, *Losing My Cool*, 38.

not immersed himself in these black classics of his own volition; his father forced him to read these books for practical reasons. First off, he wanted to connect his son to the historical black experience. Moreover, these books were intended to inform both his racial identity formation and political imagination. Finally, Williams's father hoped to prepare his son for the college entrance exams after school. Ironically, the younger Williams continued to adhere to his understanding of anti-literate hip-hop blackness, even after he performed well on the SAT.[103]

Williams reports on the consequences of his decision to venture outside of hip-hop culture after matriculating into Georgetown University. When his black colleagues ostracize him from the black campus community, he spends time with his white dorm mates. Their companionship allows him to question his understanding of blackness and masculinity. Deciding to humble himself and get to know a white colleague from a truly privileged background, Williams begins to question his past attitudes. Describing the anxiety induced by his new companions and their academic, cultural, and social explorations, he refers to his pre-Georgetown mentality:

> We met each other somewhere in the middle. Still it was difficult to venture off my own turf and to engage people [white students] like Playboy on their terms. The ice-grill mask of black cool and default membership within hip-hop culture predicated on street sensibilities, elaborate shape-concealing costumes, and esoteric 'hood vernacular had shielded my boys and me from ever having to face up to the fact that we were not invincible or always in control of things. Rather than know ourselves, we cloaked our ignorance. . . .[104]

One of his experiences is visiting Dean and Deluca, an upscale grocery store. Playboy suggests that they eat cheese with a baguette. Williams agrees to grab the baguette but realizes that he does not know what that is. He writes, "It hit me: 'Baguette' must just be French for 'little bag.'"[105] Upon returning with a plastic handbasket, Williams is forced to admit his ignorance. This encounter is a rupture. The language of a foreign food illuminates Williams's ignorance. Instead of getting defensive, he silently drops his shield and implicitly admits his ignorance.

At that moment, he opens up himself to an alternative future by becoming curious about his new environment. Although his black friends ate different kinds of food, "no one ever talked about cheese."[106] As he ponders why this is, he discloses how attending a college and engaging other cultures, food, and people from diverse backgrounds and experiences creates an opening. He writes, "Real niggas didn't talk about cheese because, for whatever the reason, cheese ain't real. To be straight up, cheese is corny. Sneakers are real, not cheese; cognac is real, not wine; rap is real, not jazz; expensive cars are real, not expensive educations."[107] Williams's inner dialogue reflects the binary grammar of hip-hop culture. He distinguishes authentic black culture based on contemporary hip-hop and street culture. Yet, he decides not to veil his ignorance by striking the "cool pose." Choosing to go beyond the unknown into the threshold that Georgetown has offered and experience more of the world, he rejects defensiveness.

At its most basic level, Williams's narrative contains educational transformations that occur as simultaneous culture crossings as he moves into young adulthood. Once Williams begins the shift from hip-hop culture to normative academic life, the reader can revisit his earlier metamorphosis to uncover how racial trauma inaugurated his movement from early childhood to a more self-aware adolescent. This traumatic event leads to his misguided miseducative agency as a form of self-protection. Williams writes a narrative that contradicts the mistaken belief that education is confined to the school and necessarily equals progress. Martin describes Malcolm X's experience in similar terms: "His own experience taught him that many of society's educational agents—in which category fall school, home, church, neighborhood and, indeed, all the other institutions of society—are profoundly miseducative."[108] Martin argues that narratives such as Malcolm X's also contradict the idea that education is a predictable, linear, and cumulative process that leads to intellectual and moral development. So, it seems in *Losing My Cool.*

Throughout the narrative, Williams is a voracious learner. He learns race in binary terms from his parents at home. By reading *Malcolm X's Autobiography* at the age of seven, Williams discovers that racism has led to violent, murderous acts against black people. On the way to the barbershop, he has a miseducative moment when he's called a honky, and then he begins to recognize that others don't take his blackness for granted. "It was not enough, simply to know and to accept that you were black—you had to look that way, too. You were going to be judged by how convincingly you could pull off the pose."

106. Williams, *Losing My Cool,* 96.
107. Williams, *Losing My Cool,* 97.
108. Martin, *Educational Metamorphoses,* 49.

Consequently, he begins to study black men at the barbershop, on the basketball court, and in rap videos. On this phase of his life, he explains that "in retrospect appears a lot like the fervency of the convert, the zealously born-again, I consciously learned and performed my race, like a teacher's pet in an advanced placement course on black masculinity."[109] This profoundly miseducative process could have ruined his ability to take advantage of educational opportunities. Martin explains that "in daily bombarding young people with unwholesome, antisocial models of living and in making these appear fatally attractive, the print and electronic media are guilty of doing precisely this."[110] Fortunately, Williams's father makes sure that his son reads books and prepares for college exams.

On the surface, the younger Williams seems committed to a narrow notion of black masculinity. In parochial school, he experiences a deep ambivalence around his literacy performance due to his father and mother foregrounding literacy in their home and enforcing a consistent study regimen to prepare Williams for the SAT. Moreover, his father protects him from the hoop dreams common to young black men by taking him to a practice session of a team of the best and hungriest basketball players in the nation, according to Williams. One might argue that reading set up Williams for ongoing self-reflection that enabled him to perceive his father's intentions. In the aftermath of this experience, he became even more reflective and realistic about his sports aspirations.

In short, Williams's memoir details his ability to learn in almost every context. Unfortunately, much like Malcolm X, Williams's encounters with racism and narrow images of blacks and blackness—from peers and in books, music, and social contexts—were profoundly miseducative. Martin describes Malcolm X's life as demonstrating "that educational [encounters and] transformations do not always add up to progress."[111] Moreover, Martin writes:

> Malcolm's metamorphosis into a hustler was not brought about by a wave of a wand or the administration of a drug. Nor can it be chalked up to human development pure and simple. On the contrary, it was due to education in the broadest sense of that term—the sense that recognizes school as but one of education's agents, and that acknowledges that education can be either educative or miseducative.[112]

109. Williams, *Portrait in Black and White*, 48.
110. Martin, *Educational Metamorphoses*, 59.
111. Martin, *Educational Metamorphoses*, 51.
112. Martin, *Educational Metamorphoses*, 49.

While Williams does not evolve into a street hustler, drug dealer, or criminal, he does develop ambivalence toward literacy and speaking Standard English. Fortunately, because of his father's SAT study sessions, he accumulates the knowledge he needs to perform well in school. However, he fails to maintain a sufficient "cool pose" in social contexts.

In the end, it is at Georgetown University that Williams has a mostly positive educational transformation that leads him beyond his narrow understanding of blackness and masculinity informed by hip-hop culture. After being ostracized from the black community, he begins to read more seriously and experiences a culture crossing with his new, more privileged friend, Playboy. He writes:

> For all my powers of projection, though, *I failed to anticipate the extent to which daily exposure to serious ideas and methods of thinking would alter me*. I didn't realize that once you leave home and see new and more complex things, you might just lose the desire to measure yourself by the old, provincial standards; they cease to motivate you even when you want them to; you set your eyes on new and higher (though they used to seem lower) sights.[113]

Williams's description of his metamorphosis here includes multiple educational agents. This narrative is nothing short of an educational transformation account spurred by the many components—intellectual and emotional—accompanying immersion in higher education. Martin connects such whole-person changes to "events in the life cycle."[114] Here I see a connection to Hughes's experience of going to college. While a Columbia student, Hughes developed a deep ambivalence about prior commitments to the world of books and letters. Williams, however, begins to embrace the life of the mind. Martin explains, "Becoming a mother is not the only event in the human life cycle that [can potentially] give rise to an educational metamorphosis. In addition to the metamorphoses occasioned by being born and by the process of dying, there [is], for example, the transformation of a small girl into a young woman and a small boy into a young man."[115] In college, Williams has several encounters that intersect to promote a second whole-person transformation. His burgeoning maturity and his time at the university provide a respite from his obsession with hip-hop culture. A grocery store encounter with his white dorm mate Playboy would suggest that culture crossings have played a critical role in precipitating a whole-person

113. Williams, *Losing My Cool*, 151; emphasis mine.

114. Martin, *Educational Metamorphoses*, 91.

115. Martin, *Educational Metamorphoses*, 94.

change. And as Martin theorizes, these evolutions are non-linear and leave the future more open-ended than closed. Nothing less than a different chronology of changes seems foreseeable for Williams. He became a cultural critic and journalist living in New York until he married a French national and moved to Paris, France.

## Conclusion

Jane Roland Martin's analysis of educational metamorphoses offers tools for identifying and interpreting the sources of ambivalence in a few prominent African-American male literacy narratives. Her understanding of educational agents and the typology of whole-person transformation illuminates the academic trajectory of Frederick Douglass, Langston Hughes, Vershawn Ashanti Young, and Thomas Chatterton Williams. In deploying her lenses, we discover the educative agents and transformations that account for the angst-ridden relationships these black men have had with literacy.

The first significant site of anxiety is the individual's transition from a "creature of nature" to a "creature of culture." All of these men, including myself, learned to read in a racialized context. They absorbed ideas about race and class at the feet of family members; besides, the authors' diverse racial contexts contributed to diverse literacy forms.

In Douglass's case, he began to read and engage the dominant culture late enough that he was able to consciously expose his own thoughts to our analytical lens to show us how thinking about race, literacy, and educational metamorphoses gradually created the ambivalence that he passed through on his way to a more secure position. One might imagine that an ambiguity emerging from intellectual and social immaturity might lead to insecurity and intolerance. But with maturation and intellectual growth, individuals can develop a more expansive notion of the self and the other, making ambivalence more tolerable. Each of the literacy narratives discussed deals with race at the most formative moments of the author's identity formation. From them, we learn that at the foundation of literary ambivalence and anxiety is a fixation with racial thinking that remains unresolved in our society—a society in which we find that the discourse of race has been complicated by the discourse(s) of assimilation and authentic blackness, lending their own difficulties to the transition from a creature of nature to a creature of culture.

On another level, the last of these literacy narratives render legible issues related to an immersion into undergraduate education, a life-cycle event that leads to educational metamorphoses. Because Martin regards educational metamorphoses as evolutionary processes in which an individual's life consists of a series of changes, she gives us the license to view coming-of-age as an educative force. Nor does this transformational period conclude with adulthood. With Douglass, Hughes, and Williams, we find that whole-person changes took place not only in each man's earliest formative moments as they crossed the boundary from creatures of nature to creatures of culture, but educational metamorphoses recurred in adolescence and continued beyond young adulthood. And in each case, the authors were able to tolerate ambivalence in a positive manner by allowing for forbearance and ambiguity.

Upon close analysis of the educative mechanisms that triggered whole-person changes in these men's lives, it becomes clear that multiple agencies were at work and that many of those agencies were miseducative. Since the journey from nature to culture involves caretakers and custodians, it makes sense that we find each author reading literacy through the lenses provided him by his family and community of origin. These perspectives led to positive, negative, and ambivalent feelings about literacy. Douglass, for example, found himself inspired by his mother's and Sophia Auld's ability to read. But Hugh Auld's miseducative "philosophy of slavery" provoked transformations in both Auld's wife and the young Douglass. While Douglass maintained a positive sense of the power of literacy, learning about abolitionism and coming to a more profound recognition of his own social status created inner turmoil.

In the next century, Hughes was turned on to literacy and a liberating form of blackness that allowed him to embrace both Standard English and the Black English Vernacular. Nevertheless, he developed ambivalence about the meaning of literacy in the context of discourses concerning black responsibility and familial piety. And at Georgetown University, Williams was exposed to art, music, literature, philosophy, and other cultural experiences that launched him into a whole-person transformation. Yet, while he moved beyond ambivalence to embrace mainstream literacy, he also developed negative attitudes regarding the black vernacular.

One of the most surprising things that Martin allows us to uncover is how "passing" in the age of colorblindness contributes to a new form of ambivalence. Williams and Young were both aware that they were expected to participate in the discourses of assimilation and social mobility as they moved through grade school and university. However, they felt the need to cross into new cultures—to pass either as middle-class or hypermasculine black men—that created ambivalence and anxiety about competence in their blackness, literacy performances, and masculinity. In the end, Martin helps us see that multiple educative agencies—both negative and positive—contribute to educational metamorphoses. In my case, Martin allows me to appreciate, comprehend, and sympathize with the ambivalence some black males experience regarding the life of the mind and their literacy performances.

From such a colonial encounter between the white presence and its black semblance, there emerge the question of the ambivalence of mimicry as problematic of colonial subjection.

—Homi Bhabha, "Of Mimicry and Man"

There is really nothing more to say—except why. But since why is difficult to handle, one must take refuge in how.

—Toni Morrison, *The Bluest Eye* (1970)

Until you make the unconscious conscious, it will direct your life and you will call it fate.

—Carl G. Jung

San Diego State University, San Diego, California (c. 1984)

Northwest Washington, DC (c. 1984)

## CHAPTER 4

# Code-Switching
### The Life of a Preppy Hustler

THE PRESUMED CORRELATION BETWEEN black male literacy and racial equality has persisted from the time Frederick Douglass declared that reading was his path to freedom. Michelle Alexander, the author of the provocative *The New Jim Crow: Mass Incarceration in the Age of Colorblindness*, has been inundated with questions about the relationship between literacy and mass incarceration in a manner that conveys our deep commitment to the literacy myth.

During a lunch conversation between talks in Seattle, Washington, Alexander shared that—following lectures on the repercussion of the War on Drugs for black males—educators, politicians, and community members would typically ask whether prison administrators and government officials were conducting "research" on the standardized test scores of nine-year-old black boys to determine whether they are reading at grade level. Supposedly, this data is meant to help government officials predict future prison populations and prepare accordingly. It turns out that this question on the antecedents of the school-to-prison pipeline is based on an urban myth grounded in racial assumptions about black male youth, assumptions given credibility by auspicious settings and the authority of the speakers gathered for these forums. According to the literature, however, our educational system does function as a pipeline "that drastically increases the likelihood that [black] children will end up with a criminal record rather than a diploma."[1] India Geronimo explains:

1. Kim, Losen, and Hewitt, *School-to-Prison Pipeline*, 1.

The school-to-prison pipeline is the nationwide trend where poor and minority students are funneled out of the education system and into the criminal justice system. Increases in school-based arrests, student suspensions and expulsions, the adoption of zero tolerance policies, the use of disciplinary alternative education programs, and the criminalization of students for minor schoolyard misconduct are symptoms of the school-to-prison pipeline.[2]

Along the same lines, Alexander and Geoffrey Canada, president and CEO of the Harlem Children's Zone, have discussed a similar concern: whether more undergraduate-aged African Americans are incarcerated than those on college campuses.[3] While elements of these concerns are real, the literature makes it clear that the assumption/expectation that poverty, racial disparities, and a culture of punishment rather than prevention and early intervention are key forces driving "the cradle to prison pipeline" tainted by misunderstandings, embellishments, and urban myths. More importantly, the appropriation of the literacy myth during the era of what Alexander calls "The New Jim Crow" perpetuates the belief that if underclass black boys would only learn to read, then they would abandon their outlaw behavior and transcend the social ills that lead to poverty and mass incarceration.

In other words, in our post-civil rights era, the literacy myth has morphed into urban myths about educational policies that restrict efforts to improve poor blacks' conditions. Ironically, these efforts are based on a genealogy of ideas about black inferiority and criminality originating in the justifications for the enslavement of Africans and then reconstructed to limit the black freedoms as well as imprison African Americans under pretenses throughout the twentieth century. The invocation of this urban legend, concerning late-twentieth and early twenty-first century mass incarceration, at once seems to promote racial uplift and advance African Americans as a group. Simultaneously, it generates intergroup marginalization due to myths about cognitive abilities and the base morality of poor blacks who refuse to conform to bourgeois cultural norms. However, the school-to-prison pipeline has been "initiated by the War on Drugs and has trickled down to numerous policies that attempt to take a hardline approach to misconduct."[4] My conversation with Alexander reveals African-American anxieties related to criminalization and literacy.

2. Geronimo, "Systemic Failure," 281–82.
3. Alexander, *New Jim Crow*, 185.
4. Geronimo, "Systemic Failure," 291.

To reveal that ambivalence is a prominent feature of African-American literacy narratives, I investigate the cultural and social contexts surrounding black males' literacy acquisition and introduce four more theoretical lenses. The first two are Michael C. Dawson's notion of "linked fate" and Evelyn Brooks Higginbotham's work on the "politics of respectability." In the following chapters, I use Toni Morrison's "Africanist idiom" and Cathy Cohen's theory of "secondary marginalization." These lenses enable us to see the external sources of ambivalence's inner experience. These realities have impacted African-American writers from slavery to the present day, including Frederick Douglass, Langston Hughes, Vershawn Ashanti Young, and Thomas Chatterton Williams. Before presenting and exploring the uses/limits or applicability/inapplicability of these theoretical lenses, I must first tell a story about myself to reveal the importance of this chapter in my own life. Far beyond conducting an impersonal analysis, I examine myself and my actions as a black man who has felt a deep ambivalence about being literate.

I became more conscious of my own ambivalence after a graduate school professor compelled me to confront the persistent voices inside my head: the voices of authority figures who invoked the conflicting ideas of W. E. B. Du Bois and Booker T. Washington regarding my literacy aspirations and social advancement.[5] Shortly after that, amid my own self-reflection, I was invited by the Clowes Center for the Study of Conflict and Dialogue at the University of Washington to deliver the Veterans of Intercommunal Violence lecture. Jim Clowes had been a mentor when I was an undergraduate student. Brilliant and down-to-earth, he had made a significant impact on campus through his leadership of the Comparative History of Ideas Program alongside its director John Toews, a MacArthur Fellow. In truth, I was ambivalent about giving the talk. A few of my peers among the minority students pressured me to reconsider speaking about my experiences in "the game" or "street life" because it would risk casting our minority groups in a negative light. This concern carried an implied threat that speaking would have consequences for my career. I was not a team player, some said. Others accused me of enabling tokenism. But my life experiences had accustomed me to elite and middle-class-aspiring minorities prejudging me, putting me down, getting in my way, and blocking opportunities. In the 'hood, we would have called these folks out for "player hating." But I was ambivalent for reasons that went beyond class conflict. It seemed to me that both W. E. B. Du Bois and Booker T. Washington would have wanted me to represent the African-American community in the best possible light.

5. Du Bois, "Of Mr. Booker T. Washington and Others," 79–95.

In the back of my head was another nagging consideration: I did not think that I was up to speaking to an audience in one of the largest lecture halls on the UW's campus. Prior speakers had come from South Africa, Sri Lanka, and Guatemala. My story seemed less significant than those of individuals who had experienced social and political upheavals of global proportions. Yet, I had grown up amongst police brutality and street violence requiring national and international attention. Lessons in the "code of streets" and occasional violence were a part of my earliest childhood memories. Even in our family, we were encouraged to adhere to the "no-snitching" guideline enforced in the streets. I had grown up during a period when street gangs began to increase in Southern California, and I had matured into manhood at the height of the War on Drugs. While I might have come from a family with black bourgeois aspirations, my mom's brothers had all done hard time. According to sociology and Yale Professor Elijah Anderson, "One person may at different times exhibit both decent and street orientations, depending on the circumstances. Although these designations result from social jockeying, there do exist features that define each conceptual category."[6] But I was never committed to street gangs as a lifestyle. My childhood had been informed by black and white films with debonair actors who dressed to the nines and the black buppies' take on the disco era with cardigan sweaters, Pierre Cardin clothes and cologne, and foreign cars.

While I was a teen, *Gentlemen's Quarterly* had been my bible; Richard Gere's portrayal of Julian Kaye in *American Gigolo* was my model of modern-day dandyism. It's true that even as I aspired to emulate the life of a pampered playboy, violence and crime were a part of the palm tree-lined urban landscape. Still, the most significant brutalities I remember experiencing—the violence of abandonment, illegitimacy, structural racism, and poverty—were clichés too well-worn to talk about in public, and seemed trite compared to struggles outside our nation. My hesitation was further related to the fear that audience members might read and interpret my biography as confirming the master narrative—the belief in African Americans' cognitive and moral deficiencies. Abolitionists, black intellectuals, community activists, black educators, preachers, and race leaders in the black community had fought to counter the ideas promoting a belief in white supremacy for centuries.

As I wrote out my biography in preparation for the talk, the details of a million relevant events from childhood, my collegiate years in Southern California, and drug dealing days in Washington, DC, spun in my head. As

6. Anderson, "Code of the Streets," 82.

an undergraduate at San Diego State University, I became more aware of apartheid in South Africa and the significance of being a member of a marginalized group of young African-American males even within the black community. In my young imagination, South Africans and poor African Americans experienced a form of marginalization that was equivalent to social death in previous historical epochs.

Meanwhile, the faculty in the African-American studies program at San Diego State University exposed me to class and ideological differences among the black intelligentsia, the black aristocracy, diverse race leaders, and the black folk. It was upon learning about these class, culture, and ideological differences that I began to feel ambivalent about the American Dream and the myth of literacy as a part of that vision of the good. In time, I'd drop out of college. Even as I deliberated leaving school, I became a street hustler, an undercover player. Preparing for my talk, I wanted to discern the personal and external forces that created the tension I felt and led to the decision to pursue an alternative path to social mobility. "What in the world had happened to me?" I asked myself. "How had a fairly good and somewhat soft kid got caught up in the game?" Finding myself unable to come up with a convincing answer, I probed my story more deeply. I had to confront the ghosts of Du Bois, who promoted a black elitism, and Washington, who sought more practical changes, and to go beyond both my biography and the early twentieth-century debates about the path to racial progress.

Back in the day, I could better relate to the emerging "street gangster rappers" than to gang bangers. Schooly D and Ice T were hustlers that rhymed and reflected a more strategic street ethos, like my own. In the foreword to Colton Simpson's book *Inside the Crips: Life inside L.A.'s Most Notorious Gang,* Ice T explains:

> We were hustling. We didn't expect to live past twenty-five. It was "go do it right now and fuck whatever happens." We had all the fineries of youthful hustlers: Fila sweat suits, Porsches, gold jewely as big as a dinner plates hanging around our necks. Along with all the hustlers. I would rap . . . I rapped about our lives. That's all I could do; that's all I knew.[7]

These guys told stories about life in the streets and of ruthlessly pursuing the same emblems of the American Dream as the starched-shirts-wearing finance guys on Wall Street: exotic women, expensive watches, and sports cars. My boys and I admired the ruthlessness perceived in Wall Street arbitrageur John Grey; the character played by Mickey Rourke in the film *9 ½ Weeks.* Rourke's swagger wasn't half bad, either. Later, Gordon Gecko,

7. Ice T, "Foreword," xvi.

played by Michael Douglass in Oliver Stone's *Wall Street*, would take greed
mainstream. Our utopian vision was more in line with Social Darwinists
and Greek Epicureans than the Puritans or the Victorians.

Although ambitious and hardworking, we were quite different from
Du Bois, Washington, and the earlier generations of African Americans
who had fought legal battles, sat at lunch counters, or adhered to black nationalist ideologies to advance black liberation. Before the golden age of rap
neo-black nationalism, Run-D.M.C. gave voice to our intuitive understanding of black activism when they rapped black pride, racism, and resistance
to white supremacy. *Tougher Than Leather* signaled the rap group's refusal
to conform to music industry norms and broader societal values. The album
presaged the emergence of gangster rap music and ratchet street culture as
a performative strategy to create a social space beyond respectability politics. It unintentionally created a path towards a more egalitarian society.
While Martin Luther King Jr. had a dream of racial equality to be attained
by peace, and Malcolm X advocated retaliation, both men had ended up as
casualties in the struggle for black liberation. Yes, we wanted equality "by
any means necessary." Malcolm had been our "shining black prince," but we
were dark and unseen street kings. Coming of age in the eighties and nineties, I respected the struggle that I witnessed among black men who worked
regular jobs. Yet, I did not see myself submitting to their depleting work-
place experiences that culminated in partying on the weekend as catharsis.

Run-D.M.C. captured our generation's reinterpretation of this militant
ideology when rapping demands that other rappers and the broader society
give us respect. The generation inventing hip-hop culture had inherited the
street orientation witnessed in the Black Power movement. The streets resonated with our normative thoughts on culture, politics, and social mobility.
"Where once the means to freedom was thought to be literacy or reclaiming the principles of the Declaration of Independence or utilizing the legal
system—or taking up guns [in self-defense]—for hip-hop entrepreneurs,
the means, according to Simmons, is hardheaded capitalism, and the goal,
massive profits."[8] Gangster rap music and hip-hop culture voiced the radical demand for unconditional cultural and personal respect. Run-D.M.C.
had captured our generation's reinterpretation of this militant ideology in
their song, "King of Rock." We in the streets, too, reigned in a feudalistic
pecking order. Young kings and princes sold powder and rock cocaine, and
the pauperish smokers used fire to burn the product out of which we were
attempting to build our fiefdoms. Our goal was to avoid acquiescing to the
mind-numbing working-class mediocrity acceptable to older relatives and

8. Gates, *America Behind the Color Line*, 6.

community members or becoming unappreciated casualties in the war on racism and poverty.

In short, we refused to go out like suckers. We wanted the freedom that we believed we could only buy with the almighty dollar. So many of our fathers had abandoned us in figurative and literal terms, and somehow the street hustlers had helped us become men. In Southern California, a youth who grows up in this environment could not avoid participating in the street culture and learning the "code of the streets": a set of informal rules governing interpersonal public behavior, including violence. The rules prescribe both proper comportment and a proper way to respond if challenged.[9] Our circumstances required that we participate in street culture where "everybody knows that if the rules are violated, there are penalties," but we wanted to participate in the square economy as well.[10] The rapper Ice T contextualizes masculinity and respect in regard to "the codes of the street." He explains,

> We're just trying to survive and prosper in our own way. In the 'hood, we don't have the brother who went to Harvard who makes us proud, who makes us feel good about ourselves. So we work on what we do have. Masculinity is at a premium. The toughest kid on the block becomes the role model. Not the richest kid, or the smartest kid. But the toughest kid. Pride is based on violence and aggression. That's how we define wealth. In the 'hood, we define wealth by strength.[11]

Individuals organize in gangs to avoid becoming a causalty. These "survival units" provide power, protection, and social capital.[12] bell hooks writes,

> Patriarchal manhood was the theory, and gangsta culture was its ultimate practice. No wonder then that black males of all ages living the protestant work ethic, submitting in the racist white world, envy the lowdown hustlers in the black communities who are not slaves to white power. As one young gang member put it, "working is weak."[13]

Under this emerging street-oriented masculinity regime, we earnestly began to re-imagine and synthesize respectability based on black bourgeois

9. Anderson, "Code of the Streets," 82.

10. Anderson, "Code of the Streets," 82.

11. Ice T, "Foreword," xvii.

12. Ice T, "Foreword," xviii.

13. hooks, *We Real Cool,* 25.

aspirations and the "code of the streets." According to sociologist Dr. Elijah Anderson,

> These two orientations—decent and street—socially organize the community, and their coexistence has important consequences for residents, particularly children growing up in the inner city. Above all, this environment means that even youngsters whose home lives reflect mainstream values—and the majority of homes in the community do—must be able to handle themselves in a street-oriented environment.[14]

Our aspirations created the contexts to recognize the strength in both white male patriarchy and street-based masculinity performances.

We learned to adhere to a hustler's epistemology, a way of meaning-making and operating in the world that mainstream individuals would describe as "living by one's wits." Recognizing the factors informing my past, I decided to speak about the mindset that steered me and others into the dope game, which culminated in our translating our street knowledge into mainstream achievement. The hustler's epistemology had allowed us to rise in the ivory tower, the private and public sectors, and the church in the same stealthy way as we did on the streets. Today, we are authors, business owners, entrepreneurs, inventors, professors, and scientists. This counternarrative exemplifies the rise of neuroscientist and Columbia Professor Carl Hart. He rose from the streets to become a professor, or the architect of gangster rap, audio engineer, entrepreneur, hip-hop mogul, and record executive, Dr. Dre. My talk would be titled "Gangster Epistemology: Urban Crime and the American Dream." Yet, while I had settled on a topic, I still needed to understand the external forces that led me—a bookish, geeky, on occasion androgynous boy from the ghetto—to reject the common sense and morality that his "Grandmamma had taught him" to pursue the life of a street hustler. Context is everything. "Sophisticated cats wearing bifocals may be incognito shot callers utilizing nerd camouflage to elude identification by the pigs, who believe that all gangbangers wear sunglasses, have bulging muscles and have 'Loc' in their name," according to notorious L. A. Crip Colton Simpson.[15] Hence, I set out to historicize myself to understand my own narrative and tell a substantive story about how young black men become ambivalent about education as a means to attain the American Dream.

I grew up in the projects under the blinding skies of Southern California, experiencing "the economic disintegration of late-twentieth-century

14. Anderson, "Code of the Streets," 82.
15. Simpson, *Inside the Crips*, 98.

black urban life" described in the Moynihan Report and repeatedly portrayed in the media. Nevertheless, I emerged from childhood amid street gangs and a weak school system with my love of learning intact, becoming both a university student and a student of "the game." I studied at the local state university during weekdays. When not at school, I was a part-time playboy, blue-collar worker, petty thief, and entrepreneur. On weekends, I went to high school games, partied, and hung out in the streets with the "fellas." As a preppy hustler, I had an expanded notion of education, as described by Jane Roland Martin.

I knew that "important as school has become, it is still only one of society's educational agents. Home is another."[16] In addition, my street epistemology enabled me to recognize how institutions, organizations, public spaces, social contexts, and media are educative. I understood that "education is both formal, within the confines of traditional schools, and informal within the confines of the [street corners] and the game [i.e., outlaw life]."[17] An inherent non-conformist, I knew that I'd incorporate both the classroom and the streets in self-reinvention and transcendence. As a child, I intuitively understood that education requires cultural crossings and that I would need to reinvent myself to be successful.

Early on, I somehow believed that reinvention was a part of the African-American experience. On weekends, I'd witness how blue-collar workers would become fly hustlers and foxy ladies. I also knew by experience that identity transformation promoted by educational growth could lead to "alienation, inner conflict, accusations, betrayal, and anxieties about going home again."[18] In our ghetto, a highly credentialed black person was an outlier. Doctors and lawyers would commute to the neighborhood to fill our cavities and file our lawsuits, but college-educated philosophers were uncommon. Certain kinds of reinventions were more suitable than others.

Moving between formal and informal educational environments, I readily synthesized what I was learning to make practical advances in both the streets and society. However, I had not matured enough to maintain optimism in social progress. Moreover, my constant crossing of boundaries as a cultural vagabond led to internal duress. Parallel to Malcolm X's experiences, my educative encounters on the street created the context for numerous self-reinventions. Eventually, the criminal world asserted the stronger call, and I turned to full-time drug dealing in both elite and street circles in Boston, Los Angeles, San Diego, and Washington, DC.

16. Martin, *Educational Metamorphoses*, 56.
17. Beliveau and Bolf-Beliveau, "Posing Problems and Picking Fights," 91.
18. Martin, *Educational Metamorphoses*, 8.

Initially, I thought I could lead a double life. The money I made from selling drugs would allow me to become a black ghetto prince, a foppish urban precursor to the trap lord, and slave to fashion, A$AP Rocky. With "product" in tow, I stealthily moved through the 'hood and among the black upper class and the mid-level street princes. However, I could not escape a deep sense of guilt that I was destroying the black community time and time again. I recalled the eyes of children whose parents bought the product from me while they stood by watching. In the midst of drug transactions, I often felt like I was taking food out of their mouths. I moved up "in the game" and began to travel. But the new "get tough on crime" rhetoric fueling the War on Drugs brought me to recognize that the game had changed, and I couldn't remain a street player forever. Growing up in a community once full of spiritual seekers who lived among the other ghetto inhabitants, I began to investigate faith as a vehicle to transcend the disillusionment and despair that had made a life of crime so appealing. My search took me through a number of religions, including Rastafarianism, until I moved beyond my sense that Christianity was a marginalizing factor in the black experience.

This convoluted trajectory prevents my narrative from either conforming to a simple Horatio Alger Jr. narrative or a straightforward educational metamorphosis with a single transformation. To tell my complicated story for the Clowes lecture, I had to make sense of the structural violence and feelings of marginalization that led me to become first a 'hood soldier in the War on Drugs, complicit in the genocide of urban black communities in the United States. In preparation for my lecture, I first realized the importance of the four theorists upon whom I draw in this and the following chapter. It was as if my experience brought these theorists to my side. In my lecture, I employed their ideas to understand how my ambivalence about literacy, writ large, had shaped the state of mind that led to consent to violence and the underground economy as a legitimate path to achieve the American Dream (i.e., respectable hedonism). These same frameworks allowed me to move beyond a paralyzing ambivalence to a much more tolerable one. Now, as I continue to explore literacy narratives among African-American men in this project, the words of these theorists ring true in a broader discussion of black male ambivalence, just as they have rung true in my own personal narrative.

## Dawson's Idea of Linked Fate

At the heart of the ambivalence among African-American males regarding the significance of Standard English and the utility of the Black English

Vernacular is a profound belief, or an ontological assumption, that our "imagined community" consists of African-American individuals whose destinies are linked due to a shared experience of racial oppression.[19] In response to the stereotypes that justified racial exclusion, African-American leaders have promoted mainstream literacy and shunned the Black English Vernacular in order to undermine slavery, Jim Crow, and other forms of racial exclusion. In the early nineties, the political theorist Michael C. Dawson took up questions about the class basis of black political behavior stating, "What must be determined is whether this current level of racial discrimination and harassment in the economic and social spheres is sufficient to keep race the most politically salient identity for African Americans [as opposed to class, gender, or sexuality]."[20] He investigates this issue in two volumes: *Behind the Mule: Race and Class in African-American Politics* and *Black Visions: The Roots of Contemporary African-American Political Ideologies.*

Dawson argues that the idea of race as an ideology of difference supports the structural barriers obstructing the advancement to social equality in our nation. Consequently, racism has been an important factor in shaping hyper-awareness among African Americans leading to a "black utility heuristic."[21] According to Dawson, this approach to social reasoning is based on the assumption that it is "more efficient to use group status as a proxy not only because a piece of legislation or a public policy [can] be analyzed relatively easily for its effect on the race but also because the information sources available in the black community . . . all reinforce the salience of racial interests and would provide information about racial group status."[22] What is the source of this political calculus? He writes, "In the historically risky environment within which African Americans have lived, procedural rationality would tend to reinforce the salience of racial identity."[23] Dawson acknowledges that not all African Americans give consistent precedence to group interest over their personal interests or preferences by developing this procedural rationality that makes race salient.[24] Nevertheless, generally speaking, as long as African Americans believe that their life options are over-determined by race, the theory of linked fate predicts they will develop

19. Anderson, *Imagined Communities,* 6.

20. Dawson, *Behind the Mule,* 57.

21. Dawson, *Black Visions,* xi–xii.

22. Dawson, *Behind the Mule,* 10–11.

23. Dawson, *Behind the Mule,* 62.

24. Dawson, *Behind the Mule,* 62.

a cost-benefit analysis, so to speak, that contrasts individual and group interests.

Although linked fate suggests homogeneity in African-American political behavior and choices, *Behind the Mule* describes its persistence among the heterogeneity in black political thought and social behavior due to three prevailing factors.[25] First, although class stratification produces diverse social experiences among African Americans, race is still the principal lens shaping black political thought. Second, due to an experience of oppression and social exclusion, African-American social reasoning prioritizes the group over the individual, according to Dawson. Third, inside the plurality of African-American ideologies are an inner logic informed by the assumption of common interests. Dawson's heuristic, based on the notion of linked fate, provides a communal approach to political and socioeconomic thought that contradicts our Western political tradition's supposed individualistic political assumptions.

In a liberal democratic society in which the individual defines the political unit, the idea of a black utility heuristic elucidates a seemingly irrational adherence to a way of thinking that shaped black political thought prior to the civil rights movement in the sixties. This political calculus emerges from a belief that life chances are over-determined by ascriptive identity. Thus, it has been most efficient for blacks to act based on their group status. Here, social psychology comes into play. "As long as African Americans' life chances are powerfully shaped by race, it is efficient for individual African Americans to use their perceptions of interests of African Americans as a group as a proxy for their own interests," Dawson explains.[26] Moreover, the historical memory of the African-American community—as perpetuated by communal, institutional, and media networks—makes ascriptive identity more salient and produces a sense of an ever-present threat against the group, and thus the racialized individual. For many (if not most) African Americans, the enduring relationship of white domination to black subordination creates social tensions that cause group interest to be perceived as much more rational than placing one's individual needs over the group.

Dawson argues that structural realities make it prudent for individuals to rely on race-informed rationality in the social arena instead of pursuing individual interests.[27] These findings contradict political theory regarding class stratification that would lead researchers to expect social cleavages to define intragroup relations among blacks. Rather, social psychology

25. Dawson, *Behind the Mule*, 63.

26. Dawson, *Behind the Mule*, 61.

27. Dawson, *Behind the Mule*, 62.

provides a calculus that explains the individual identification (self-categorization) with other African Americans as a racialized group.[28] Dawson's notion of the black utility heuristic enables him to expose the relationship between perceptions of linked fate and socioeconomic subordination.[29] He explains, "If one believes that blacks as a group are in a subordinate position, one's belief in the linked fates of individual African Americans should be strengthened. Furthermore, if one perceives the fates of individual blacks as linked to that of the group, it is at least in part because one perceives blacks as a subordinate group in American society."[30]

The social theory would suggest that social mobility—increased income and education—would diminish the perceptions of African-American *group* interests and socioeconomic issues. Unexpectedly, Dawson has found quite the opposite effect. He reports that "the more education one had, the more likely one was to believe that blacks were economically subordinate to whites, and consequently, the more likely one was to believe that one's fate was linked to that of the race."[31] Thus, black institutions and networks have played a critical role in promoting a racialized worldview. While one finds different viewpoints among different classes within the African-American community, in general, social mobility increases the perception of linked fate and black economic subordination, producing, in turn, a decision-making calculus that informs judgments and dictates political and social thought.

Dawson claims that "linked fate" has combined with a diversity of ideological perspectives over time, historically leading to competing visions of freedom within the black community. These debates go as far back as the antebellum period when Frederick Douglass argued with Shields Green about liberating slaves through armed conflict. Dawson asserts that the one constant is that political blacksmiths have persistently used the concept of linked fate as the material with which to construct those ideologies. In our era, "this sense of linked fate is a product of the individual's interactions within both informal and formal African-American sociopolitical networks"—networks that provide narratives about both a common black identity and competing ideologies.[32] Based on this, Dawson concludes that a belief in linked fate does not mean complete ideological agreement. Conflict may be attributed to differing assumptions about the terms of racial

28. Dawson, *Behind the Mule*, 11, 76.

29. Dawson, *Behind the Mule*, 76, 80.

30. Dawson, *Behind the Mule*, 80.

31. Dawson, *Behind the Mule*, 81.

32. Dawson, *Black Visions*, 11.

unity and opposing ideologies. While social cleavages may not always oc-cur around class per se, they do occur according to ideological approaches influenced by class, gender, neighborhood, and information networks. Most importantly, Dawson provides a theoretical framework that illuminates how ambivalence regarding literacy reveals ideological differences among African-American individuals even as they adhere to a belief in a linked fate requiring a monolithic and unified black community.

## "Linked Fate" and Black Male Literacy Narratives

Reading the literacy narratives under consideration in this project through the lens of linked fate makes it apparent that African-American men have historically described their literacy in the context of a black utility heuristic, based on the belief that their life chances are over-determined by race. Hav-ing grown up on a plantation and having advanced his literacy to learn about abolition, Frederick Douglass cast his condition to the group's situation. As a child, he "learned by degrees the sad fact . . . that not only the house and lot, but that grandmother herself . . . and all the little children around her, belonged to this mysterious personage [old master]."[33] This knowledge began to tutor Douglass in the workings of the racial caste system, illumi-nating the general condition of blacks. Slavery bound all the black people in his environment and disrupted the relationships of the extended family network on their aggregation of plantations. The reality of bondage made it clear that blackness itself determined that one's lot was to be the property of one old master or another.

Douglass's narratives convey an increasing awareness of the relation-ship between his own fate and the circumstance of black slaves in the United States. As recounted in *My Bondage and My Freedom* in Baltimore, he was exposed to a philosophy of slave making and management that made the relationship between his race and his condition increasingly conspicuous. "Learning would spoil the best nigger in the world," Hugh Auld warns his wife.[34] Auld's words lend credence to Dawson's research, which connects education with a clearer, more profound perception of systemic injustice.[35] After overhearing his master's speech against educating slaves, Douglass finally understood "the *white man's* power to perpetuate the enslavement of the *black man*."[36] The increase in knowledge has "bitter, as well as sweet

33. Douglass, *My Bondage and My Freedom,* 142.

34. Douglass, *My Bondage and My Freedom,* 217.

35. Dawson, *Black Visions,* 69.

36. Dawson, *Black Visions,* 218; emphasis mine.

results. The more [he] read, the more [he] was led to abhor and detest slavery."[37] Later, Douglass would teach other slaves to read and encourage them to escape to the North before eventually escaping himself and then becoming a prominent abolitionist. Dawson's "lens" of linked fate helps us see that, as a result of his social station and self-education, Douglass developed a keener perception of racial injustice as a common racial destiny.

At the earliest dawning of his social awareness and quest for literacy, Langston Hughes, too, appears to have had a profound sense of linked fate. As a child in knickerbockers, Hughes would be placed on his grandmother's lap and told stories of ancestors who had risen to be illustrious as well as infamous. These tales of the lives of progenitors who wanted to "make the Negroes free" communicated a narrative of salient racial identity, historical racism, and racial hierarchy that implied linked fate. Interestingly, in *The Big Sea* Hughes precedes the discussion of his family tree with a painful memory of his visit to Africa—a pain that Dawson's concept of linked fate helps us to understand. He writes, "But there was one thing that hurt me a lot when I talked with people. The Africans looked at me and would not believe I was a Negro."[38] The individuals Hughes encountered in Africa understood their identity in unambiguous terms that emphasized the biological dimensions of race and de-emphasized the shared experience of racial subordination. Like many African Americans, Hughes had a tangled, multiracial genealogy. The Africans he encountered took his curly hair and light complexion to be a white man's characteristics, which caused Hughes pain, a sign of his indoctrination into the concept of linked fate.

How are we to understand this pain? Why would it be so crucial for Hughes to see himself as Negro rather than as the racial mix represented in his genealogy? With Dawson's lens of linked fate, we can see that more significant than biology in Hughes's mind was the perception of a common struggle against racial subordination—a perception that linked fate renders explicable. He had landed on the West Coast of Africa in 1923. West Africans were waiting for Marcus Garvey to liberate them from colonialism. Hughes tried to commiserate, but his interloper rejected him. He writes, "'Our problems in America are very much like yours,' I told the Africans, 'especially the South. I am a Negro, too.' But they only laughed and shook their heads and said, 'You, white man! You, white man!'"[39] It hurt Hughes to no end that Africans identified him either as white or with the condescending foreign blacks who served white mission efforts. The notion of

37. Dawson, *Black Visions*, 227.
38. Hughes, *Big Sea*, 11.
39. Hughes, *Big Sea*, 103.

linked fate meant more than an abstract ideology; it had been absorbed into his identity. His childhood memories had been linked with the pain of the group; while sitting on his grandmother's knee, Hughes deeply empathized with all black people's political struggle. This observation offers an operative interpretation for how the concept of linked fate both informed and found expression in Hughes's earliest literary aspirations.

At the height of racial tension in the early twentieth century, Hughes began to write jazz poetry that wedded art to history and language to a black identity, in camaraderie with the black underclass migrating north. He respected African-American soldiers' bravery and the fugitives from the South who struggled for freedom and liberty under a regime of racial discrimination and violence. He believed African Americans were "the gayest and the bravest people possible."[40] On the way to visit his father, he pondered "his [father's] strange dislike of his own people."[41] He continued, "I didn't understand it, because I was a Negro, and I liked Negroes very much."[42] Dawson enables us to recognize that Hughes implies a robust race-consciousness beneath this declaration of solidarity, one that emerges in his poem imagining the relationship of rivers to the African-American experience—a consciousness that Dawson's notion of linked fate helps us see in bold relief.

Let us read Hughes further through the lens of linked fate. The inspiration to write "The Negro Speaks of Rivers" came during the Red Summer of 1919, when African Americans across the nation clashed with whites following the Great War. His words reflected a historical consciousness and his imagining a common black identity. The poem makes apparent how "individual political and social attitudes are formed partly as a response to individual perceptions of the status of the group."[43] Hughes writes:

> I've known rivers:
>
> I've known rivers ancient as the world and older than the flow of human blood in human veins.
>
> My soul has grown deep like the rivers.
> I bathed in Euphrates when dawns were young.
> I built my hut near the Congo and it lulled me to sleep.
> I looked upon the Nile and raised the pyramids above it.

---

40. Hughes, *Big Sea*, 54.
41. Hughes, *Big Sea*, 54.
42. Hughes, *Big Sea*, 54.
43. Dawson, *Behind the Mule*, 62.

I heard the singing of the Mississippi when Abe Lincoln went
down to New Orleans, and I've seen its muddy bosom turn all
gold in the sunset.

I've known rivers:
Ancient, dusky rivers.

My soul has grown deep like the rivers.[44]

In "The Negro Speaks of Rivers," Hughes connects the enslavement of
African Americans to the historical black experience. The poem portrays
rivers in ancient Egypt and villages in the Congo. Moving beyond Africa,
Hughes descends into the American slave experience.[45] Because this poem
launched the young Hughes's literary career, the prodigy's literacy act is
evidence of the profound sense in which the historical black experience
and the interconnectedness of the black Atlantic shaped the construction
of black identity among literate African Americans at the beginning of the
twentieth century. This literary imagination persists in constructing black
art, identity, and thought.

Dawson has pointed out that historical memory has repercussions for
African Americans developing a deep sense of black consciousness and the
calculus of linked fate. At seventeen, Hughes had already written a poem that
cultivated historical memory and created an imaginative space in which he
constructed a black utility heuristic that united his personal experience of
racial subordination with blacks in America and blacks in Africa. As noted
above, Hughes would experience painful rejection years later when Africans
rejected his claims on blackness.

Similarly, during their formative years, Vershawn Young and Thomas
Chatterton Williams both strongly identify with African Americans as a
group, in a manner that seems to point toward a belief in linked fate based on
a shared experience of racial subordination. As Dawson predicts, education
enhanced their already heightened awareness of a common experience of
oppression with a consequential sense of obligation. In a black barbershop,
Young felt anxious about how his "language and demeanor often mark[ed
him] as educated, separating [him] from those who exemplify the stigmatized . . . black male profile [and] the plight that follows that image."[46] Nevertheless, a sense of linked fate lingered. Young writes, "I am troubled because
black men who suffer most from the educational and judicial systems are

44. Hughes, *Big Sea*, 54–55.
45. Hughes, *Big Sea*, 54–55.
46. Young, *Your Average Nigga*, xiii.

poor, from the underclass, from the ghetto, like me."[47] Education and social mobility did not negate his sense of connection; they only heightened his perception that his destiny was tied to other black men's life chances.

Williams's racial awakening began with his parents telling him of his identity as a black man and with the knowledge that his father grew up in Texas during the Jim Crow era. As a seven year old, Williams's father had him read *The Autobiography of Malcolm X*. Sleep would evade him at night as he thought about how the Klan had killed Malcolm's father and left "his cranium cracked open like a coconut husk."[48] Despite his mixed-race heritage, he learned from the book, and his life began to paint race relations in such a dark light that Williams rejected the contribution of his mother's white heritage. He recalls:

> I didn't want to resemble in any way whatsoever those men who do such things to other men. It was a fortunate thing for me, too, that I didn't want to be white. It was fortunate because I really didn't have much choice in the matter. My parents were right: Around white kids, I simply was not white.[49]

Williams also witnessed his older brother's uneasy relationship with his white friends in their suburban neighborhood. In response to his observations, reading, and social experiences, as a mere child, he began to identify with the most relevant black men in the lower-class black institutions—the black media sources and sports arenas—and developed a myopic perception of the black social world.

Drawing on hip-hop culture, Williams even altered his mannerisms to ensure others interpreted him as "black"—an ambiguous term. He describes the significance of urban black identity performances during the early nineties in this way: "It was not enough simply to know and to accept that you were black—you had to look and act that way, too. You were going to be judged by how convincingly you could pull off the pose."[50] He took cues from the younger men at the barbershop, *Rap City* on Black Entertainment Television, and hip-hop movies such as *New Jack City*.[51] Reminiscent of the protagonist in Tupac Shakur's song "Shorty Wants to Be a Thug," Williams began using expletives and performing "a certain way of moving or gesticulating that went with whatever was said." Put differently, Williams's

47. Young, *Your Average Nigga*, xiii.
48. Williams, *Losing My Cool*, 6.
49. Williams, *Losing My Cool*, 6–7.
50. Williams, *Losing My Cool*, 11.
51. Williams, *Losing My Cool*, 11.

childhood effort to appropriate blackness based on his observation of street literacy performances directly coincided with his developing a black utility heuristic based on lessons in his home and observations in the street about blackness.

These examples make it evident that particular individuals perceive a relationship between their racial identities and their literacy acquisition within the broader contemporary and historical African-American experience. Literacy emerges as an option in the context of a racialized social order. As a child, Douglass learned that his condition as a slave was tied to his family and the broader black community. Hughes, too, tied his untutored pan-Africanism to his family history and penned poetry that reflected this perspective. Young and Williams both yearned to connect with other black men who struggled with both social challenges and literacy due to their lower socioeconomic status and urban conditions. Young's reflection on his complicated thoughts concerning his relationship with other African-American men reveals a deep-seated ambivalence. However, the young professor's own struggles led him to develop a substantial degree of empathy. Williams's parents used literacy and family discussions to reinforce their son's black identity. In the streets and in schoolyards, both Young and Williams grew up believing that authentic black masculinity involved something other than race, politics, ideology, intellectual pursuits, and social uplift. For them, blackness was demonstrated by performing the "cool pose," talking street, and engaging in certain masculine activities—rapping, playing basketball, and street fighting—that was dominated by black males in their social worlds, according to Williams. In the end, their amorphous grasp of linked fate provided a foundation for their commitment to a depoliticized cultural conception of blackness, a commitment that had implications for their evolving notions of literacy.

Dawson's concept of linked fate makes legible the palpable belief among African Americans that the well-being and destiny of the individual are tied to the good of the group in a way that requires conformity to some prevailing form of blackness. In other words, one must demonstrate one's blackness in a manner that confirms a commitment to the idea of a monolithic black people. This cultural agenda became an unquestioned assumption among black youth growing up in the post-civil rights era. "Those ensconced in the hip-hop culture, which is also commonly described as the hip-hop nation, do not entirely ignore the earlier dominant themes of race and nation that were so central to twentieth-century black intellectuals and leaders along a continuum," Murray Forman explains.[52] A comprehensive

52. Forman, 'Hood Comes First, 63.

discussion of black male ambivalence toward literacy demonstrates that linked fate provides the grounds for an analysis of the relationship between the individual and the group and reveals a cultural assumption that the individual's identity and behavior must conform to an agreed-upon cultural norm. Evelyn Brooks Higginbotham, writing on the activities of African-American women in the National Baptist Convention USA around the turn of the twentieth century, provides further insight into the influence of linked fate on the relationships among education, racial uplift, and class politics. On the foundation of linked fate, black women and men in the Baptist church promoted assimilation through literacy, cleanliness, and respectability.

## Higginbotham's Idea of the "Politics of Respectability"

In *Righteous Discontent: The Women's Movement in the Black Baptist Church, 1880–1920*, Higginbotham details how, during the "nadir" in American race relations, African-American women and men exercised their individual and communal agency by gathering under the auspices of the church to fight against the prevailing racial politics in broader society. These endeavors included establishing women's auxiliaries and a separate national denomination within the Baptist Convention. These women believed that they should found black women's colleges and, eventually, a Baptist Women's Convention. African-American churchwomen collaborated with white women and taught their class politics in home mission societies to promote racial uplift. According to Higginbotham, the black Baptist women were both black nationalists and feminists to the core. While *Righteous Discontent* tells the story of African-American women's theology, ideology, and activism in response to racism and sexism, I am primarily interested in how their commitment to assimilation informed their guiding strategy. Higginbotham labels "the politics of respectability."[53] She argues that this ideological approach eventually generated a bourgeois class of African Americans. They sought to elevate their underclass brethren into the political body to achieve racial equality.

These black Baptist women's optimistic and nationalistic response to Jim Crow and narratives of black inferiority led them to promote "middle-class ideals among the masses of blacks in the belief that such ideals ensured the dual goals of racial uplift and respect from white America."[54] According to Higginbotham, "The Baptist women's preoccupation with

53. Higginbotham, *Righteous Discontent,* 14–15.
54. Higginbotham, *Righteous Discontent,* 14–15.

respectability reflected a bourgeois vision that vacillated between an attack on the failure of America to live up to its liberal ideals of equality and justice and an attack on the values and lifestyle of those blacks who transgressed white middle-class propriety."[55] Their ranks included teachers, ministers' wives, and missionaries, who defined their lives by bourgeois values and aspirations. Higginbotham writes, "Duty-bound to teach the value of religion, education, and hard work, the women of the black Baptist church adhered to a politics of respectability that equated public behavior with individual self-respect and with the advancement of African Americans as a group."[56] Already committed to this strategy, this emergent class of leaders gained the psychological assent of the poorer and less "respectable blacks."[57]

Higginbotham argues that the politics of respectability—a response to racism and segregation—is important in several ways. These women encouraged the poor to live frugally and rely on self-help within the black community. This ideology fueled the growth of the black middle-class. The promotion of bourgeois women's values meant transforming "the culture of the 'folk'—the expressive culture of many poor, uneducated, and 'unassimilated' black men and women dispersed throughout the rural South or newly huddled in urban centers."[58] Higginbotham describes the Baptist women's social movement as vacillating between criticizing whites for not fulfilling the tenets of democracy and underclass blacks for their poor behavior. The pendulum of respectability swung between radical politics and conservative social norms. The women's conservatism shone through "when they attributed institutional racism to the 'negative' public behavior of their people—as if rejection of 'gaudy' colors in dress, snuff dipping, baseball games on Sunday, and other forms of 'improper' decorum could eradicate the pervasive racial barriers that surrounded black Americans."[59] Black elites found it difficult to perceive the lifestyles and agency exercised among lower-status blacks, who rejected white middle-class values. "While adherence to respectability enabled black women to counter racist images and structures, their discursive contestation was not directed solely at white Americans; the black Baptist women condemned what they perceived to be negative practices and attitudes among their own people," Higginbotham writes.[60] The bicultural context contributes to the politics of black distinc-

55. Higginbotham, *Righteous Discontent*, 15.

56. Higginbotham, *Righteous Discontent*, 15.

57. Higginbotham, *Righteous Discontent*, 15.

58. Higginbotham, *Righteous Discontent*, 15.

59. Higginbotham, *Righteous Discontent*, 15.

60. Higginbotham, *Righteous Discontent*, 187.

tion. It is informed by "Yankee, neo-Puritan, Victorian and middle-class" attitudes that sought social, political, and economic progress and bourgeois respectability but shunned the hedonistic behavior and high society whites pursuing materialism and the "idleness and vice" of the black folk.[61]

Leaving aside the participants' economic realities in home missions, because bourgeois politics have a racial valence, the black churchwomen's appropriation of white America's behaviors and values as a means to promote self-help and racial uplift caused them to perpetuate racism toward the black folk unwittingly. "[The] conservative and moralistic dimension [to their uplift rhetoric] tended to privatize racial discrimination," Higginbotham explains, "thus rendering it outside the authority of government regulation."[62] She cites Nannie Burroughs's 1913 speech on blacks' poor housing conditions in Chicago, Illinois. Burroughs was an advocate of euthenics, a science concerned with bettering their condition by improving their environment. Advocates of euthenics promoted schooling and education concerning personal and environmental hygiene. In Burroughs's 1913 speech, she vociferously condemned the government but left the burden of structural change on African Americans. She complained,

> In Washington City there is much talk about getting the seventeen thousand Negroes out of the alleys. To the student of euthenics, who believes that the shortest cut to health is by creating a clean environment in which to live this plan is most feasible, but to do a work that will abide we must first "get the alley" out of the seventeen thousand Negroes, and it will not be an easy task to get them out of the alley.[63]

Clearly, in Burroughs's mind, it is not environmental racism that produces unhealthy living conditions, but the street *within* urban black communities that creates harmful environmental conditions. Thus, while she tries to bring about social and political equality, her rhetoric reveals that she, too, had internalized stereotypes that condemned poor black people for having brought their circumstances upon themselves through their disreputable conduct.

The adherence to middle-class respectability was a religious and ideological and political strategy whose contradictions led to the marginalization of underclass folks. First, it engaged a range of discourses: "[These black churchwomen] contested the racist discourses and rejected white America's depiction of black [men and] women as immoral, childlike, and unworthy

61. Higginbotham, *Righteous Discontent*, 95, 187.

62. Higginbotham, *Righteous Discontent*, 203.

63. Higginbotham, *Righteous Discontent*, 203.

of respect. . . ."[64] In doing so, the women "condemned what they perceived to be negative practices and attitudes among their own people."[65] In waging a battle against white supremacy, black Baptist churchwomen acquiesced to a standard of behavior based on a racial logic that implied black inferiority and that supported the racial hierarchy, then and now. Marginalization occurred when these missionaries attributed negative behaviors to unchurched, underclass blacks and constrained them to the lowest social tier.

Regarding the black folk who were less inclined to participate in regular church attendance, "their assimilationist leanings led to their insistence upon blacks' conformity to the dominant society's norms of manners and morals. Thus, the discourse of respectability disclosed class and status differentiation,"[66] Higginbotham asserts. Nevertheless, *Righteous Discontent* lays bare the unintended repercussion of their adherence to the politics of respectability and assimilation as a subversive strategy. These churchwomen did not intend on accommodating a racist society and its structures, but their subversion had cultural and material consequences for unconverted blacks, then and now.

## Seeing with the "Politics of Respectability"

Frederick Douglass developed a response to enslavement that presaged Higginbotham's conceptual construct of "the politics of respectability." Douglass's attempt to educate and raise the sociopolitical awareness of other enslaved blacks represents the germ of respectability politics. Nearing manhood, Douglass moved from student to teacher, slave to liberator. A black minister had told him that the Lord had great work for him to do.[67] He prepared for this "great work" by studying Scripture. As a hired hand, Douglass began to teach other slaves to read the Bible. He writes, "They very soon mustered up some old spelling-books, and nothing would do but that I must keep a Sabbath school. I agreed to do so, and accordingly devoted my Sundays to teaching these my loved fellow-slaves how to read."[68] Douglass reports that his students "came because they wished to learn. Their minds had been starved by their cruel master."[69] This theological work had political repercussions. He writes, "I taught them, because it was the delight of my

64. Higginbotham, *Righteous Discontent*, 184.
65. Higginbotham, *Righteous Discontent*, 187.
66. Higginbotham, *Righteous Discontent*, 187.
67. Douglass, *Narrative of the Life*, 68–73.
68. Douglass, *Narrative of the Life*, 72.
69. Douglass, *Narrative of the Life*, 72.

soul to be doing something that looked like bettering the condition of my race."[70] In addition to teaching the slaves how to read and write, Douglass sought "to imbue their minds with thoughts of freedom."[71] The literacy aspirations of these slaves bring to light the reality that, on the plantation, a few slaves subscribed to an unarticulated self-help ideology as a means of both personal edification and communal uplift. On the surface, this appears similar to Dawson's linked fate. Due to social uplift efforts, their approach to education contains the seeds of respectability politics.[72]

Hughes spent part of his impoverished childhood living among and learning from European immigrants, but he also worked in the local black community where he identified with poor African Americans. During his teen years, "Negroes were coming in a great dark tide from the South," and he began to spend more time among them.[73] The aspiring young writer began to experience a strong identification and solidarity with them. His happiest moments were the hours he worked at a soda fountain "in the heart of the colored neighborhood. People just up from the South used to come in for ice cream and sodas and watermelon."[74] Hughes was fascinated with the migrants from the South. He admired the courage of the black soldiers returning from overseas to face racial oppression in the states and reveled in the stories of black Southerners who had fled racial violence. This burgeoning social awareness informed his political imagination and prompted him to begin writing about the black folk's lives, using the black vernacular.

Hughes began to work out his literary agenda in his second book of poems, *Fine Clothes to the Jew*. He writes, "It was . . . more about other people than myself. . . . It made use of the Negro folk-song forms, and included poems about work and the problems of finding work, that is always so pressing with the [poorer] Negro people [sic]."[75] Hughes considered the collection his best writing, thus far. The white press received it well. But the black establishment hated it. They called his writing "trash" and the author a "sewer dweller."[76] Describing the literary politics of the black aristocracy, Hughes writes: "The Negro critics and many of the intellectuals were very sensitive about their race books. In anything that white people were likely to read, they wanted to put their best foot forward, their politely polished

70. Douglass, *Narrative of the Life*, 72.
71. Douglass, *Narrative of the Life*, 83–84.
72. Higginbotham, *Righteous Discontent*, 14–15.
73. Hughes, *Big Sea*, 54–55.
74. Hughes, *Big Sea*, 54–55.
75. Hughes, *Big Sea*, 263.
76. Hughes, *Big Sea*, 266.

and cultural foot—and only that foot."[77] This is a concern that persists to this day, as Bill Cosby and others have shared their concerns about the state of black America in articles, books, interviews, panels, and speeches made at prominent events. Yet, even during the Harlem Renaissance, Hughes was ambivalent about black distinction politics. While he sympathized with and understood the political goals of the critics, he felt that he "didn't know the upper class Negroes well enough to write much about them."[78] In the end, Hughes ignored the critics and their racial politics, choosing instead to write about the masses "who had [not] been to Harvard, or had heard of Bach."[79] Higginbotham helps us to see that by leaving behind respectability in his writing and lifestyle, Hughes departed from a norm prevalent among the black upper class. This conspicuous cultural shift reveals class tensions as a source of ambivalence regarding literacy.

Reading literacy narratives from the other end of the twentieth century, I again draw on Higginbotham to explore how the politics of respectability continues to influence African-American black culture, but at the same time conflicts with an increasingly influential black street culture practiced by a group of black men born after the civil rights and Black Power movements. Vershawn Ashanti Young and Thomas Chatterton Williams exemplify the black youth who consider rejecting and subverting the politics of middle-class distinction (i.e., the politics of respectability) to show fidelity to black culture and black masculinity.

Young first encountered the intersection of race and class in middle school when he read E. Franklin Frazier's *Black Bourgeoisie* and Harold Cruse's *The Crisis of the Negro Intellectual*. Reading these classic black sociological texts as a schoolboy, he learned that he wasn't part of the assimilationist bourgeois society because he was too dark and lived in the projects. Living up to his confrontational self-image as a student, he angered one teacher when he shared his feelings about the black middle class:

> I made sure I let that teacher know I didn't want to be bourgeois; they weren't any good. They didn't like us [poor blacks]. And I asked her why members of the black bourgeoisie came to teach us ghetto kids, anyway, if we could never be counted among them. I was sent home and told not to return without my mother.[80]

77. Hughes, *Big Sea*, 266–67.
78. Hughes, *Big Sea*, 267.
79. Hughes, *Big Sea*, 267.
80. Young, *Your Average Nigga*, 32.

We see his early resistance to the class ideology and assimilationist lean-ings of the black elite that Higginbotham refers to as respectability politics. Young believes that black elites had rejected lower class, uneducated, and dark-skinned African Americans. Consequently, it is not surprising then that he found himself in conflict with the only other fair-skinned black teacher at an event at Columbia College in Chicago.[81] As a tenure-track professor, he was asked to give a lecture to roughly sixty part-time writ-ing instructors and wanted to promote his theory of code-meshing with Black English Vernacular as a means to endorse literacy. In the process of advancing this new position, he came into conflict with a black middle-class colleague who was committed to the politics of respectability.

Young knew in advance that most of the instructors uncritically endorsed code-switching and a superficial valuation of the Black English Vernacular. He forecasted a misunderstanding concerning his promotion of a "seamless mixture of BEV and [White English Vernacular] that leads to a more natural, less artificial, well-expressed prose."[82] Predictably, the most vociferous opponent was the only other African-American in the room: Diane, an account executive in a marketing firm and part-time English instructor. She and Young were usually on collegial terms. However, when Young advocated using the Africanist idiom, Diane fumed. She pointed out that Young had advanced in life due to his mastery of Standard English instead of "ghetto literacy."[83] Young, who consistently describes his own be-havior throughout his narrative as ambiguous and as rejecting a wholesale middle-class self-identification, was tempted to go "ghettomatic" on Diane and "signify"[84] on her middle-class pretensions, including her wearing a fur coat in November and "ultraproper racial speech performance."[85] Here, Hig-ginbotham's assessment of racial politics in terms of class, race conscious-ness, and the unintended consequences of the war on racism can bring the ambivalence of some African Americans around literacy into sharp focus.

At the turn of the last century, black churchwomen "endeavored to implant middle-class values and behavioral patterns among the masses of urban blacks who retained folkways of speech, dress, worship, and other distinct cultural patterns."[86] These church women's spirit has endured in their socially mobile daughters like Diane, who is seen grasping her white

81. Young, *Your Average Nigga*, 107.

82. Young, *Your Average Nigga*, 106.

83. Young, *Your Average Nigga*, 108.

84. Young, *Your Average Nigga*, 108.

85. Young, *Your Average Nigga*, 108.

86. Higginbotham, *Righteous Discontents*, 196–97.

pearls of respectability, having taken up the mantle of racial uplift through schooling and adherence to white middle-class norms. Although both Diane and Young shared the goal of helping students learn to write, in their heated argument, Diane espoused assimilation strategies—a move that disregards the difficulty poorer black students find with code-switching. Young believes it leads to further ambivalence about school in general and literacy. Diane's professional experiences and class commitments are revealed in her closing statement. She declared, "I don't make the rules [of dominant society]; I just follow them."[87] Indeed, Young opines that she failed to recognize "how [a new] politics of race should inform the way we teach writing."[88] He writes, "This difference [in opinion] led her to contend that my advocacy . . . sells black students short; it suggests that they can't master the standard dialect."[89] Diane, indeed, thought that allowing black students to speak the Black English Vernacular would limit "the chances for success of any minority student, especially underprivileged Blacks who need to learn the language of public communication to make it in this world."[90] Consequently, in their debate and Young's frustrated reflection, we witness a manifestation of the conflict between the politics of respectability and the culture of the streets in the guise of a new politics of race.

In contrast, Williams was attracted to his high school paramour Stacey because she represented the antithesis of respectability politics. In his imagination, Stacey embodied an anti-intellectual and oppositional blackness enslaved to the commercial hip-hop regime that he believes will help him appropriate a believable street literacy performance as a sophomore in high school. Williams confesses that he chose Stacey as a girlfriend because "winning her attentions authenticated my blackness and justified my swagger."[91] Decades later, he explains, "The way a weaker jogger will strive to match the pace of a stronger partner, I strove to meet her at her level of cool."[92] Williams's father had problems with their relationship and definitively represents the politics of black distinction. Of his father, Williams writes, "All Pappy ever wanted to do in his life was to distinguish himself, to be a man capable of commanding respect in a world that was madly hostile to anyone who looked like him."[93] While Williams understands his father's

---

87. Young, *Your Average Nigga*, 108.

88. Young, *Your Average Nigga*, 108.

89. Young, *Your Average Nigga*, 108.

90. Young, *Your Average Nigga*, 108.

91. Williams, *Losing My Cool*, 49.

92. Williams, *Self-Portrait in Black and White*, 50.

93. Williams, *Losing My Cool*, 72.

concerns, he believes that Pappy's world was as "unrecognizable to Charles [his friend] and me as ours was to him."[94] The difference in their world-views helps us interpret the tension in Williams's discourse of ambivalence. "Pappy and I saw the world through different lenses," he writes. As a more reflective adult living in Paris, Williams explains that "he was concerned by the idea of increasing my own physical and cultural blackness, of less-ening any dilutions."[95] Williams's concern about his literacy and gender performances in opposition to his father's politics makes the discourse of ambivalence legible. Ironically, as we will see later when he moved on to Georgetown University and began to pursue his scholastic potential and respectability and embrace academic literacy, his girlfriend Stacey served as his foil. Attending Georgetown prompted Williams's transition toward the politics of distinction and respectability. This shift included adopting elite white sociocultural norms and speech patterns. As one might predict for someone at his developmental level and psychological temperament, Wil-liams developed a dismissive attitude toward his high school friends and the African-American students at Georgetown that remained committed to a more hybrid identity and literacy performances.

Higginbotham illuminates how the politics of respectability played out in the literacy aspirations of Douglass, Hughes, Young, and Williams. In response to master narratives about black inferiority, black males have often sought to appropriate and redefine what it means to be literate. In Doug-lass's case, he equated the acquisition of letters with political freedom. This association allows us to imagine that, for Douglass, there was an implied connection between the study of the Bible and improving one's spiritual and moral character and a germinal political philosophy akin to the politics of respectability. In this sense, Douglass was committed to communal uplift through helping other slaves attain literacy and develop a religious outlook and a political consciousness.

Hughes had a different response to the politics of respectability. The poet understood the relationship between literature and propaganda in the African-American experience. He broke free of the agenda of the African-American literati, which required that he write about the lifestyles of the black elite. These lifestyles sought to emulate the cultural and moral norms of upper-class whites. This agenda was nothing new. According to Hig-ginbotham, "It was the positive image of respectable African Americans that the [black] Baptist women sought to promote by means of 'distinc-tive' literature, their term for literature written by black authors. Virginia

94. Williams, *Losing My Cool*, 72.
95. Williams, *Self-Portrait in Black and White*, 50.

Broughton ... explained the need for a 'distinctive literature' in 1902 when she declared that blacks must publish their side of history in order to contest racist discourses and instill pride in their people."[96] Hughes claimed to have not known many "upper-class Negroes."[97] Whether or not it was true, he wrote about the lives of African Americans who had not attended elite colleges and did not listen to classical music. In their engagement about black cultural representations and the black vernacular, one finds a fascinating discourse of ambivalence about the criteria for African-American literature and literacy performances.

At the beginning of the twenty-first century, the literacy debates go beyond arguments about what constitutes politically correct African-American literature. The most significant discussions return to the idea that personal development through literacy acquisition deconstructs racist narratives and promotes individual growth, racial progress, and solidarity among African-American people. Ironically, these discussions have happened among the black aristocracy—Bill Cosby, C. Delores Tucker, and Barack Obama—and continue through black youth in the context of dialogues about acting and talking white (or gay).

Young's literacy narrative concedes that his promotion of what his colleague deemed "ghetto literacy" contains within it an implicit ambivalence about race, gender identity, and literacy myths. Young is clear about how his proposed literacy model vacillates between identifying and (dis)identifying with the urban males who refuse to speak "white English Vernacular."[98] Elite blacks chose literacy to achieve "respectability" as a cornerstone of racial uplift, and never tolerated a double standard of behavior.[99] Young observes that the conflation of gendered differences in both behavior and political strategies exacerbates the gender realities of black males. In one sense, "the difference between black boys and white boys is that black boys not only feel coerced to give up their masculinity if they do well in school, but they feel forced to abandon their race—the ultimate impossibility," Young writes.[100] But social pressure also leads to another form of coercion. According to Young, "it may be more accurate to say that if those black males do not exhibit other behaviors considered to be masculine, such as displaying the pimp walk, playing sports, or engaging in sexual banter with females, they

96. Higginbotham, *Righteous Discontent*, 194.

97. Hughes, *Big Sea*, 267.

98. Young, *Your Average Nigga*, 90–91.

99. Higginbotham, *Righteous Discontent*, 185.

100. Young, *Your Average Nigga*, 90.

will inevitably endanger [perceptions about] their black maleness."[101] These tensions reveal how the agenda of black distinction creates ambivalence among black males by ignoring gender dichotomies of which young men are quite aware.

Lest one finds hyperbole in Young's analysis, Williams suggests that an identical social pressure shapes his literacy narrative's trajectory. Early on, he chose to learn and interpret blackness that rejected respectability politics and sought to distinguish itself from the dominant white culture. He closely observed the attire, behavior, and mannerisms of Rashawn, a street thug, and don on the basketball court with a real black name, as a model to develop his identity.[102] Reflecting on Rashawn, William writes:

> The loose-fitting jeans falling from our hips, the unlaced kicks [shoes] adorning our feet, the slang encrypting our speech, the slow roll choreographing our strides, the funky-ass hairstyles embellishing our domes, the hip hop sound tracking our days, the pigment darkening our skin—all these disparate elements congealed into a kind of glue that invisibly but definitively united people like Rashawn and me.[103]

Williams defined his racial identity based on hip-hop as a synonym for (empowered) blackness in contrast to respectability politics. Instead of academic and cultural distinction, he chose feigned illiteracy and hyper-masculinity. Regarding books, he writes, "[Street masculinity] was a wicked genie that I, too, [like Rashawn] could summon if I chose, if I was just willing to play down the things [like books and literacy] I saw in my father's study—things that only put distance between Rashawn and me—and to play up the things I saw on BET, on the street, and ESPN."[104] As discussed earlier, Williams admits that dating Stacey in order to assert his own racial and gender identity was in contradistinction to his father's politics of respectability. On a number of levels, his behavior and literacy narrative embodies the tensions experienced among males in the black community between literacy and respectability, on the one hand, and a black street identity, on the other, creating a discourse of ambivalence.

Dawson's concept of linked fate exposes one of the factors that influence African-American males' interpretation of the relationship between black identity and literacy acquisition. The idea of linked fate is critical to misperceptions regarding the existence of a monolithic African-American

101. Young, *Your Average Nigga*, 91.
102. Williams, *Losing My Cool*, 24–25.
103. Williams, *Your Average Nigga*, 24.
104. Williams, *Your Average Nigga*, 24–25.

community and the belief that it pursues ideological homogeneity as a social and political goal. Apart from Douglass, each of the men learned about
the significance of literacy in the black experience at an early age. Douglass's narrative is a critical historical precedent to the continuing linkage
between literacy and black liberation. The contrarian Hughes rejected the
idea that black literature had to be imitative or reflect respectability. Young
and Williams, however, remind us that more recent generations of black
males inhabit a world in which the choice between mainstream and street
literacy performances is not taken for granted. Higginbotham's thesis reveals that social programs promoting education and conservative behavior
and values as a path towards personal and racial uplift have contributed to
literacy ambivalence among code-switching black males, such as Hughes,
Williams, and Young.

In the next chapter, I will explore Toni Morrison's and Cathy Cohen's
theoretical frameworks illuminating the relationship between the notion of
a deficient African-American literacy in our cultural imagination that had
been deployed as a means of defining whiteness and the aspirations of black
and community-based literacy. Those frameworks will help us examine how
the black community has sought to acquire literacy by repressing images
and behavior among African Americans that might connote illiteracy or
disreputable behavior.

This is race talk, the explicit insertion into everyday life of racial signs and symbols that have no meaning other than pressing African Americans to the lowest level of the racial hierarchy. Popular culture, shaped by film, theater, advertising, the press, television, and literature, is heavily engaged in race talk. It participates freely in this most enduring and efficient rite of passage into American culture: negative appraisals of the native-born black population. Only when the lesson of racial estrangement is learned is assimilation complete. Whatever the lived experience of immigrants with African Americans—pleasant, beneficial, or bruising—the rhetorical experience renders blacks as noncitizens, already discredited outlaws.

—Toni Morrison, "On the Backs of Blacks" (1993)

# NEW **CHID** FOCUS GROUP
## *COMPARATIVE HISTORY OF IDEAS*

6'6"
6'0"
5'6"
5'0"
4'6"
4'0"
3'6"
3'0"

# YOUR AVERAGE
# NIGGAS:
## CHID 496K

CLOSE READINGS OF THE NEW JIM CROW AND
OTHER NARRATIVES OF MASS INCARCERATION(S)
IN THE AGE OF COLORBLINDNESS

Authors: Michelle Alexander, Linda Tucker, Michel Foucault, Martha Nussbuam, Toni Morrison,
Thomas Chatterton Williams, Vershawn Ashanti Young, Jeff Henderson,
Sanyika Shakur aka Monster Kody, and Stanley Tookie Williams

*Facilitators:*
MAX HUNTER
AND EDDIE MOORE JR

Autumn 2010
*Time:* TBA
*Contact:* **chid@uw.edu** for add codes

**W**
UNIVERSITY *of*
WASHINGTON

CHAPTER 5

# Blackness Out of Bounds

## Remixed Literacy in the Black Experience

IN THE WAKE OF winning the Nobel Prize in Literature in 1993, novelist Toni Morrison published "On the Backs of Blacks" in *Time* magazine. This article argued that for immigrants to receive full inclusion into the political economy of the United States, dominant society mandates that they internalize a racial logic and rhetoric that marginalizes African Americans.[1] In this chapter, I build on my previous discussion of the relationship between the notion of linked fate and the politics of respectability in order to reveal the power of what Morrison terms "race talk," or racial rhetoric, to shape both African-American politics and the psyches of black males to create ambivalence regarding literacy. It's from Morrison that a connection can be seen between literature and the conception of self as literate or illiterate in relation to an imagined black other. The tension between viewing the self through the lens of a deficient blackness on the one hand, and, on the other, reinventing the self in opposition to a mediated black other in order to migrate across the color-line into the land of opportunity and renewal contributes to the palpable ambivalence or double-consciousness found in black male literacy narratives.

In *Playing in the Dark: Whiteness and the Literary Imagination,* Morrison probes the hidden assumptions about the meaning and significance of blacks in American literature. She helps us understand how the dichotomy outlined above emerged in our nation and evolved to create ambivalence among black males pursuing erudition. Morrison's analysis lays bare the close-knit relationship between racial ideologies and the North American

1. Morrison, "On the Backs of Blacks," 57.

literary imagination in signifying black as illiterate and white as literate. She explains, "Cultural identities are *formed and informed* by a nation's literature, and . . . what seemed to be on the 'mind' of the authors in the literature of the United States, at its founding [and throughout our history, was] the self-conscious but highly problematic construction of the American as the new white man."[2] At the intersection of our dominant racial logic and the American novel is an attitude of neglect that allows literary critics to ignore race's role in our literature. According to Morrison, "Like thousands of avid but non-academic readers, some powerful literary critics in the United States have never read, and are proud to say so, any African-American text."[3] This attitude toward black literature and the black subject has led to obliviousness to how "a carefully observed, and carefully invented, Africanist presence" informs our native literature and the conceit of the white American.[4] These Africanisms are hidden rhetorical moves that signify blackness (or illiteracy) and, by implication, whiteness (literacy).

Suppose Morrison is correct about the white literary imagination, as I believe she is. In that case, I'd argue that, regardless of race, many learned and lay readers of the American canon have been indoctrinated into a literary imagination that participates in the denial and marginalization of black subjectivity—a process dependent on what Morrison calls an "Africanist presence" and the "African idiom" at the center of the American canon, literary imagination, and political thought.[5] These conventions of signification inform black males' reflections on their own literacy by setting up a polarity buried deep in the American literary imagination. I start with the assumption that the literary imagination informs political ideation. In Morrison's words, "Black slavery enriched the country's creative possibilities. For in that construction of blackness and enslavement could be found not only the not-free but also, with the dramatic polarity created by skin color, the projection of not-me."[6] In this chapter, I continue to probe the thoughts of Frederick Douglass, Langston Hughes, Vershawn Ashanti Young, and Thomas Chatterton Williams to uncover these authors' strategies for defining their own identities within a context that implies that the black male was/is characterized by a marginalized American Africanism.[7]

2. Morrison, *Playing in the Dark*, 39; emphasis mine.
3. Morrison, *Playing in the Dark*, 4–5.
4. Morrison, *Playing in the Dark*, 6.
5. Morrison, *Playing in the Dark*, 51.
6. Morrison, *Playing in the Dark*, 51.
7. Morrison, *Playing in the Dark*, 17.

Morrison's perspective enables us to see how an Africanist presence functions in the literacy narratives we consider. Africanisms are "the denotative and connotative blackness that African peoples have come to signify, as well as the entire range of views, assumptions, readings, and misreadings that accompany Eurocentric learning about [black] people [in the United States]."[8] Morrison suggests that our literature draws on a normative racial lexicon that either depicts blackness as invisible or employs it as a means to reproduce racial hierarchies and myths that inform the dominant group's understanding of the superior white self and that mediate its self-reinvention. Indeed, the core of Morrison's examination attempts to elucidate the literary and moral imagination of "a nation of people who decided that their worldview would combine agendas for individual freedom and mechanisms for devastating racial oppression [against enslaved Africans and their descendants]."[9] Within the American canon, Africanisms are constructed to empower white males and inscribe them with freedom. She writes, "The very manner by which American literature distinguishes itself as a coherent entity exists because of this unsettled and unsettling population."[10] American writers have crafted a distinctive national identity "through significant and underscored omissions, startling contradictions, heavily nuanced conflicts, through the way [they] peopled their work with the signs and bodies of this [Africanist] presence—one can see that a real or fabricated Africanist presence was crucial to their sense of Americanness [or newness]."[11] To be clear, I am claiming that the Africanist presence and the Africanist idiom, as Morrison identifies them in white American literature, also appear in the narratives of the African Americans male authors I examine in this project.

Moreover, these black male authors—and the theories through which we have viewed and will view their narratives—deploy the Africanist idiom in self-reflection, mediation, and reinvention of the *new exceptional black self*. In other words, in the conscious renegotiation of their own literate identities, we find them failing in their ability to transcend the idiom due to the need to negate and distance themselves from the less erudite African Americans. This black male ambivalence is related to the black literati's presence and views of African-American leadership committed to respectability.

In *Playing in the Dark*, Morrison appraises the narratives created for the New World setting. An Africanist presence was appropriated to serve as a surrogate for a new nation and a new man. The New World offered "a

8. Morrison, *Playing in the Dark*, 6–7.
9. Morrison, *Playing in the Dark*, 38.
10. Morrison, *Playing in the Dark*, 6.
11. Morrison, *Playing in the Dark*, 6.

once-in-a-lifetime-opportunity not only to be born again but to be born again with new clothes, as it were. The new setting would provide new raiments [*sic*] of self."[12] On the psychic and political necessity to construct a European American identity, Morrison writes:

> In the absence of real knowledge or open-minded inquiry about Africans and African Americans, under the pressures of ideological and imperialistic rationales for subjugation . . . an American brand of Africanism emerged: strongly urged, thoroughly serviceable, companionly, ego-reinforcing, and pervasive. For excellent reasons of state—because European sources of cultural hegemony were dispersed but not yet valorized in the new country—the process of organizing American coherence through a distancing Africanism became the operative mode of a new cultural hegemony.[13]

As a result, when the American novel includes a black character, the prose often shapes itself around the literary construction of this "American Africanism," using it as a surrogate for the formation of new [American] identity.[14] On black surrogacy in the romantic genre, Morrison writes:

> There is no romance free of what Herman Melville called "the power of blackness," especially not in a country in which there was a resident population, already black, upon which the imagination could play; through which historical, moral, metaphysical, and social fears, problems, and dichotomies could be articulated. The slave population, it could be and was assumed, offered itself up as surrogate selves for meditation on problems of human freedom, its lure and its elusiveness.[15]

Mark Twain's Huckleberry Finn provides a matchless example of the canonical texts that fit this reading. Morrison argues, "The agency . . . for Huck's struggle is the nigger Jim, and it is absolutely necessary . . . that the term nigger be inextricable from Huck's deliberations about who and *what he himself is—or, more precisely, is not.*"[16] In other words, slavery is tied to freedom, black to white, powerless to powerful, disenfranchised to enfranchised, illiteracy to literacy.

12. Morrison, *Playing in the Dark*, 34.
13. Morrison, *Playing in the Dark*, 8.
14. Morrison, *Playing in the Dark*, 8.
15. Morrison, *Playing in the Dark*, 37–38.
16. Morrison, *Playing in the Dark*, 55; emphasis mine.

Morrison's framework can be used to explore how the literary construction of American Africanisms enables not only white authors but also
the black authors of our four literacy narratives to perceive themselves and
other blacks as "other." Morrison proposes four areas of the American canon—and, by extension, of these black literacy narratives—in need of further
research: first, we must seek to understand how "the Africanist character
[has been used] as surrogate and enabler"; second, we must understand "the
way an Africanist idiom is used to establish difference or, in a later period,
to signal modernity"; third, we must study "the technical ways in which an
Africanist character is used to limn and enforce the invention and implication of whiteness"; and finally, we must explore "the manipulation of the
Africanist narrative . . . as a means of meditation—both safe and risky—on
one's own humanity."[17] In *Playing in the Dark*, Morrison provides an analytical framework to render transparent and then decipher this broad subject,
in which "silence and evasion have historically ruled the discourse."[18] Our
current liberal, supposedly post-racial environment suggests that "noticing
[race] is to recognize an already discredited difference. [Yet] to enforce its
invisibility through silence is to allow the black body shadowless participation in the dominant cultural body."[19]

In reading the material that follows, a critical reader might complain
of Morrison's lens's overly general application, contending that my usage
seems formulaic and should draw out more social, historical, and literary
differences across the centuries. However, I would argue that Morrison has
constructed a theory of the American literary imagination that captures the
history of the entire canon. In testing the elasticity of her analytical framework, I must keep front and center how the Africanist idiom establishes the
difference between whites and blacks, as well as between blacks and blacks.
We must pay attention to how Morrison writes,

> The dialogue of black characters is construed as alien. . . . The
> Africanist language practices are employed to evoke the tension
> between speech [literate] and speechlessness [illiterate]; how it
> is used to establish a cognitive world split between speech and
> text, to reinforce class distinctions and otherness as well to as-
> sert privilege and power; how it serves as a marker and vehicle
> for illegal sexuality. . . . Finally, we should look at how a black
> idiom and the sensibilities it has come to imply are appropriated

17. Morrison, *Playing in the Dark*, 51–53.
18. Morrison, *Playing in the Dark*, 9–10.
19. Morrison, *Playing in the Dark*, 10.

for the associative value they lend to modernism—to being hip, sophisticated, ultra-urbane.[20]

In other words, I am arguing that the Africanist idiom has broad literary and historical application when considering the literacy ambivalence of black males across time and different contexts. The illiterate and inarticulate black slave, as well as the modern American student to whom normative schooling introduces the North American canon, are indoctrinated into the white literary imagination, as well as into the perception that it is to "a self-reflexive contemplation of fabricated, mythological Africanism" that one must accommodate oneself in order to "become American."[21]

While invoking the Africanist idiom has historical origins, it continues into our historical moment and across diverse contexts. According to Morrison,

> Popular culture, shaped by film, theater, advertising, the press, television, and literature, is heavily engaged in race talk. It participates freely in this most enduring and efficient rite of passage into American culture: negative appraisals of the native-born black population. Only when the lesson of racial estrangement is learned is assimilation complete. Whatever the lived experience of immigrants with African Americans—pleasant, beneficial or bruising—the rhetorical experience renders blacks as noncitizens, already discredited outlaws.[22]

It is in tracking this process and reflecting on the ongoing Africanist presence—as a factor external to the black community that contributes to the broader discourse of racial ambivalence—that one can observe the development of an internal ambivalence about the relationship between blackness and mainstream literacy.

## The Black Self and the Othered with the Africanist Presence

Borrowing from Morrison, we can see how the black male writers in this study use the Africanist trope to expose and deconstruct the racial ideology that shapes society. Further, in constructing their own literate selves in light of the Africanist idiom and then subverting that trope through their appropriation, they reveal their own ambivalence toward literacy. Morrison helps us perceive that Frederick Douglass describes the relationship

20. Morrison, *Playing in the Dark*, 52.
21. Morrison, *Playing in the Dark*, 47.
22. Morrison, "On the Backs of Blacks," 57.

between whites and blacks on the big plantation in a manner that draws on the Africanist idiom to reinvent himself. As described by Douglass, slave life fits all the clichés of ambiguous parentage, a nonexistent nuclear family, and growing up among other parentless pickaninnies on the yard. Yet, Douglass also writes about the institutional sources of the slave's abhorrent condition. Rejecting the innate inferiority implied in the Africanist idiom, he emphasizes how slave life had been shaped by the dictates of labor over the needs of slave families. Describing his mother's literacy and love, he disrupts the Africanist trope by describing her as profoundly caring. She demonstrated her self-agency and motherhood by rescuing Douglass, giving him "a large piece of ginger cake [and reading his tormenter] Aunt Katy [the riot act]."[23] In addition, he reveals that he'd later learn that his mother was literate. He fails to divulge the source of her literacy, however.

The genre of the formal autobiography requires Douglass to be discreet. Still, the careful reader can heed the subtle innuendoes Douglass makes regarding his own literacy as well as that of his mother. One can imagine that it was in the context of an intimate relationship that she learned to read, perhaps the same relationship in which her biracial son was conceived. While acknowledging that a literate field hand presents a mysterious anomaly to racial expectations during slavery, Douglass nonetheless challenges the racial lexicon built on the illiterate and mute black's silence. The mother's act of care is an actual and literary form of resistance to the trope of the black mother without agency, who is acted upon as a sexual object and then separated from her child. Moreover, reading between the lines of her literacy attainment, one can imagine that her mysterious literacy is a function of the social context on the plantation or the literal relationship that produced Douglass. In linking her agency and an implied intimate relationship with the master's household out of which Douglass's mother conceives him, he deconstructs the Africanist idiom. He inserts literacy at the foundation of his biological origins.

Describing his childhood, Douglass demonstrates his awareness of the distancing black trope and the racial logic that constructs African Americans as bestial and carefree and then contradicts it. He constructs himself as a carefree child and yet full of cares due to his social awareness. His slave status, mysterious paternity, and the inevitable relational losses that accompany being enslaved all lead to his fretting about his future in relation to his people's condition. At the same time, he describes his preliterate state as "spirited, joyous, uproarious, and happy."[24] Being a neglected slave child

23. Douglass, *My Bondage and My Freedom*, 154.
24. Douglass, *My Bondage and My Freedom*, 145.

had some advantages, as black children were exempted from the challenges of socialization experienced by their white peers. A slave child "is never expected to act like a nice little gentleman. . . . He literally runs wild; he has not pretty little verses to learn in the nursery; no nice little speeches to make . . . for aunts, uncles, or cousins to show how smart he is."[25] Then, in the Auld home in Baltimore, Douglass crossed the boundary (or color-line) of oblivious and mute blackness to appropriate the raiment of literacy to become a new man. Yet, the new Douglass became suicidal and, looking backward, invoked the Africanist idiom. "In moments of agony," he writes, "I envied my fellow slaves for their stupidity. I had often wished myself a beast."[26] Comparing himself to the illiterate slaves, he inscribes them with both silence and illiteracy, and reinscribes himself with the capacity for literacy, speech, and thought. One draws on the African idiom when adopting or assuming a European or Western perception of black folk wittingly or unwittingly. In other words, he enters into the tropes of Africanism to define himself. Thus, in writing a narrative involving his trajectory from slavery to freedom, Douglass demonstrates the Africanist idiom's power to inscribe difference and produce a new man or reinvent oneself as distinctive.

Morrison gives us another angle on understanding Langston Hughes as well, also in light of the Africanist presence and idiom. In *The Big Sea*, Hughes conveys with subtlety an understanding of the role that blackness plays in the white literary imagination, to borrow Morrison's phrase, by relating his ambivalent relationship with Charlotte Osgood Mason. A white patron of African-American arts, she supported historically black colleges in the South and the New Negro artists and writers.[27] She was not necessarily progressive in her racial thinking, however. Mason was a downright conservative racial thinker:

> Concerning Negroes, she felt that they were America's great link with the primitive, and that they had something very precious to give to the Western World. She felt that there was a mystery and mysticism and spontaneous harmony in their souls, but that many of them had let the white world pollute and contaminate that mystery and make of it something cheap and ugly, commercial and, as she said, "white."[28]

Hughes moves on to describe how Mason provided him with a degree of comfort unusual for an African-American at the beginning of the Great

25. Douglass, *My Bondage and My Freedom*, 144.

26. Douglass, *Narrative of the Life*, 42.

27. Hughes, *Big Sea*, 315.

28. Hughes, *Big Sea*, 316.

Depression, but that he began to feel guilty about her request that he produce art to demonstrate the black primitive. He writes, "I did not feel the rhythms of the primitive surging through me, and so I could not live and write as though I did."[29] Mason inscribed Hughes and other black Americans with a primitive blackness. Because Hughes could not fulfill this role, the pair reached an impasse that required his extracting himself from their friendship and patronage. More interestingly, Hughes's refusal to accommodate her fantasies of the black primitive distinguishes his appropriation of Black English in his poetry from the Africanist idiom in American literature and racial thought.

Vershawn Ashanti Young's and Thomas Chatterton Williams's narratives, however, can be regarded as using the "Africanist idiom to establish difference."[30] This idea may at first seem counterintuitive. But as we have seen with the previous two narratives, the dichotomy between white and black, literate and illiterate, creates space for us to recognize the trope in black narratives. My interpretation of Morrison's thesis would have us understand that the Africanist presence is in all American literature and that it cannot help but shape the broader culture.

Through Morrison's lens, we can see that Young deploys Africanist language in his narrative and dialogue to "evoke the tension between speech and speechlessness; how it is used to establish a cognitive world split between speech and text, to reinforce class distinctions and otherness as well as assert privilege and power. . . ."[31] In doing so, he unintentionally reproduces the very categories that he is trying to erase. He writes, "Since BEV ain't goin' nowhere, it only makes sense that we should allow students to combine it with the discourse we're required to teach, a strategy I call code-meshing."[32] While *Your Average Nigga* seeks to offer an innovative pedagogy of black literacy to eliminate education-induced schizophrenia, it is important to balance that intention with Morrison's observation that in the white literary imagination, the Black English Vernacular is used to contrast the articulate (white) and the inarticulate (black).[33] When an author deploys or discusses black speech, she or he implies differences in cognition, in orientation toward texts and the written word, in class, and in a manner that signifies an unbridgeable otherness. If the chasm is bridged, it will require a seemingly anomalous elevation of mainstream literacy among

29. Hughes, *Big Sea*, 325.

30. Morrison, *Playing in the Dark*, 52.

31. Morrison, *Playing in the Dark*, 52.

32. Young, *Your Average Nigga*, 105.

33. Young, *Your Average Nigga*, 12.

black males.[34] Young and Williams provide exemplary narratives for revealing this dynamic.

Young underscores the unity between the prevailing literacy norms
and the middle-class black conformity that reveals vestiges of Africanist
literary conventions. When Young comments on his verbal altercation with
Diane, a black-upper class part-time English instructor, he employs the Africanist template. He draws on the same language and analytical framework
when discussing Shelly Eversley's anecdote in her book, *The Real Negro*. In
the story, Eversley discusses her experience with self-consciousness and inadequacy as a black academic when talking about sexism and homophobia
in a black barbershop.[35] He wonders aloud: "Had she become the twenty-
first-century incarnation of Du Bois's double-consciousness, an embodi-
ment of racial schizophrenia? One moment she spoke as an 'imitation white
woman,' and after a switch of the tongue, she became an authentically black
one."[36] Morrison's theory of the dichotomous construction of blackness is
apparent here. According to Young, Eversley is either an "imitation white
woman" or an "authentically black one."[37] In other words, in the imagined
African-American community, real black people are not articulate (i.e.,
don't speak mainstream English), and African Americans who speak Standard English are counterfeit. Finally, he describes Eversley as embodying
double-consciousness, the well-known form of schizophrenia. Morrison's "Africanist idiom" illuminates the tension created for some African
Americans who aspire to move into dominant society through education
but possess a cultural imagination that makes racial determinations based
on a person's literacy performance. Young asks a few questions: "What endowed the barbers with the authority to make her feel race-fake and then
authentic? Did her [literacy] performance really have such transformative
power?"[38] And he then concludes, "Whatever the answers to these questions
are, it's clear that Eversley [felt] compelled to contend with the consequence
of her [literacy] performance: the transformation of her political commitments into identity ambivalence."[39]

There's a bit more irony here, however. The unintentional implication
of Young's analysis is that real black people are inarticulate, and those appropriating academic and mainstream literacy performances are beyond

34. Young, *Your Average Nigga*, 12.
35. Young, *Your Average Nigga*, xiii.
36. Young, *Your Average Nigga*, xiii.
37. Young, *Your Average Nigga*, xiii.
38. Young, *Your Average Nigga*, xiii.
39. Young, *Your Average Nigga*, xiii.

the bounds of blackness. Bolstering the dichotomy further, Young goes into great detail about the new form of racial passing that requires "that you be black but act white, erasing the requirement of racial concealment and stressing racial performance."[40] Finally, from this perspective, he describes Eversley as embodying double-consciousness, a form of racial schizophrenia first characterized by W. E. B. Du Bois. Morrison's "Africanist idiom" illuminates the tension created for some African Americans like Diane, Eversley, and Young. They aspire to move into dominant society through education but possess a racial imagination that makes a racial distinction based on literacy performances.

Morrison's "Africanist presence" enables us to see anew Williams's (reverse) code-switching. He moved between his middle-class neighborhood and the academia that he began to embrace at Georgetown University and the hip-hop poser identity he cultivated at school, barbershops, and basketball court.[41] Williams's high-school sweetheart Stacey functions as an Africanist trope, catalyzing his ability to achieve "American coherence through a distancing Africanism."[42] Stacey embodies an anti-intellectual and oppositional blackness that defined aspects of the hip-hop regime. Having decided to abandon his street-defined black authenticity politics meant that Stacey's identity, as sublimated Africanist trope, would inhibit Williams's efforts to obtain his literacy potential in his gilded academic setting. In brief, Stacey had unwittingly become a surrogate for her boyfriend's blackness. Likewise, he will juxtapose his literate self to her unknowing 'hood identity performance to become a new American man. Williams's catharsis and literary deconstruction of Stacey provide an outlet for him to regulate "love and the imagination against the psychic costs of guilt and despair." As a foil, Stacey enables Williams to abandon his hip-hop-poser identity, minus the guilt, to reinvent himself into an authentic and transparently literate de-racialized person.[43] In other words, Williams never has to deal with his perceived deficiencies or failures as a black male; instead, his emotional energies and racial longings are mediated through Stacey's body and street persona. Using Morrison's notion of the Africanist presence, we can interpret her as a surrogate, mediator, *and* foil for Williams—or as ushering to the new raiment Williams puts on to become an authentic (black) man. He predictably discards her in becoming something more transcendent: the new African-American man.

40. Young, *Your Average Nigga*, 45.

41. Morrison, *Playing in the Dark*, 7.

42. Morrison, *Playing in the Dark*, 35.

43. Morrison, *Playing in the Dark*, 52.

Having gained a modicum of cosmopolitanism and sophistication during his first semester at Georgetown, Williams describes Stacey in demeaning and binary terms regarding her literacy and morality. On the way home, Stacey puts Williams down for "running around using 'big-ass words' and dressing 'like a fag fresh out the village.'"[44] He writes that Stacey also attempts to insult him by confronting him with her pregnancy by someone she has designated as a more authentic black man—even though, ironically, the couple had sex in the car before driving over to his friend's party. Williams says he then asked her what the father did for a living and reports her response and behavior: "'Nigga, he sells crack!' she shrieked. . . . 'He is on the block. What the fuck you do, huh? Fuck you! You think you better than niggas 'cause you fucking go to college? Fuck you!'"[45] Recounting their conversation allows Williams to invoke the Africanist presence. The conversation continues to capture his abdication of hip-hop culture and Stacey. The demeaning narrative is deployed to justify his neglecting the emerging moral compass implied in his academic interest in philosophy and the life of the mind. One might expect his cultural and intellectual growth led to an increased capacity for empathy, intersubjectivity, and maturity, culminating in remorse and recognition of Stacey's humanity and others who participate in hip-hop culture and the streets. Instead, Williams cast her in a demeaning black archetype to appropriate her street credibility and then discarded her to bolster his sense of superiority and transcendence.

Morrison's analysis that "cultural identities are formed and informed by a nation's literature" illuminates the relationship between Williams's portrayal of his break up with Stacey and the "self-conscious but highly problematic construction of the American as a new . . . man" in our literary canon.[46] *Playing in the Dark* suggests that, unwittingly, Williams deploys his pen to transform Stacey into an Africanist idiom that, in juxtaposition to his burgeoning intellectualism, defines his own transformation into a new literate black man and, in doing so, she serves as a surrogate, again, providing the bridge for him to cross over into the land of academic literacy on his path to cosmopolitanism, respectability, and social mobility. Through an implicit comparison with Stacey, whom he has just used as a sex object, we see Williams becoming a new man. As a high school student, Williams describes believing that he could gain street credibility by pursuing a romantic relationship with Stacey and mimicking her hip-hop style during high school and then attempting to own her body to the point of engaging

44. Williams, *Losing My Cool*, 115.
45. Williams, *Losing My Cool*, 116.
46. Morrison, *Playing in the Dark*, 39.

in domestic violence. After his poser status is exposed at Georgetown, Williams then discards Stacey. He elevates himself by defining her as culturally and morally inferior in relationship to out-of-wedlock pregnancy and a new partnership with an uneducated criminal drug dealer at a moment that his reader might be moved with compassion.

As a mere freshman at Georgetown University, he can contrast his own academic literacy use with her illiteracy and black-street vernacular. In making inarticulateness seem innate to Stacey, whose family he describes in more middle-class terms, Williams recalls one of many conversations with his father about her. Williams's "Pappy" had cautioned his son, saying, "I'm afraid that girl will never do the kind of work it takes to put that mind to any good use."[47] Williams then adds his own cynical assessment, which renders her the ultimate modern Africanist idiom: "By eighteen she was a statistic: another undereducated, unwed black teen mother doing her small part to bolster the 70 percent single-mother birthrate everyone bemoans."[48] Here we witness his tapping into a trope pervasive in the white literary imagination to construct Stacey as an Africanist other who facilitates and reflects his own newfound sense of self-dignity and worth based on his new deeper appreciation for the literacy promoted in his parents' home. "Once he has moved into that position, [Williams and others are] is resurrected as a new man, a distinctive man—a different man. And whatever his social status in [our racial hierarchy or global economy], he is a gentleman. More gentle, more man. The site of his transformation is within rawness: he is backgrounded by savagery [uncivilized blackness]" as implied in Morrison's theoretical framework.[49]

Using Morrison's lens, we can see a rhetorical strategy here that makes Stacey a symbolic scapegoat in Williams's move to abandon the hip-hop community. Morrison helps illuminate how this encounter works to depict hip-hop literacy as burdened: "Africanism is the vehicle by which the American self knows itself as not enslaved, but free; not repulsive, but desirable; not helpless, but licensed and powerful; not history-less, but historical; not damned but innocent; not a blind accident of evolution, but a progressive fulfillment of destiny."[50] In this light, Stacey embodies a deterministic view of urban hip-hop blackness that implies that black youth who embrace this culture, though intelligent, lack the character to attain or appreciate literacy. More importantly, her presence mediates Williams's knowledge of his own

47. Williams, *Losing My Cool*, 118.
48. Williams, *Losing My Cool*, 118.
49. Morrison, *Playing in the Dark*, 44.
50. Morrison, *Playing in the Dark*, 44.

difference and superiority. Young, too, moves between similar polarities, shuttling back and forth between defining himself in contradistinction to the illiterate Africanist presence and the new African-American male who must come to terms with his privilege and license to transcend illiterate and mute blackness.

## Cohen's Concept of Secondary Marginalization

Cathy Cohen's theory of marginalization creates a frame in which it becomes clear that the intersection of the Africanist idiom, the concept of linked fate, and a commitment to an authentic, narrowly defined, one-dimensional blackness—predicated upon the dependence on a single black ideology— creates a political ethos that marginalizes the most vulnerable in the imagined African-American community.[51] Identifying the processes that lead to this marginalization provides a powerful heuristic for recognizing the sociopolitical forces that contribute to literacy ambivalence discourse among African Americans.

In *The Boundaries of Blackness,* Cohen seeks to understand the slow response to the HIV/AIDS crisis in the African-American community. In doing so, she challenges the mainstream commitment to a belief in the existence of a broad and consensus-based political agenda in the (monolithic) African-American community.[52] Cohen argues that fidelity to a coherent black political agenda, based on the notion of linked fate, creates layers of marginalization in a community increasingly fragmented around issues of class, gender, sexuality, and social mores. She contends that the black utility heuristic is a questionable principle that props up the mistaken belief in a common political agenda, exposing the ideological fault lines in the black community uncovered in Michael C. Dawson's scholarship. "Where once consensus issues dominated the political agendas of most black organizations, these concerns are now being challenged and sometimes replaced by cross-cutting issues and crises rooted in or built on the often hidden differences, cleavages, or fault lines of marginal communities," she explains.[53] Cohen goes on to examine the virtual non-responsiveness of the black political and institutional elite to the AIDS crisis in New York City, tracking the portrayal of the epidemic in African-American newspapers and media

51. Cohen, *Boundaries of Blackness,* 11–19.

52. Cohen, *Boundaries of Blackness,* 11–19.

53. Cohen, *Boundaries of Blackness,* 9.

to expose inconsistencies in the tenet of linked fate and cleavages in the black community because of "cross-cutting" issues.[54]

Cohen claims that the ongoing commitment to consensus politics accounts for the failure of African-American political leaders to mobilize their communities and silences and isolates minority communities within the black community, resulting in secondary marginalization. Marginality is central to the experience of non-elite blacks. With the AIDS crisis, one finds a narrative about black sexuality at work that performs secondary marginalization against forms of sexuality that do not fit within the bounds of black respectability. Cohen seeks to demonstrate how cross-cutting issues expose diverse life circumstances within the black community. Regarding sexuality, Cohen argues, "We must remember that . . . throughout the history of the United States, images and ideas of reckless black sexuality have been used to sustain the exploited position of black people, especially black women."[55] The black elite has always feared activities, behavior, and images that might provide evidence of black moral or cognitive inferiority. Hence, the well-worn colloquialism: my color but not my kind.

During the AIDS crisis, homophobia fueled the assimilationist black elites' fears, according to Cohen. Accordingly, these leaders relied on exclusionary systems to protect a section of the black community imagined to be pathological and permanently incapable of assimilating into the social order due to the stigma of AIDS. Consequently, "to understand the response to AIDS and other cross-cutting issues by African Americans, we need a more complex theoretical model—one that . . . incorporates the historical experiences of exclusion and marginalization that have so forcefully shaped the experiences of African Americans."[56] Drawing on Dawson's theory of linked fate, Cohen argues that African Americans are subject to a twofold psychological process that first involves an experience of injustice based on race, followed by seeing one's destiny tied to the fate of the group. Thus, African-American identity and black consciousness provide a framework for mobilizing the group. Therefore, the black-owned media and institutions promote a monolithic view of blackness and communicate the idea that particular issues are significant to the entire black community. Yet, Cohen is specifically interested in how black elites respond to cross-cutting issues: "those concerns which disproportionately and directly affect only certain segments of a marginal group."[57]

54. Cohen, *Boundaries of Blackness*, 53–55.
55. Cohen, *Boundaries of Blackness*, 35.
56. Cohen, *Boundaries of Blackness*, 35.
57. Cohen, *Boundaries of Blackness*, 13.

According to Cohen, consensus issues "are often the most visible segments of the black political agenda, and they often receive the bulk of resources and attention from black political leaders and organizations."[58] In reality, these issues take on significance due to privileged community leaders and political entrepreneurs who frame them as having repercussions for the entire community. Consensus issues are those having a comprehensive impact. On the other hand, cross-cutting issues tend to impact a marginalized segment of the black society. Cohen defines these as "issues such as AIDS and drug use in black communities, as well as the extreme, isolated poverty disproportionately experienced by black women—all issues which disproportionately and directly affect poor, less empowered, and 'morally wanting' segments of black communities—fall into this category of political issues."[59] On the disregarded, she explains that

> those subpopulations of marginal communities that are the most vulnerable economically, socially, and politically, and whose vulnerable status is linked to narratives that emphasize the "questionable" moral standing of the subpopulation. These [cross-cutting] issues challenge for prominence in the public imagination the middle-class persona put forth by community leaders attempting to legitimize marginal group members and their concerns to dominant institutions and groups.[60]

In the end, these issues expose the complexity of identity in a way that forces questions about the worthiness of broad-based community responsiveness based on a common ascribed identity. The tendency has been to continue to describe black identity and community in monolithic terms, ignoring heterogeneity and differences in power within the black community.

Because African Americans have assimilated into every social arena, one can observe at least two distinct class experiences among them. In the context of the bifurcation in the African-American community between the elite and marginalized, Cohen uncovers class-based competition among African Americans for power and the ability to define the black political agenda. In this contest for power, the black elite's concern about the circulation of stigmatizing public images leads them to limit marginalized blacks' access to resources and media technologies. Moreover, bifurcation leads to the further fragmentation of the behavior, political thought, and social norms of poor African Americans. It follows that the upsurge of disreputable or stigmatized identities within a community historically defined by

58. Cohen, *Boundaries of Blackness*, 11.
59. Cohen, *Boundaries of Blackness*, 14.
60. Cohen, *Boundaries of Blackness*, 14.

an imagined unified identity and political consensus threatens to result in increased disjuncture among African Americans.

Of course, challenges to the notion of a cohesive and monolithic African-American community are not new. American history reveals that differentiation among African Americans—religious, political, and economic—is at the core of the black experience. These distinctions imply that an imagined homogeneity has long existed alongside an undeniable diversity within the black community. But power and access to resources dictate which subgroup's agenda gets beyond the black public sphere to the broader public arena. This counter-discourse represents "that sphere within a sphere that has always existed as a facet of American society but has been systemically rendered invisible, secondary, or problematic within dominant discourse and inquiry."[61] Throughout black history, one finds African-American elites policing the public sphere and black counterpublic to ensure that their agendas are "legitimate, respectable, and ready for public inspection."[62] In other words, the black elite tends to endorse issues that reflect dominant political norms and middle-class American values. And as this group has experienced growth in size and influence following the Civil Rights Act, bourgeois African-American leaders have adapted their cultural, economic, and political agendas to increase opportunities for social mobility within their group. Besides, America finds itself in a post-industrial economy where poor blacks are increasingly isolated. Thus, tensions between so-called respectable and disreputable blacks have recently become more pronounced in the public arena.

In *The Boundaries of Blackness*, Cohen attributes these tensions to the evolution of marginalization in the African-American community. Marginalization, in and of itself, is a complex and multilayered process embedded in historical relationships between dominant and subordinate groups. She sums up the evolution of power with a four-tiered theory that incorporates categorical, integrative, advanced, and secondary marginalization. The research importantly defines secondary marginalization, as we shall see when we apply her perspective of secondary marginalization to our select literacy narratives. She says:

> I assume that a group is marginal to the extent that its members have historically been and continue to be denied access to dominant decision-making processes and institutions; stigmatized by their identification; isolated or segregated; and generally excluded from control over resources that shape the quality of their

61. Forman, *'Hood Comes First*, 11.
62. Cohen, *Boundaries of Blackness*, 18.

lives. Much of the material exclusion experienced by marginal groups is based on, or justified by, ideological processes that define these groups as "other." Thus, marginalization occurs, in part, when some observable characteristic or distinguishing behavior shared by a group of individuals is systematically used within the larger society to signal the inferior and subordinate status of the group.[63]

Cohen moves on to outline three consequences of marginalization: an altered worldview; the development of indigenous organizations, information, and leaders; and complete framing of mobilization.[64] When a marginalized community enters the stage of advanced marginalization, this pattern leads to conflict, and elite leaders become more tentative about seeking transformative political agendas on behalf of those residing on the margins. Moreover, they find themselves at odds with members of the stigmatized groups, which don't adhere to the dominant social-political discourse.

## Cohen's Perspective on Marginalization in Literacy Narratives

Frederick Douglass lived in an era during which African Americans experienced *categorical exclusion*, being excluded from political and socio-economic power.[65] It's true that during slavery, a few freed blacks had access to resources and that Douglass was better off than many whites. And a study of abolitionism and, later, classic black nationalism would reveal degrees of power and influence among individuals and groups of African Americans in the first part of the twentieth century. Most blacks, however, did not have any access to political or socio-economic power whatsoever. In general, until the end of the nineteenth century and the rise of race leaders such as Booker T. Washington, one found few individuals collaborating with the dominant group in a manner that would suggest advanced marginalization in autonomous African-American communities.

Moving forward, in the narrative of Langston Hughes, one finds that African Americans had shifted into a stage of *integrative marginalization*. This new phase meant they were pressing on toward a political agenda of advanced marginalization. Hughes's father, who had lived in the United States during the backlash against the failed project to reconstruct the

---

63. Cohen, *Boundaries of Blackness*, 24.
64. Cohen, *Boundaries of Blackness*, 48.
65. Douglass, *Life and Times*, 756–61.

South, moved to Mexico, where he owned businesses and managed multinational corporations. In South America, the elder Hughes was treated as a white man within an indigenous racial caste system; he avoided social exclusion and the threat of physical violence. Experiences with categorical exclusion fueled his rejection of his son's literary aspirations. When his father asked him about his professional goals, Hughes said he wanted to become a professional writer like Alexander Dumas. Still, his father didn't see a vocation in the arts fitting with his social status in the States. He told his son, "Learn something you can make a living from anywhere in the world, in Europe or South America, and don't stay in the States, where you have to live like a nigger with niggers."[66] Hughes had to confront another issue that his father didn't reckon. He was living in an era in black history when the dominant group allowed "for the limited mobility of some 'deserving' [black] group members."[67] The black aristocratic class wanted to move their in-group toward advanced marginalization, from which vantage point they would shepherd less privileged African Americans. Hughes contended with pressure to conform to their norms, though he politically identified more with the black underclass.

In the twenties, African Americans entered a more advanced marginalization stage. The black elite and middle-class grew in number and prominence to represent themselves as the black community's chosen leaders. They led movements, dominated the core institutions in the black community and media, and functioned as an administrative, mediating class between the marginalized masses and the whites. They promoted writing that reflected white middle-class behavior, culture, and norms on artistic and literary fronts. But Hughes wanted to portray the lives of the masses unveiled and unvarnished. As discussed before, the black middle class condemned his work. "It does not matter to me whether every poem in the book is true to life. Why should it be paraded before the American public by a Negro author as being typical or representative of the Negro? Bad enough to have white authors holding up our imperfections to [the] public gaze," one black newspaper reviewer vehemently wrote.[68] The black elite believed Hughes's poetry would provide stigmatizing fodder that substantiated white narratives of racial superiority and black inferiority. More importantly, Cohen allows us to identify in this attitude the secondary marginalization taking place among African Americans in the 1920s and its creation of a discourse of ambivalence regarding literacy and literature. In light of Cohen's analysis,

66. Hughes, *Big Sea*, 62.

67. Cohen, *Boundaries of Blackness*, 26.

68. Hughes, *Big Sea*, 267.

we understand that this dynamic emerged half a century before the post-civil rights era. New social policies catalyzed racial integration and moved a portion of the black community into a phase of advanced marginalization.

Vershawn Ashanti Young's and Thomas Chatterton Williams's narratives exemplify the perspective of black males whose relationship with literacy, blackness, and masculinity has been circumscribed by the forces of secondary marginalization. These young authors participate in both underclass and elite counterpublics, requiring them to face social pressures to conform to agendas shaping ideas on authentic blackness under these diverging regimes. Much like Langston Hughes, albeit in a different city and era, Young grew up among poor folk in Chicago's Henry Horner Homes. Young's mother encouraged her children to become highly literate so that they could participate in post-Jim Crow "racial passing" to pursue social mobility and transcend stigmatizing blackness.[69] Young writes, "She didn't want me to be like some other black men—many of those I grew up with—who were dead, in jail, selling drugs, working for minimum wage or not at all."[70] Here we see class and racial ideologies creating the context for exclusion and marginalization. "Marginal communities faced with dominant definitions of themselves as inferior and 'other' constructs an indigenous and often oppositional group identity—redefining themselves for their group members and the larger public," Cohen explains.[71] Young's frustration with black elitism makes legible "the indigenous construction and policing of group identity and membership that serves as the site of local power struggles within the pattern of secondary marginalization."[72] Young's mother sought to counter the adverse effects of race-based ideologies by teaching her children to be just as good as whites and, as black elites, to deconstruct the visible characteristics that lead to material and social exclusion.

Young's mother's plan was successful to a degree but ultimately fell short. In his narrative, Young reveals that he makes some progress toward a dominant class literacy performance but retains elements of the Black English Vernacular in his speech and shades of the ghetto in his personality. He also has difficulty keeping a job and gets arrested at one point. In short, the ambivalent college professor stands with one foot on each side of a social cleavage created by secondary marginalization. Young attributes his inability to perfect his literacy performance—either as a ghetto or middle-class—as

69. Young, *Your Average Nigga*, 42.

70. Young, *Your Average Nigga*, 85.

71. Cohen, *Boundaries of Blackness*, 70.

72. Cohen, *Boundaries of Blackness*, 70.

the source of his inner and outer conflict. He is anxious about being perceived as gay or as a race traitor gung-ho about assimilating whiteness in a black barbershop. Based on his logic, if black men, and broader society, equate blackness with authentic black manhood, then rejecting street blackness is equivalent to embracing a scholarly identity with neutered masculinity, at best, or effeminacy and homosexuality, at worst.

The logic informing these gender and race-based dichotomies did not originate in the African-American community. In the United States, racial concepts based on an assumption of innate differences in cognitive and moral agency led to a binary ideology establishing a belief in black inferiority and white superiority. Young's "ghetto-to-black-middle-class identity" creates issues in the university as well. Secondary marginalization hangs him out to dry as he tries to connect with his more street-savvy students in the classroom. He confronts the "juxtaposition of ghetto versus black middle-class black[ness]" which tempted him to "get street" on a black middle-class colleague to taunt her "ultraproper racial speech performance."[73]

As it turns out, this presentation demonstrates several of Cohen's concepts. As Young recounts in Your Average Nigga, his presentation argues for a new approach to teaching English to black students due to his awareness that speakers of Black English Vernacular are denied "access not only to dominant resources and structures but also many of the indigenous resources and institutions needed for their survival."[74] His attempt to negotiate the marginalized's ability to access resources demonstrates the phenomenon of secondary marginalization. Although Young is on the faculty and his opponent, Diane, is a part-time instructor, her black elite values and literacy performance, which buy into the dominant society's essentialist narratives, enable her to shut him down during his presentation at the faculty meeting. He writes, "Everyone knew that, despite our both being black, Diane was espousing a different position from mine on how the politics of race should inform the way we teach writing."[75] The narrative conveys the sense that Diane's invoking the dominant narrative on black deficiency enabled her to capture Young's audience effortlessly. Because she invoked the literacy myth as a path to social achievement, Diane was able to interrupt the tendency toward critical deconstruction and analysis that is normative in most academic settings. Young's narrative renders transparent the African-American elite's ability to define the black community's social agenda. More interestingly, he portrays Diane's ability to draw on her own

73. Young, Your Average Nigga, 89.

74. Cohen, Boundaries of Blackness, 75.

75. Young, Your Average Nigga, 108.

narrative of socialization as a form of authority to gain the ear of whites in advocating suitable strategies for an educational agenda. Once again, Diane bolsters her power to correct Young in her articulateness, upper-class status, and facility articulating the literacy myth.

In doing so, Diane appeals to both middle-class ideas of black authenticity and elite literacy, offering herself as the acceptable model for African Americans. They have desired to acquire mainstream literacy as the path to social mobility. In the literacy myth, illiteracy is a barrier to the American Dream. Diane makes an example of her black student interns at the advertising agency where she works full-time. She claims that they cannot write themselves out of a paper bag. Hence, she has returned to the university to prepare them. Diane argues that Young's theory of "code-meshing sells black students short; it suggest[s] they can't master the standard dialect."[76] Lacking her facility in speech or deftness in the literacy myth genre. Young is left mute:

> I stood in front of the room, trying unsuccessfully to don the same stony disposition that Diane had displayed earlier. I managed to hear Diane without getting too hot, that is, until she announced: "I'm black too. And I'm quite familiar with the codes of BEV. I know them better than anyone here might suspect. But I also know when and where to use them. No business out there is going to allow students or me to bring those codes to work, so we shouldn't allow them here." Then she added, "I don't make the rules. I just follow them. I want to teach my students how to do so as well."[77]

Diane's actions reflect the tendency of the African-American community to improve itself by "self-regulations of individual black people, but also . . . significant policing of black group members."[78] On the other hand, Young wants to go "ghettomatic" on her, yet lacks her facility with code-switching between standard English and the BEV. Moreover, Diane was correct; Young's desired behavior would have undermined his academic authority. According to the narrative, Diane can transform her identity and speech performance with the flip of a switch. In this instance, she, not Young, receives applause from his peers by arguing that "underprivileged blacks . . . need to learn the language of public communication in order to make it in this world."[79] In the end, a member of the black elite publicly polices

76. Cohen, *Boundaries of Blackness*, 107.

77. Young, *Your Average Nigga*, 70.

78. Cohen, *Boundaries of Blackness*, 71.

79. Young, *Your Average Nigga*, 107.

and marginalizes a member of the black underclass (albeit one with more credentials, expertise, and professional mobility) in his professional setting.

Williams's story also reflects the relationship between literacy and secondary marginalization among African Americans in society. Although he has a white mother and lives in an upscale community, Williams's highly educated parents tell him when he is still young that he is a black male in preparation for the struggle for racial equality and racial distinction that he will face. Williams, developmentally not ready for abstract thought or ideological reasoning, receives their message in the most literal manner. After being confronted by African Americans and whites, who misread Williams's complex identity and misread him based on simplistic blackness conceptions, he begins to feel racially deficient as a black male. A clever young boy, Williams covertly decides to reject assimilation and the traditional approaches to education that his father promotes in his college prep courses. Instead, while still adhering to a conventional notion of monolithic blackness, Williams develops a hip-hop conception of black masculinity based on his encounters with hip-hop devotees and other black youth he encounters on basketball courts and television at the black barbershop. In other words, Williams's racial imagination is limited to books, boys, and hip-hop videos and movies.

The memoir reveals his limited participation in elite black clubs, institutions, and organizations until he visits Howard University once he begins to attend nearby Georgetown University. One can imagine that he had no interaction with real middle-class and upper-middle-class individuals emerging from elite black communities or with black professional parents until he encountered them in college. Williams's narrow sphere of social interactions is critical to his fundamental conception and description of the African-American community and black identity. Under the gaze of the black youth-oriented media and street-identified youth, he prepares to present himself as an authentic black man, as defined in hip-hop films, music, and videos. This gaze is critical to the shift in his literacy aspirations changing after high school.

Once Williams begins studying at Georgetown, he gradually accepts cultural assimilation as a superior model for blackness and masculinity and thus sheds his stigmatized identity. He begins to recreate himself in an image similar to past generations of black elites who "reconstruct themselves for the white gaze, formulating their own indigenous definition of blackness," to draw on Cohen's phrasing.[80] We then see Williams ceasing to

---

80. Cohen, *Boundaries of Blackness*, 74.

vacillate between street literacy and Standard English literacy performances
and begin to conform to middle-class linguistic and literacy norms.

At the end of his memoir, Williams presents a scathing appraisal of
hip-hop culture and its adherents to discourage and police the behavior of
his peers and the black community. He does so when discussing his new
status as "persona non grata in Georgetown black society."[81] Williams earns
his new status, as a literary fact, after an impulsive moment, humiliating
Ashley. According to him, she is a "tall, buxom, high-yellow girl from the
South, who belonged to a clique of pretty, upper middle class black female
freshmen, whose weakness for thugs, athletes, and rappers became the stuff
of legend in the greater metropolitan area."[82] Williams justifies humiliating
her with a Super Soaker water gun based on assumptions about her background. He speculated that "The daughter of dentists, probably a debutante,
very Jack and Jill of America style—she was the kind of bourgeois black
girl who never really had black friends or dated black guys growing up."[83]
Losing My Cool outlines his attempt to appropriate a child's and teenager's
interpretation of black culture, blackness, and black masculinity.

At Georgetown, the black community's complexity thwarts his efforts
to move stealthily between his academic and street personas. After Ashley's
basketball player boyfriend and his friends threaten Williams for his act of
disrespect, Williams finds himself ejected from the black community. He
writes, "Thrust into my new role as persona non grata in Georgetown black
society, the more I marinated on the significance of this random, patheti-
cally melodramatic turn of events in my life, the absurdity of the situation
started to press its full weight upon me."[84] As a college freshman, the young
Williams, based on limited experience and knowledge, describes Georgetown's black community as "a microcosm of the wider black world outside
the university gates."[85] He explains,

> In many ways, it was the negative of the surrounding white so-
> cial order (a white order the likes of which I surely hadn't seen
> before): the top of this obsidian pyramid where the students
> who remained closest to the street or whom the scent of show
> business was most detectable. In the roughly descending order,
> this black Brahmin class compromised: (a) the men's basketball
> team . . .; (b) the alpha females who hung out with, fought over,

81. Williams, Losing My Cool, 107.
82. Williams, Losing My Cool, 100.
83. Williams, Losing My Cool, 100.
84. Williams, Losing My Cool, 107.
85. Williams, Losing My Cool, 84.

and [slept with] the men's basketball team; (c) the blossoming
R&B singer Amerie and some of her friends . . .; (d) certain
members of the football team . . .; (e) one or two members of
the track team . . .; and (f) the truly thugged-out non-athletes
for whom affirmative action was either a godsend or Sisyphean
curse.[86]

The memoirist confesses a desire to defile Georgetown's black undergraduate community. One might reason *Losing My Cool* is a subversive extension
of the scheme to undermine the rising elite black students, or "black Brahmins class," as he refers to them. Williams's assessment exemplifies Cohen's
observation that "as dominant players attempt to remove themselves or are
removed from the direct regulation of marginal communities, newly elected
officials, traditional leaders, public intellectuals, and other members of marginal groups are *given* or *take on* the role . . . of policing the community."[87]
*Losing My Cool* reveals Williams's attempt to dismiss and discipline, through
literary means, the black community, as he'd imagined it. He writes,

> When I had attacked Ashley with my water gun, I couldn't really
> say why I hated her so much; the feeling was far more visceral
> than it was rational. I acted on a whim, an unthinking desire.
> Had I been in the presence of another black friend, I am sure
> I would have suppressed it completely. But standing there with
> Playboy, an outsider, a [white] guy who couldn't understand all
> the vagaries of the caste system I lived in, I felt all of a sudden
> moved to rebel against the hierarchy, not just reject it but also
> to defile it. I think I felt compelled to reject and defile whatever
> part of myself there was that still believed in [blackness and
> ghetto masculinity].[88]

This fascinating facet of Williams's memoir reveals the power of racial
politics and secondary marginalization to create cleavages within marginalized groups. These community leaders and self-appointed public intellectuals enact marginalization when seeking to promote racial uplift, mostly
through enforcing behavior and culture norms, yet, in doing so, further
devaluing and stigmatizing the most vulnerable subgroups within the African-American population. As a graduate student at New York University,
Williams continues his rejection when writing a harsh critique of hip-hop
for the *Washington Post* that launched his career as a public intellectual. The
essay marks his abandonment of a marginalized identity to the movement

86. Williams, *Losing My Cool*, 84–85.

87. Cohen, *Boundaries of Blackness*, 70; emphasis mine.

88. Williams, *Losing My Cool*, 107.

toward the elite's position. He completes the act, later writing an adult version of *Losing My Cool* that outlines his rejection of affinity groups based on race in *Self-Portrait in Black and White: Family, Fatherhood, and Rethinking Race* (2020).

## Conclusion

To understand how the dimensions of the social and cultural contexts of African-American male literacy acquisition shape personal and communal ambivalence, I have drawn on concepts constructed by four prominent African-American social and literary theorists: Michael C. Dawson's notion of "linked fate," Evelyn Brooks Higginbotham's work on the "politics of respectability," Toni Morrison's "Africanist idiom," and Cathy Cohen's theory of "secondary marginalization."

Now comes the most crucial question: How does viewing these literacy narratives through these analytic lenses help us to account for the phenomenon of ambivalence toward being black and literate that we find in the stories of Douglass, Hughes, Young, and Williams? As I attempt to lay out the significance of these four theories for understanding others' literacy narratives, I return to my quest to understand myself and my own actions as one black male who feels deeply ambivalent about his own literacy.

As I think alongside these theorists about my own encounters with ambivalence in the African-American community, it becomes apparent that the story I began in chapter four contains numerous racial discourses. When the Clowes Center at the University of Washington offered me the opportunity to speak about my former life as a preppy hustler, I felt uncertain about accepting the invitation. In my caution, I can now see the results of a lifelong experience of secondary marginalization—tied to the notion of linked fate—as well as the expectations of black respectability that would disallow my reproducing Africanist idioms by talking about myself as a criminal and a black man from the ghetto or, like Hughes, about the life of black folk. I was uneasy about sharing my disreputable experiences in an academic community in a manner that might shame the African-American community.

As I prepared for the talk, I met resistance from black, brown, and yellow colleagues who had themselves adhered to a politics of respectability based on some vague but implied notion of linked fate. One can imagine their concern was that, amid a community established on the foundations of intellectual prowess and meritocracy, I would reproduce another Africanist idiom validating a belief in the cognitive and moral inferiority of African

Americans and suspicions about affirmative action. These colleagues were prepared to fight class-based contests—within their own races—for power and the ability to define the political agenda. As mentioned earlier, Cohen remarks that stigmatizing public images led black elites to limit underclass blacks' access to the media and other resources. On a meta-level, my speaking in the academy provides a case study of how the multiplicity of identities within a minority community, historically defined by an imagined unity and political consensus, threatens to fragment the group further. My presence and narrative represented blackness out of bounds.

My literacy narrative and ambivalence have revolved around seeking social mobility in the midst of a life of abandonment, illegitimacy, structural barriers (class and race), and poverty in urban America. Exhibiting many of the same qualities as Langston Hughes's grandmother, my grandmother tutored me into a worldview forged by the idea of linked fate and racial uplift contingent on the politics of black respectability. These ideologies were intended to deconstruct the Africanist idiom, even as that idiom was invoked in community dialogue and the black media as an archetypal nemesis. With black nationalism in the air, the community sought to prepare intelligent and educated black youth for a future where integration and geographic mobility were options. Our job was to fulfill the promise of the civil rights movement. But the dream and program of black elites didn't consider the personal and structural challenges that kids like me had (and have) to deal with to transcend our situations. My recognition of mainstream society's failure—white and black—to appreciate the nuances within my marginalized experience led to frustration and ambivalence.

This ambivalence followed me when I became a hustler in the drug trade, frustrated by how secondary marginalization had cut me off from resources. I found allies, resources, and freedom in the streets—yet no escape from my ingrained belief in linked fate and Huxtable-like black propriety as the ultimate American lifestyle. While I participated in the underground economy, where I found support in my quest for social mobility, I eschewed the literal streets and the gangs that roamed them, knowing (though not in so many words) that my criminal colleagues were less concerned about literacy performances and middle-class respectability. Even as a drug dealer and street hustler, much of the time, I'd try to act in a decent manner that defied the idiom of the stupid, illiterate, licentious, and criminal black male. I clung to the same ideas about blackness and masculinity as my assimilationist excluders in the midst of marginalization. I gravitated toward a model of hustling that only approximated street-savvy hyper-masculinity, and a base, hedonistic approach to the American Dream.

In the end, my education in the underground economy culminated in my learning, on a deeper level, that the prospects of underclass black males for social mobility were over-determined by their race. My sense of linked fate became much more palpable as a result. By seeing what "moves on the margins," as Toni Morrison would say, I gained a greater awareness of the reality of commonality amidst heterogeneity within the black community.[89] In her Nobel acceptance speech, Morrison shares a series of queries from imagined visitors:

> Tell us what it is to be a woman so that we may know what it is
> to be a man. What moves at the margin. What it is to have no
> home in this place. To be set adrift from the one you knew. What
> it is to live at the edge of towns that cannot bear your company.[90]

My experience among perpetual outlaws revealed the depth of beauty and existential truth within a criminalized community of poor black folks excluded from both dominant and black society that could not bear our presence. It pricked my conscience and led to deep-seated feelings of guilt about my participating in an enterprise that exploited those on the furthest margins. Although educational and social experiences have increased my historical, political, and socioeconomic connection to African Americans as a group, studying the social and ideological cleavages described by academic theorists has compelled me to identify most acutely with black underclass males. I continue to experience marginalization and a seeming social death in this group.

While working in juvenile detention, I recognized, like Young, that the "black men who suffer most from the educational and judicial systems are poor, from the underclass, from the ghetto, like me."[91] As Cohen explains, marginalization occurs when observable characteristics and distinguishing factors signify the inferior and subordinate status. When I realized in college how class differences within the African-American community further limited my possibilities, I began to feel ambivalent about respectability, the American Dream, and the myth of literacy as part of that dream. My ambivalence experience started with a story about a black male committed to literacy and pursuing a respectable life who yet became a drug dealer. These narratives force me to acknowledge my current ambivalence concerning class, education, literacy, and social mobility.

89. Morrison, *Nobel Lecture*, 28–29.
90. Morrison, *Nobel Lecture*, 28–29.
91. Young, *Your Average Nigga*, xiii.

On some level, I understood that my initiation into the black under-world might offer me, in Morrison's words, a "once-in-a-lifetime-opportu-nity not only to be born again but to be born again with new clothes, as it were. The new setting would provide new raiments of self."[92] Morrison described blackness's unspoken yet intended power to provide a surrogate for either an authentic black self or a new, transcendent black man. I found myself identifying with Schooly D and Ice T, who viewed the streets (i.e., the underground economy) as a kind of more "honest" antithesis to Wall Street. My comrades "in the life" worked to synthesize a new Africanist idiom that fused a Puritan work ethic, the Victorian right to self-invention, and an ability to exercise authority in the streets, and appropriated a post-modern form of hedonism that allowed us to enjoy the spoils of our labor fully. That is, I could disaggregate my own upward socioeconomic quest from the African-American historical narratives. In the struggle for racial uplift, our forbearers had fought with weapons of respectability, honest labor, and fierce black nationalism. With the black community moving beyond advanced marginalization to secondary marginalization, I sought to synthesize the tensions "between speech [literate] and speechlessness [il-literate]" and at the same time construct myself as "being hip, sophisticated, and ultra-urbane."[93] Through that effort, I have come to both appropriate and shun the Africanist idiom in my black masculinity and literacy perfor-mance. On some occasions, I turn up my blackness to make it clear where I am coming from regarding my class and racial politics. But in my quest for social mobility and racial uplift as a black professional, I feel obligated to an academic literacy performance. While I strive to comport myself in the manner worthy of a black Ivy-league-trained intellectual, my academic, psychological, and sociological awareness creates an unspoken yearning to perform a more authentic integrated identity that generates an inner *Sturm und Drang*.

In the university setting, I refer to my bridging the gap between as-similation and marginalization as "gangster epistemology": a street ethos that uses whatever is available—abandonment, illegitimacy, marginaliza-tion, hedonism, American Africanisms, and the dream of social mobility—to create meaning and navigate between the worlds of underclass blacks and the starch-collared world of the elite. Dawson, Higginbotham, Morrison, and Cohen make legible the external forces that led a bookish boy to seem-ingly reject everything his grandmother had taught him when in reality, secondary marginalization had created an ambivalence that could only

92. Morrison, *Playing in the Dark*, 34.
93. Morrison, *Playing in the Dark*, 52.

be dealt with through reconciling and deploying outwardly contradictory black ideologies. I continue to grapple, however, with these diverse black and non-black ideologies. This gangster epistemology has enabled me to climb the rungs of the ivory tower and higher education. Although I have an esteemed academic pedigree, I remained an underclass black male dependent on the patronage of elite blacks and whites to survive financially, nurture a family, and promote social justice. I navigate diverse agendas daily—negotiations that regularly create an inner ambivalence toward my various projects and the ideological contexts that require me to code-switch in and out of different personas. Since I began reflecting on black male literary narratives, I've launched out on my own to become an independent black man. As I hit my fifties, I began to yearn for the liberty and prosperity that I experienced "in the life."

In the next chapter, I pull upon the work of philosopher and psychoanalyst Jonathan Lear to help comprehend how the aforementioned racial discourses and social trauma can deform the psyche and soul in a manner that makes it difficult to understand the method in the madness of literate black males prone to experience ambivalence regarding their love of books and words. Within our seemingly irrational actions, I find a rational underpinning that indicates a potential mode of healing and the possibility for diverse literacies during the search for authentic black masculinity. I examine how racial trauma causes the mind to respond with both acuity and resistance to the potential of novel possibilities and perspectives. My goal is to understand the madness that leads to ambivalence and later recommend a methodology for achieving a robust sense of literacy and wholeness.

Though this be madness, yet there is method in't.

—William Shakespeare, *Hamlet*


The ambivalence of colonial authority repeatedly turns from *mimicry*— a difference that is almost nothing but not quite—to *menace*—a difference that is almost total but not quite. And in that other scene of colonial power, where history turns farce and presence to "a part" can be seen the twin figures of narcissism and paranoia that repeat furiously, uncontrollably.

—Homi Bhabha, "Of Mimicry and Man"


[The fog of war is] the state of ignorance in which commanders frequently find themselves, as regards the real strength and position, not only of their foes, but also of their friends.

—Lonsdale Augustus Hale, *The Fog of War*

Rock Creek Park, Washington, DC (c. 1985)

# CHAPTER 6

# Method to the Madness

## *Ambivalence under Analysis*

As I PONDER THE bewildering and convoluted trajectories of the African-American male's literacy narratives in this project, I am struck by the fact that racial trauma is critical to each author's perceptions about race, racism, gender, and literacy. Frederick Douglass, Langston Hughes, Vershawn Ashanti Young, and Thomas Chatterton Williams show us how American racism creates a context that compels black males to assume certain kinds of literacy performances in response to Africanisms and criminal caricatures in the popular imagination—performances that draw on implied notions of linked fate, racial progress, social mobility, and black authenticity. Hughes's, Young's, and Williams's literacy stories are embedded in approaches to civil rights assimilation that are predicated upon the ideology of black distinction in response to propaganda fostering a belief in black inferiority.

Critical race theorist E. Patrick Johnson has investigated efforts to define and police the boundaries of authentic blackness in a manner that illuminates the social context shaping literacy ambivalence among black males. In *Appropriating Blackness: Performance and the Politics of Authenticity*, he explains, "In contemporary society, one of the most palpable examples of the arbitrariness and politics of authenticity is in language use. Particularly among young black American and white American youth, whose cultures overlap in multiple and complicated ways, there exists a crisis of blackness involving language use that remains a permanent schism in identity politics."[1]

---

1. Johnson, *Appropriating Blackness*, 5–6.

In *Appropriating Blackness,* Johnson further illuminates the fact that within the African-American canon, which grants us access to black male literacy narratives, one finds an undeniable ambivalence connected to a palpable fascination with blackness, whiteness, and racial identity due to formative events in the lives of the authors that often produce racial trauma. According to Johnson, concerns about literacy performance create social cleavages in the African-American community:

> [A black youth's] inner-city cousins may ridicule the young black professional who lives in the suburbs because, according to them, he talks like a "white" man. In this instance, talking "white" is equivalent to speaking Standard English and talking "black" is equivalent to speaking in the black vernacular. The black American who either chooses not to or simply cannot speak in the (black) vernacular is cast as a traitor to the race— indeed, as "white."[2]

This narrative describes how many African-American males find themselves in a social condition that leads to their fixating on the relationship between literacy performances and masculinity. The fluidity in identity is captured in the racist construction of blackness defined by behaviors and language and the subsequent move of some whites to reappropriate these racially marked performances. Johnson points out that "for their part, whites construct linguistic representations of blacks that are grounded in racist stereotypes to maintain the status quo only to reappropriate these stereotypes to affect a fetishistic 'escape' into the 'other' to transcend the rigidity of their own whiteness, as well as to feed the capitalist gains of commodified blackness."[3] As a cultural observer, I am writing amid a hip-hop race-related feud between African-American rapper, singer, songwriter Azealia Banks, and Australian recording artist and Southern-based rapper Iggy Azalea; I concur with Johnson's argument that black and white youth cultures are mutually constitutive, on numerous levels. It is clear that "there exists a crisis of blackness involving language use that [creates a seeming unbridgeable] permanent schism in identity politics."[4]

Language, however, creates both the breach and the bridge over these troubled waters. Individuals code-switch back and forth across the cultural divide. For a subset of black males, their movement between cultures and tongues produces literacy ambivalence. The goal, thus far, has been to demonstrate that literacy ambivalence and social cleavages are a consequence

2. Johnson, *Appropriating Blackness,* 5.

3. Johnson, *Appropriating Blackness,* 5.

4. Johnson, *Appropriating Blackness,* 5.

of race and class schisms, among other things, and not vice versa. Jonathan Lear's scholarship in the field of psychoanalysis retells Sophocles's play, *Oedipus Rex*, in a manner that enables us to reveal the sources of a mindset loyal to authentic blackness and then reinterpret the single-minded commitment to a street-inflected literacy performance that creates the literacy ambivalence outlined in this book.[5]

The fascination with blackness, and sometimes with black masculinity among black males articulating double-consciousness in the literacy narratives discussed so far, is linked to an often-unarticulated essentialist notion regarding what it means or should mean to be black and male. In excavating the sources of ambivalence as a form of double-consciousness that leads to what Lear might describe pejoratively as "knowingness" in some African-American males, I include here W. E. B. Du Bois's *The Souls of Black Folk* and Claude Steele's *Whistling Vivaldi: And Other Clues to How Stereotypes Affect Us*. Du Bois coined the term "double-consciousness" to describe apparent and burdensome metacognition that involves "a peculiar sensation, this [inordinate self-awareness], always looking at oneself through the eyes of others, of measuring one's soul by the tape of the world that looks on in amused contempt and pity."[6] Lear describes knowingness as an overreliance on reason and the strict adherence to common-sense narratives in daily life and norms or established standards in one's profession. This inability to question long-held beliefs, practices, and assumptions impedes growth and development.[7]

In the American context, African-American males experience double-consciousness due to dominant social norms and standardized tests, which lead to distorted assessments and a pervasive knowingness about their educational intentions. Consequently, some black boys internalize our educational and cultural knowingness to develop ambivalence towards mainstream literacy. Richard Wright appropriated Du Bois's concept of double-consciousness to describe the "dreaded objectivity" or "frog perspective" that African Americans possess.[8] His explanation illuminates their ambivalence:

> "Frog Perspectives." This is a phrase that I've borrowed from Nietzsche to describe someone looking from below upward, a sense of someone who feels himself lower than others. The concept of distance involved here is not physical; it is psychological.

5. Lear, *Open Minded*, 40–41.
6. Du Bois, *Souls of Black Folk*, 45.
7. Lear, *Open Minded*, 4.
8. Wright, *White Man Listen*, 5.

It involves a situation in which for moral or social reasons, a person or groups feels that there is another group above it. Yet physically they all live on the same general plane. A certain degree of hate combined with love [ambivalence] is always involved in this looking from below upward and the object against which the subject is measuring himself undergoes constant change. He loves the object because he would like to resemble it; he hates the object because his chances of resembling it are remote, slight.[9]

Wright's analysis would evolve to consider the benefit of this "double-vision."[10] Yet, subsequent scholarship suggests that "the 'second sight' that Du Bois professed blacks to have—the ability to see through the distortion of racial bias—has in contemporary society mutated and multiplied."[11] Consequently, social psychologists have felt compelled to study the distortion that emerges from perceiving oneself through Du Bois's "veil" of racial self-awareness.[12] Steele's interest, however, was born from experience and research. He is concerned about how "identity contingencies"—contingencies created when a stereotyped environment interacts with a particular social identity—lead to "stereotype threat."[13] He writes, "I believe stereotype threat is a [common] predicament of life. It springs from our human powers of intersubjectivity—the fact that as members of our society we have a pretty good idea of what other members of our society think about lots of things, including major groups and identities in society."[14] Lear's theoretical framework illuminates the relationship between ambivalence, double-consciousness, and injurious intersubjectivity.

## The Logic of the Black Soul

In analyzing ambivalence in this chapter, I offer an alternative perspective that attempts to define another approach to understanding that cognitive dissonance: a course of action that neither ignores the necessity of "ascriptive identities" (based on an unchosen social marker that makes individuals feel the need to promote the good of their ascriptive identity group), nor pretends that Toni Morrison's explanation of American Africanisms is just a

9. Wright, *Pan-Africanism or Communism*, 11–14.

10. Wright, *Outsider*, 129.

11. Oliver, *Double-Consciousness*, 1.

12. Du Bois, *Souls of Black Folk*, 44.

13. Steele, *Whistling Vivaldi*, 5, 68.

14. Steele, *Whistling Vivaldi*, 5.

literary conjecture, nor contends that the politics of respectability is a mere theory about the middle class, nor claims that Cathy Cohen's description of advanced marginalization describes an inevitable situation within the African-American community.[15] I return to my own literacy narrative to apply the psychoanalytic lens of Jonathan Lear to explore what he describes as the irrational motivations that lead to a knowingness that can close the student to pluralism regarding literacy. My goal is to identify the underlying rationality that might inform an individual's psyche, leading to ambivalence as it develops for black men who live in a social order that ranks people according to an overt hierarchy based on both literacy and race.

Lear enables us to consider some black males' ambivalence toward being literate anew. In particular, Lear helps us understand how unexpected tutors have initiated many black youths into racial consciousness in a traumatic manner that has caused them to fixate on their racial identity, masculinity, and literacy performances. Here, I will present Lear's notions of "knowingness" and "thinking with abandon," which emerge in his analysis of Oedipus's mental states as illustrated in Sophocles's play. These ideas shed light on the black male authors' literacy narratives, which we have been considering, revealing how trauma can lead some black men to obsess over conceptions of blackness and manhood. Out of those traumatic experiences, generations of black men have sought to either adhere to middle-class literacy performances that mimic some form of whiteness or execute street masculinity and Black English Vernacular or juggle both the "cool pose"—"a ritualized form of masculinity that entails behaviors, scripts, physical posturing, impression management, and carefully crafted performances that deliver a single message: pride, strength, and control"[16]—and middle-class respectability. The cool pose is a coping mechanism that renders black males visible and creates social capital that males in other communities derive through educational pedigree, high-status careers, and wealth accumulation. Majors and Billson explain:

> The cool pose is constructed from attitudes and actions that become firmly entrenched in the black male's psyche as he adopts a façade to ward off the anxiety of second-class status. It provides a mask that suggests competence, high self-esteem, control, and inner strength. It also hides self-doubt, insecurity, and inner turmoil.[17]

15. Gutmann, *Identity in Democracy,* 117.

16. Majors and Billson, *Cool Pose,* 5.

17. Majors and Billson, *Cool Pose,* 5.

Regardless of my subjects' choices, Lear helps us see how the anxiety and ambivalence among black males pursuing the American Dream or participating in hip-hop informed street culture are not illogical but entirely rational. "For many blacks, life is a relentless performance for the mainstream audience and often for each other. Creating the right image—the most impressive [one]—is part of acting in a theatre that is seldom dark," according to Majors and Billson.[18] Hence, the stakes are high.

My own experience of being improperly detained and accosted by the police almost weekly in San Diego further heightened my awareness and sensitivity to race and led me to become ambivalent about literacy and traditional interpretations of the American Dream. Over and over again, the police and other white officials made me feel vulnerable in a manner that prompted me to find the quirkiest methods for retaliating, for asserting my manhood. Through Jonathan Lear's theories of knowingness and motivated irrationality, I can better understand how being humiliated by police at the Abbey Road nightclub was the genesis of my ambivalence toward being black, male, and literate.

## Emasculating Policing

The police stop presaged growing attitudes towards police depicted in the rap group NWA's song "Fuck the Police." "Nigger, where's the drugs?! Nigger, I said where's the damn drugs at?" the beady-eyed cop swore as he stopped frisking me and ducked back into the car to search it. It was 1979, and the red-faced police officer was destroying the last vestiges of my racial naïveté. There I was: cold, indignant, and embarrassed, standing in my freshest designer jeans, and topsiders, drenched in Ralph Lauren cologne beneath a heavily starched button-down, legs apart and hands on the trunk in front of the only all-ages disco in the city. We had stopped in front of the club to meet the girls who would exit when it closed.

Back then, I thought it was all Norman El-Amin's fault. One of Norm's friends from across town had just turned twenty-one, so we had met at one of the guys' apartments, smoked a joint, and imbibed some whiskey before heading out in two cars. That night we had hit the skating rink, taken in a couple of parties, and landed at the front door of the Abbey Road disco. It was my first time to the famous club, and nothing about the street looked like the Beatle's album cover, as I'd imagined. Shortly after we arrived, the police pulled up behind us and turned on the lights. As they searched our

18. Majors and Billson, *Cool Pose*, 5.

car for drugs over and over, I was scared to death. Kiese Laymon describes a similar bullshit stop in *Heavy: An American Memoir.*

Although the pint-sized officer's badge and gun made me feel completely powerless, imagining the wrath of my mother if I got hauled into juvenile detention scared the crap out of me even more. When the officers relented and let us go, we got in the car, and all the guys began laughing at me. One of the older brothers in the front seat looked in the backseat and said, "Nigga, the police had your heart." What could I say? It was true. The police had enacted a scene scripted for a seventies Blaxploitation film, and I felt humiliated on several levels.

What bothered me the most, however, was that the old heads from across town had taken it for granted that the police could get away with calling me a nigger, enunciated not in a soulful way, but in a derogatory (white) practice, in front of a group of black onlookers that included beautiful black women. Norm had told me that these guys were committed to black consciousness. They all had names reflecting a connection to the Five-Percent Nation. Powerful sounding names like Divine, Supreme, and True God, but not one felt outraged or violated. I couldn't comprehend their nonchalance, their silence—for the most part, it was the first time that I had rolled out of the community with *older* cats. After that, as I began to leave our 'hood to go out to more bougie parties in other parts of the city, the rationale behind their passive response became more apparent: nearly every weekend, the police stopped us no less than twice an evening. We had been lucky to have the police stop only once that first night.

In the tenth grade, around the time I began to hang with Norm, I started to feel more in touch with the ever-present weight of being a black man. Norm was a bit different from the rest of us. He didn't wear an Afro, Jheri Curl, or shag hairstyle. Instead, in the Nation of Islam's tradition, Norm kept his hair groomed close to his scalp in a style that foreshadowed the popular East Coast fade. Plus, he tried to dress like a model in *Gentlemen's Quarterly.* Because we weren't familiar with players like Norm, some fellas would say, "*GQ* means Just Queer."

Nevertheless, inspired by his *savoir faire*, Moms began to bring *GQ* home for me. She wanted me to dress like Bernard Edwards, Niles Rogers, and Tony Thompson in the band Chic. She hoped that I'd carry myself with a bit more sophisticated swagger than "ignant niggas" in the 'hood. More importantly, Norman's religious heritage informed his conversation. Over time, I began to feel the burden of black manhood.

Norm and his Pops were different from the homies. His mother had died in a car accident, so he lived with his father, a black Muslim. When we weren't hanging out in the streets, we'd spend hours listening to Mr.

El-Amin's views on everything from chess to women to government surveillance strategies. He had a special gift for making the most delicious patty
melts and popcorn. He'd sit in his recliner with a fastidiously folded-down
paper bag full of his puffy, yellow booty. Although he'd share only the last
morsels of the bag, he would drop science—teach us—about some deep
stuff. After undergoing the incident at the disco and spending more time
with Mr. El-Amin, everything around me began to look different. While I
had talked with family members and men in the community about historical racism and black nationalism before, somehow, the confluence of these
events made the scales fall from my eyes. When police officers began to
jack us around regularly, I developed a nagging insight into the reality of
being a black man in America. On that brisk fall night in front of the Abbey
Road disco, I had gone through a rite of passage into black manhood, one
in which the police took my still somewhat innocent heart and replaced it
with a colder and darker one.

Other things were happening in my world that made the weight of
being black and male more palpable. In 1979, desegregation was a lopsided
enterprise in San Diego. Only a few white students were bussed to schools
in our neighborhoods to magnet programs. It seemed that students from
Southeast San Diego were commuting. Moreover, it didn't feel like our suburban teachers were invested in us on the surface. We seemed to be a conundrum that needed to be watched to protect other students and the school.
The ratio between non-white and white students guaranteed that we would
never have enough political power to shape student government or decide
what kinds of music we had at school dances. Middle-school-aged black students from the 'hood weren't great organizers. We were overwhelmed with
the long commute between the 'hood and American suburbia. Although our
school was integrated, we were out of the dating pool for non-black girls and
many other non-academic experiences. Most African-American girls were
like our cousins or sisters; we had grown up with each other through all our
awkward phases and gone to school with them for years. To be honest, I had
my eyes on a surfer girl or two. If an Asian, Latino, or white suburban girl
did take a black brother guy seriously, she was called a "nigger lover." And
the humiliation didn't stop there.

On weekends, Norm and I would go out to the well-heeled neighborhoods in the north part of the city to paint home addresses on curbs. As a
child, I had been in these same neighborhoods with my grandmother when
she did domestic work. Now, I noticed how rich these people were and how
poor we were. I saw other differences. We were treated differently in retail
outlets. Our presence in predominantly white communities seemed to inspire unintended fear. On occasion, store clerks seemed so afraid that they

routinely overpaid us in change when we stopped in at neighborhood mar-
kets. Oddly, their fear made me feel powerful. Yet, the police kept this sense
of power in check. Inevitably, officers would show up to interrogate us when
fearful neighbors called the police. They'd then wait for a city bus to arrive
at the stop and escort Norm and me onto the bus headed back to Southeast
San Diego. Later, we'd go out to house parties, skating rinks, or clubs, and
the police would stop and harass us on the way there and on the way home.
It was a weekly ritual. In a matter of months, I began to view racial encounters as mundane for me as they were for the guys I had been drinking with
when the police stopped us in front of Abbey Road. On another level, the
fear and harassment that I encountered as a teenager began to color the lens
through which I read the world.

During that chilly winter of 1979, immediately after my Abbey Road
experience, I understood my grandparents on a deeper level. They had a
profound distrust of white people. It seemed that they didn't ever want to
see us improve our lives, let alone help us substantively make economic and
social progress (I've been burned almost every time I let my guard down).
The civil rights movement and bussing didn't appear to have disrupted historical and structural racism. Extended family members, educators, social
workers, police officers, and Mr. El-Amin were consciously and unconsciously teaching me that being a black man meant living under whites' gaze
and implied control. We were vulnerable to their whims, our needs placed
on the margins. So when a black man referred to me as a brother, I began
to feel a sense of solidarity with him in a whole new way—catching the bus
to a school where I wasn't a part of things started to feel overtly humiliating
and disingenuous.

During my sophomore year in high school, the reality of being a poor
black boy who lived in the projects began to cast a shadow over our he-
roic black past and my dreams for the future. Oddly, however, the darkness
became a motivating factor. On the last day of school that June, I got on
the yellow bus at Clairemont High School—the Clairemont of *Fast Times at
Ridgemont High* fame—for the last time. Over the summer, I transferred to
Lincoln High, the predominantly black school in my neighborhood. Along
with the bitter winter frost, thinking about race began to overshadow my
grandparents' optimism for me to transcend our common catastrophes and
racialized existential dilemma, instilled by the Civil Rights Act.

## Not Insanity, Motivated Irrationality

In *Open Minded: Working Out the Logic of the Soul*, Jonathan Lear investigates the relationship between our humanity and our thinking, as well as how psychology has lost sight of its philosophical grounds. According to Lear, Plato believed that being fully human requires a particular habit of mind that the modern clinical thinkers might have neglected due to an overreliance on an empirical mindset. This neglected habit is the human "capacity to be *open minded*: the capacity to live non-defensively with the question of how to live," i.e., approaching each new challenge with a posture of humility and openness.[19] Sigmund Freud is an intellectual descendent of Plato, according to Lear. These philosophers "understood that the human psyche is in dynamic interaction with the cultural-political environment, and that both are fundamentally shaped by the movement of meanings from polis to psyche and back again."[20] Based on Plato's cave metaphor, Lear argues we primarily live our lives based on illusions, as our minds are perpetually active in organizing our experiences, imaginations, and thoughts. Hence, the influence of the police (our imagined communities) on our minds and vice versa is subliminal and undetected.

Freud indicated how the mind works in response to the social world, and in doing so, carried forward Plato's claim into psychoanalysis.[21] The early interest of psychoanalysis in the unconscious role in meaning-making persists in enabling thinkers to render meaning from the unintelligible.[22] Lear writes,

> It is a mistake to think of psychoanalysis and Prozac as two different means to the same end. The point of psychoanalysis is to help us develop a clearer, yet more flexible and creative, sense of what our ends might be. "How might we live?" is, for Socrates, the fundamental question of human existence—and the attempt to answer the question is, for him, what makes life worthwhile.[23]

While arguments rage about the misuses of psychotherapy, one cannot deny that "humans are inherently makers and interpreters of meaning. It is meaning—ideas, desires, beliefs—which causes humans to do the interesting things they do."[24] According to Lear, what's at stake in Freud-bashing

19. Lear, *Open Minded*, 8.
20. Lear, *Open Minded*, 10.
21. Lear, *Open Minded*, 20.
22. Lear, *Open Minded*, 19.
23. Lear, *Open Minded*, 28.
24. Lear, *Open Minded*, 24.

is his profound insights and human ontology (conception). He asks, "Are we to see humans as having depth—as complex psychological organisms which generate layers of meaning which lie beneath the surface of their own understanding? Or are we to take ourselves as transparent to ourselves?"[25] Scapegoating psychoanalysis (Freud) allows us to neglect the complexity of humans and act as if human existence and happiness were easily discernible. Yet, "this, if anything, is the Western tradition: not a specific set of values, but a belief that the human soul is too deep for there to be [an] easy answer to the question of how to live."[26] In brief, Lear argues that our concept of the human being and the depths of the mind has implications for how we inter-pret motivated irrationalities, which occur when we answer Plato's ancient question in a manner against our own self-interest. In fact, "the point of psychoanalysis [and self-reflection] is to help us develop a clearer, yet more flexible and creative, sense of what our ends might be. 'How shall we live?' is, for Socrates, the fundamental question of human existence."[27]

Lear reads Sophocles's *Oedipus* as an invaluable metaphor for under-standing black male literacy ambivalence. Investigating the implications of Oedipus's confidence in his reasoning and his self-destructive behavior, Lear finds three critical themes in both Sophocles's play and psychoanaly-sis: *knowingness*, *abandonment*, and *motivated irrationality*. These terms, in turn, have informed my own thinking regarding both how we have under-stood either the rejection of literacy or a corresponding ambivalence toward literacy. At the root is the need to grapple with the primordial existential question, "How do I live?"

In *Oedipus*, "tragedy confronted [Greek citizens] emotionally with the fact that they had to make their decisions in a world which was not entirely rational, in which rationality was sometimes violently disrupted, in which rationality itself could be used for irrational ends."[28] In a world that sometimes defies reason, we, too, must grapple with the non-linear and unpredictable nature of learning to understand the motives that inform our attitudes towards literacy. More importantly, we must reassess how educa-tors respond to ambivalence among black males by taking up an attitude of knowingness.

In Oedipus's declaration to Tiresias—"I hit the mark by native wit, not by what I learned from birds"—Lear points out "the fundamental myth of

25. Lear, *Open Minded*, 27.

26. Lear, *Open Minded*, 28.

27. Lear, *Open Minded*, 28.

28. Lear, *Open Minded*, 29.

knowingness."[29] Like modern-day philosophers and psychoanalysts, Oedipus is trapped not by literal knowledge but by a cynical attitude of knowingness (based on the logic of presumption) that blocks the possibility of considering innovative paths of inquiry and discoveries. Haughtiness and presumption present a barrier to critical reflection and distracts thinkers from asking Socrates, "In what way should one live?"[30] Lear explains, "The stance of 'already knowing' functions as a defense: if you already know, you do not need to find out."[31] The focus on presumption reveals how the emphasis on professionalism and professionalization has "instill[ed] deadness" in psychology.[32] Once a field of inquiry defines parameters, develops categories, and establishes protocols, practitioners no longer need to maintain an open-minded approach to emerging challenges. This orientation leads to an attitude of knowingness that blinds one from realizing that some things defy reason. What Oedipus "misses completely is the thought that his 'knowingness' might lie at the heart of his troubles: what he doesn't know is that he doesn't know."[33] Through this lack of open-mindedness, Oedipus involuntarily fulfills the same prophecy he set out to avoid. In this way, Lear clarifies that, when faced with problems that aren't easily solved, knowingness and hubris lead to disaster.

How did Oedipus fall into this trap of knowingness? Lear posits the concept of abandonment as an answer. Upon hearing a drunkard say that Oedipus's parents are not the man and woman who have raised him, Oedipus experiences the news as a literal abandonment and then acts out that pain by turning to his reason. Oedipus "abandons himself to thinking. . . . He acts as though thinking could compensate him for his loss, but since there can be no compensation, the thinking has to become so enthusiastic, and so thin, that it blinds him to any [real] recognition of loss. Thus 'knowingness' comes into the world."[34] In other words, trauma leads Oedipus to draw on the power of his mind to resolve his perceived problem. Still, Sophocles frames the dilemma to reveal that the reason alone cannot plumb the depths of such a profound mystery as the ruler's misery. Knowingness is the denial of tragedy, loss, and "the idea that there may be meaning opaque to human understanding."[35] In this way, *Oedipus* embodies Sophocles's proposition

29. Lear, *Open Minded*, 42.

30. Lear, *Open Minded*, 4.

31. Lear, *Open Minded*, 34.

32. Lear, *Open Minded*, 3.

33. Lear, *Open Minded*, 46.

34. Lear, *Open Minded*, 48.

35. Lear, *Open Minded*, 50.

that rational inquiry and comprehension are insufficient to provide insight into human existence and our existential dilemma.

Lear's goal in penning *Open Minded* is to move psychoanalysts and our dominant culture beyond a position exemplified by Oedipus's knowingness, which comes from the perceived lack of a *rational* alternative.[36] According to Lear, motivated irrationality has sound sources:

> Humans regularly behave in ways they do not well understand, which cause pain to themselves and others, which violate their best understanding of what they want and what they care about. And yet, for all of that, there is, as Shakespeare put it, method in their madness. These behavings are not simply meaningless intrusions into the ordinary life: they express some motivational state, they have a "logic of their own." Once you recognize the phenomenon of motivated irrationality, you are committed to there being some form of unconscious meaning.[37]

The term motivated irrationality is a behavioral expression to describe our skewed perception of a traumatic life event. The defensive response is irrational behavior that leads to further suffering and trauma. Lear's goal in penning *Open Minded* is to move psychoanalysts and our dominant culture beyond Oedipus's position of knowingness, which emerges from the perceived lack of a *rational* alternative.[38] This new reading of the Oedipus myth implies that to move beyond the discourse of knowingness, we must surrender our hubris and begin to approach the daunting challenge of understanding human behavior with awe and wonder. In doing so, we must move in a direction that allows us to gently renounce knowingness, relinquish our commitment to rationality, and abandon our research-based principles. Only then can we begin investigating the motivating irrationalities that inform individual behaviors, habits of mind, and our culture.

## "When the Shadow Swept Across Me": The Trauma of Racialization

Jonathan Lear offers a powerful lens for understanding how trauma creates motivated irrationalities (unconscious drives) that inform individual and cultural ambivalence around African-American literacy. Lear contends that "the mind is active and imaginative in the organization of its own

36. Lear, *Open Minded*, 53.
37. Lear, *Open Minded*, 54.
38. Lear, *Open Minded*, 53.

experience . . . whether the mind is trying to come to grips with painful reality, reacting to trauma, coping with the everyday, or 'just making things up.'"[39] Motivated irrationality is one way the mind deals with a traumatic event. For example, "Oedipus is abandoned by his parents, and in response he abandons himself to thinking. He thinks with abandon."[40] Stated differently, he overreacts by relying on his own thinking and counsel. If so, then we must search the African-American male literary canons for the initial trauma that leads the author to think with abandon and develop a posture of knowingness about blackness, in general, and the relationship between blackness and literacy, in particular.

I have described how some African-American males have thought and continue to think about their literacy and identity performances with blackness in the previous chapters. The writings of Frederick Douglass, Langston Hughes, Claude Steele (as a subject), Vershawn Ashanti Young, and Thomas Chatterton Williams—each of whom has experienced racial trauma—become helpful in exposing the sources of motivated irrationality in their literacy narratives.

Frederick Douglass represents a classic case of ambivalence resulting from racial trauma. Douglass's experience of ambivalence began when he overheard a candid conversation about himself. The slave boy's overhearing Master Hugh mirrors Oedipus's exposure to the drunkard's uninhibited words. Master Hugh's declaration that "If you teach a nigger . . . how to read, there would be no keeping him. It would forever unfit him to be a slave."[41] These words became a self-fulfilling prophecy. This racial incident represents a critical juncture in Douglass's formation, introducing a motivated irrationality. He writes:

> The revelation haunted me, stung me, and made me gloomy and miserable. I almost envied my fellow slaves for their stupid contentment. This knowledge opened my eyes to the horrible pit, and revealed the teeth of the frightful dragon that was ready to pounce upon me, but it opened no way for my escape.[42]

Losing his naïveté, Douglass "was no longer the light-hearted, gleesome boy, full of mirth and play," who first landed on the Auld's doorstep in Baltimore.[43] More importantly, Auld's political and psychological analysis

39. Lear, *Open Minded*, 20.
40. Lear, *Open Minded*, 48.
41. Douglass, *Narrative of the Life*, 41.
42. Douglass, *My Bondage and My Freedom*, 226.
43. Douglass, *My Bondage and My Freedom*, 227.

of literacy's impact on a slave reveals his recognition of its implication for knowingness and motivated irrationality.

It is enough to say that Douglass responded by wanting to read with abandon, a motivated irrationality, and that this same yearning for letters led to a tormenting ambivalence. He writes, "That which he [Master Hugh] most loved I most hated; and the very determination which he expressed to keep me in ignorance, only rendered me resolute in seeking intelligence [through literacy]."[44] Master Hugh had predicted that learning to read would lead to ambivalence. Douglass confesses, "I would at times feel that learning to read had been a curse rather than a blessing. It had given a view of my wretched condition, without remedy."[45] These words unveil the chief fact that being a slave is the source of his motivated irrationality. Conforming to Lear's description of Oedipus, Douglass writes, "It was the everlasting thinking of my condition that tormented me. There was no getting rid of it."[46] Decoding words and building a learned vocabulary resulted in his enthrallment with racial matters, leading to a politically informed understanding of slavery that became unbearable.

In *The Souls of Black Folk*, Du Bois provides yet another poignant example of how a racial slight led him to think through the prism of race as a motivating irrationality. While contemplating the "strange experience" of being considered a problem (or burden), Du Bois looks back on his childhood to discover his first inkling of race consciousness. He writes, "It is in the early days of rollicking boyhood that the revelation first bursts upon one, all in a day, as it were. I remember well when the shadow swept across me."[47] The incident occurred when Du Bois's classmates decided to buy "visiting-cards" and exchange them.[48] Du Bois was happily trading cards with his classmates until one particular interaction alerted him to his racial difference. Describing the subtle transaction, he writes, "One girl, a tall newcomer, refused my card—refused it peremptorily, with a glance."[49] His retelling of the event implies that her refusal traumatized the young Du Bois, who realized "with a certain suddenness that I was different from the others; or like, mayhap, in heart and life and longing; but shut out from their world by a vast veil."[50] After this abrupt introduction to racial difference,

44. Douglass, *My Bondage and My Freedom*, 218.
45. Douglass, *Narrative of the Life*, 42.
46. Douglass, *Narrative of the Life*, 42.
47. Du Bois, *Souls of Black Folk*, 44.
48. Du Bois, *Souls of Black Folk*, 44.
49. Du Bois, *Souls of Black Folk*, 44.
50. Du Bois, *Souls of Black Folk*, 44.

in a move that mirrors Oedipus's motivated irrationality, Du Bois became obsessed with race.

The numerous traumatic incidents experienced by Langston Hughes, both among blacks and whites, shaped his racial thinking. While Hughes's aloof grandmother gave him a positive racial self-image, he first experienced racial trauma as a teenager at his father's hands. As discussed in chapter 5, before writing his most famous poem, he pondered his father's "strange dislike of his own people" and recalled his father's warning to move to Europe and to not "stay in the States, where you have to live like a nigger with niggers."[51] The disdain of Hughes's father against African Americans (of all classes) opened a wound that middle-class blacks would later aggravate when they condemned his use of the Black English Vernacular in his poetry and identification with dark-skinned and underclass African Americans.

The jazz poet's writing suggests that one of his most painful memories involved a prominent literary club in Washington, DC. As a prolific young writer, Hughes, along with his mother, was invited to the club's annual dinner, where he was to read in celebration of a *Survey Graphic* dedicated to *The New Negro*. Although he had been celebrated as a prodigy and invited to read his poems, "the society ladies were careful to whisper to his mother that perhaps she'd better not come. They were not sure she would have an evening gown."[52] In this way, Hughes and his mother were slighted by the black aristocracy, who sought to imitate the social-cultural, material, and social standards of elite white society. While this intraracial offense doesn't seem to correlate to racism on the surface, Hughes retold this story multiple times, exposing the traumatic impact it had on him. This wound implicitly reminded Hughes of his father's rejection of the black folk as well. More importantly, the slight led to his ongoing hostility toward black high society and strengthened his identification with poor blacks. It reveals his grappling with "the crisis of authenticity," according to J. Martin Favor.[53]

Claude Steele had built a career on thinking about issues related to motivated irrationalities. In *Whistling Vivaldi*, he discusses a particular form of knowingness, describing it as a "highly vigilant-to-threat narrative."[54] He opens the book with his own traumatic racial awakening. Growing up in Chicagoland in the 1950s and 1960s, Steele had to deal with the color-line. He "learned that we 'black kids' couldn't swim at the pool in our area park,

51. Hughes, *Big Sea*, 54, 62.
52. Hughes, *Big Sea*, 29.
53. Favor, *Authentic Blackness*, 2.
54. Steele, *Whistling Vivaldi*, 166.

except on Wednesday afternoons."[55] He also describes a poignant racial epiphany after spending an entire day waiting to get a job at a golf course, only to be told that the job was not for an African American. Steele writes, "This is how I became aware I was black. I didn't know what being black meant, but I was getting the idea that it was a big deal."[56] These experiences informed his lifelong quest to understand identity threat and identity contingencies, "the things you have to deal with in a situation because you have a given social identity."[57] His research seeks to move beyond anecdotes and individual experiences to an analysis of racial experience in order to understand how social identity exposes humans to "stereotype threat," which causes underperformance in the classroom and broader world.[58] Steele's research on identity contingencies deeply echoes Du Bois's analysis of double-consciousness. Moreover, it manifests Richard Wright's prescient statement:

> They are going to be self-conscious; they are going to be gifted with a double vision, for, being Negroes, they are going to be both inside and outside of our culture at the same time. Every emotional and cultural convulsion that ever shook the heart and soul of Western man will shake them. Negroes will develop unique and specially defined psychological types. They will become psychological men, like the Jews. . . . They will not only be Americans or Negroes; they will be centers of knowing, so to speak. . . . The political, social, and psychological consequences of this will be enormous.[59]

Vershawn Ashanti Young, growing up in the Henry Horner Homes projects on the west side of Chicago, had an African-American principal school him on his place and race. A bright child hungry for knowledge and precocious literacy, he was accused by his teacher of having a "bad attitude."[60] After confronting a white science teacher who hadn't provided a clear explanation for entering projects into the science fair, Young tried to convince the principal that he was within his rights. But, he recalls, "The principal said I had an attitude problem and that she needed to work with me—help me out before I went to high school."[61] Although the principal was an African American, Young demonstrates a posture of knowingness

55. Steele, *Whistling Vivaldi*, 1.
56. Steele, *Whistling Vivaldi*, 2.
57. Steele, *Whistling Vivaldi*, 3.
58. Steele, *Whistling Vivaldi*, 4–5.
59. Wright, *Outsiders*, 129.
60. Young, *Your Average Nigga*, 30.
61. Young, *Your Average Nigga*, 31.

when he interprets her response. He writes, "I was supposed to affect mock humility [around white folks], know my boundaries, and accept the limitations that growing up black would place around me."[62] Young describes the principal's racial reasoning: "She also didn't want me to show too much confidence in my abilities around other black folks. They'd think I was trying to be better, trying to be white. I probably should have learned these lessons. But I refused."[63] Moving forward in his academic experience, Young continued to develop antagonistic relationships with black and white authority figures and colleagues and teachers due to his knowingness about others' racial expectations.

The exploration of knowingness or motivated irrationality might allow us to predict if we didn't already know, that Thomas Chatterton Williams, a biracial African-American male raised in a New Jersey suburb, would experience a traumatic introduction to race. Williams's experience reflects knowingness on multiple levels. On one level, Williams inherited the trauma of his father, who grew up in the Jim Crow South and believed that he had to read in the closet with a flashlight because "an educated nigger in the South was a dead nigger."[64] This story mirrors a narrative about a slave who said that he read with a hot ember under a bed.

At times, similarities between Williams's vignettes in *Losing My Cool* (and his second book) and other autobiographies and historical narratives seem uncanny. I use the term "uncanny" in its Freudian sense described in his essay *Das Unheimliche* (1919). Sigmund Freud moved beyond his psychoanalytical terrain into aesthetics when discussing *unheimlich*, derived from the word *heimlich* ("homely"). The psychologist aspired to signify how "the uncanny is that class of the frightening which leads back to what is known of old and long familiar."[65] *Losing My Cool* provides tropes that both confirm and counter views about black male erudition in their individual literacy narratives to remove novelty and promote ambivalence. Freud helps us begin to locate the sources of ambivalence through recognizing "that what is novel can easily become frightening but not by any means all. Something has to be added to what is novel and unfamiliar in order to make it uncanny."[66] Jacques Lacan further elaborates on its implications for irreducible anxiety when explaining that an aesthetic or narrative that creates a sense of the uncanny puts us into a situation "where we do not know

62. Young, *Your Average Nigga*, 31.

63. Young, *Your Average Nigga*, 31.

64. Williams, *Losing My Cool*, 126.

65. Freud, *Uncanny*, 418.

66. Freud, *Uncanny*, 418.

how to distinguish bad and good, pleasure from displeasure."[67] This art and literature can inspire an intended ambivalence that might lead us to pursue a remedy to our cognitive dissonance through uncovering the real or truth.

Williams experienced the uncanny with his own traumatic reading experience as a seven year old. It began with his parents attempting to teach a lesson on his black identity and then assigning *The Autobiography of Malcolm X*. After reading the vignette about the Klan murdering Malcolm's father, Williams couldn't sleep at night. Malcolm's storytelling conjured images of his mortally wounded father. Within proximity to that experience, a school mate heard him singing a Public Enemy song that deployed the term nigga, and inquired, "You're a nigger, too, right, so how can you say that?"[68] As if these two experiences weren't distressing enough, an incident outside the home fully ushered him into a trauma that would produce motivated irrationality.

The young Williams's second encounter with racism happened shortly thereafter as he traveled with his mother and older brother through the ghetto on a trip beyond their suburb to get a stylish haircut at a black barbershop. As Williams peered out the car window, a black woman turned towards their Mercedes and began to hurl derogatory racial epithets at them. He recounts that as a young boy, he felt as if being called a honky by the woman "had somehow stripped me of myself, taken something from me. I felt I had to protect myself from ever feeling that kind of loss again."[69] This sense of denied or mistaken identity motivated Williams to perform blackness unmistakably to compensate for an apparent lack of pigmentation. Williams's pursuit of hip-hop blackness echoes Oedipus's mistake: he thought he "knew" the geography of his sorrow and thus tried to flee from it. In doing so, Williams began a cultural quest informed by a motivated irrationality that culminated in the pursuit of authentic blackness.

## "Know What I'm Saying?": Knowingness and the Black Male Experience

In the context of the African-American male's pursuit of literacy—and I use the term broadly here—one finds a remarkably motivated irrationality in the form of the defensive social construction of identity. In this chapter, I discuss this evolving fixation with the meaning of blackness. Our discussion will demonstrate how racial trauma leads to a "knowingness" about what

67. Vidler, *Architectural Uncanny*, 224.
68. Williams, *Losing My Cool*, 2.
69. Williams, *Losing My Cool*, 9.

it means to be black and male in a way that precludes one from pondering Plato's ancient inquiries. Consequently, we will probe the "logos of the
psyche" and build a new foundation for the existential investigation into
"What is it to be minded as we are?" The answer to that question moves one
to Plato's query: how to live.[70]

My Bondage and My Freedom displays Douglass's concerns about race
and American racial politics. Born into a Southern caste system defined
mostly by race, he developed an increasing awareness of the relationship
between his race and his status as a slave. In Baltimore, he describes sitting
with his white peers and hashing over his slave status as a black child.[71] He
says, "'I wish I could be free, as you will when you get to be men.'"[72] Douglass intended to elicit pity from his peers. Yet, even their compassion didn't
disrupt his continued preoccupation with his slave status. He writes:

> When I was about thirteen years old, and had succeeded in
> learning to read, every increase of knowledge, especially re-
> specting the FREE STATES, added something to the almost
> intolerable burden of the thought—"I AM A SLAVE FOR LIFE."
> To my bondage I saw no end.[73]

As I have discussed earlier, Douglass's progress in his literacy aspirations
brought about an "almost intolerable burden of thought" that elicited an
attitude of knowingness. He explains, "It was a terrible reality, and I shall
never be able to tell how sadly that thought chafed my young spirit."[74] Although outwardly compliant, he expressed an inner stance of insubordination and rejection of the social caste system. Douglass found blacks who
acquiesced to slavery irritating:

> I have met many religious colored people, at the south, who are
> under the delusion that God requires them to submit to slavery,
> and to wear their chains with meekness and humility. I could
> entertain no such nonsense as this; and I almost lost my pa-
> tience when I found any colored man weak enough to believe
> such stuff.[75]

One can see in Douglass's observation a critique of irrationality and fatalism, which stands in stark contrast to the incessant deployment of his wit to

70. Lear, Open Minded, 8.
71. Douglass, My Bondage and My Freedom, 224.
72. Douglass, My Bondage and My Freedom, 224.
73. Douglass, My Bondage and My Freedom, 225.
74. Douglass, My Bondage and My Freedom, 225.
75. Douglass, My Bondage and My Freedom, 226–27.

undermine his status and the slave system in thought and deed. Douglass knew, and he was right, that the power of his mind would enable him to overcome both slavery and racism. Simultaneously, he on occasion neglects to appreciate that others might have equally compelling reasons to acquiesce to their condition or feign acquiescence.

In this regard, Douglass, too, was as mindful as Oedipus. Having criticized submissive fellow slaves who allowed themselves to allow whites to use religious rhetoric to keep them ensnared in slavery, something he was too clever for, Douglass eventually found himself coveting their ignorance. He writes, "I almost envied my fellow slaves their stupid contentment. . . . I was too thoughtful to be happy. It was this everlasting thinking which distressed and tormented me; *and yet there was no getting rid of the subject of my thoughts*."[76] Here we see the link between living by one's wit, mindfulness, and education, and the path to ambivalence about literacy and about being a learned slave. Although Douglass was quite critical of his slave peers, his narrative reveals how living by one's wits did not immediately free him. But it does help us see how a sense of knowingness can lead to feeling burdened and overwhelmed, leading to vacillation and ambivalence.

W. E. B. Du Bois's form of knowingness is in the same vein as Douglass's thinking. The schoolhouse incident described earlier would prompt him to develop a state of motivated irrationality (or knowingness) about how black men should respond to racism. After his unpleasant encounter with the newcomer, whose refusal of Du Bois's card indicated his difference, the young boy set out to do battle with his new adversaries. "[The] sky was bluest when I could beat my mates at examination-time, or beat them at a foot-race, or even beat their stringy heads," Du Bois boasts.[77] He conceded that whites dominated American society, but he desired to wrest a few of their prizes from them. In other words, his response to racial trauma was to beat whites at their own game. He would prove that he was more than equal. He writes, "Just how I would do it I could never decide; by reading the law, by healing the sick, by telling the wonderful tales that swam in my head— some way."[78] Coming of age in New England, he'd attend Fisk University and Harvard College and then attend graduate school at Berlin and Harvard Universities. A prolific writer, he eventually chose to dedicate himself to the "life of the mind" and to attacking the racial caste system with his wit—a modern-day Oedipus.

76. Douglass, *My Bondage and My Freedom*, 227; emphasis mine.
77. Du Bois, *Souls of Black Folk*, 44.
78. Du Bois, *Souls of Black Folk*, 44.

I suspect the location of Du Bois's racial *awakening*—the school-house—had implications for his strategy. The young boy found academic competition preferable to the conventional response of "other black boys [with whom] the strife was not so fiercely sunny: their youth shrunk into tasteless sycophancy, or into the silent hatred of the pale world about them and mocking distrust of everything white; or wasted itself in a bitter cry."[79] Early on, Du Bois had ascertained that fatalism was not a path toward political or spiritual freedom. Unlike his black peers, the scholar refused to ask, "Why did God make me an outcast and a stranger in mine own house?"[80] Instead, he relied on his reason. Du Bois's began to recognize a unique form of knowingness. Discovering an unexpected gift he described himself as "a sort of seventh son, born with a veil, and gifted with second-sight in this American world—a world which yield[ed] him no true self-consciousness, but only [let] him see himself through the revelation of the other world."[81] In these observations, we see that Du Bois understood the source of his motivated irrationality on a surface level: his awareness of white scorn. Yet, he refused to submit to their perception, seeking instead to think his way beyond their condemnation and scale the walls of his racial prison by native wit.

Although Du Bois had established a seemingly rational response to anti-blackness, he still developed ambivalence. The subsequent consideration leads him to define his psychological dilemma as double-consciousness. Du Bois's self-analysis, moreover, reveals his capacity for intersubjectivity. In reflecting upon his mental state, Du Bois's exercise excavates his motivated irrationality, knowingness, and ambivalence in a prosaic illustration. Du Bois explains:

> [Double-consciousness] is this sense of always looking at one's self through the eyes of others, of measuring one's soul by the tape of a world that looks on in amused contempt and pity. One ever feels his two-ness—an American, a Negro; two souls, two thoughts, two unreconciled strivings; two warring ideals in one dark body, whose dogged strength alone keeps it from being torn asunder.[82]

For Du Bois, the black man struggled to reconcile his two selves "to make it possible for a man to be both a Negro and an American."[83] Based on

79. Du Bois, *Souls of Black Folk*, 44.
80. Du Bois, *Souls of Black Folk*, 45.
81. Du Bois, *Souls of Black Folk*, 45.
82. Du Bois, *Souls of Black Folk*, 45.
83. Du Bois, *Souls of Black Folk*, 45.

double-conscious, or profound racial self-awareness, Du Bois experiences racism-induced schizophrenia that lies at the heart of an age-old question: How do we (African Americans) live? He argues that he would need to "merge his double self into a better and truer self."[84] This reasoning suggests merging two antagonistic selves into a higher self as a real possibility. He asserts that the black man must not "bleach his negro soul"; instead, he must be allowed to contribute his message to the world and gain opportunity. Lear's claim about the relationship between the polis and the psyche exposes how the broader social milieu impacts individual black males (and of course, black females). Du Bois's profound metacognitive and tenacious analysis produces cognitive dissonance and unresolved inner turmoil. He looked to his own wit to solve and deconstruct American racism. But surpassing his white colleagues by becoming educated did not transform his social status or obliterate the racial caste system. The inability of his wit to once and for all transform our society reveals the irrational basis of Du Bois's motivation. The myths of meritocracy and racial inferiority are fraternal twins that veil the (il)logic of a social inequality grounded in racial ideologies and supported by sedimented social structures.

Langston Hughes's approach to resolving his identity issues reflects a Lear-defined, motivated irrationality as a cognitive and cultural phenomenon. Like others in this book, his perceived commitment to "linked fate" with other African Americans, based on an imagined monolithic racial identity that obliges race-based solidarity, led to a Lear-defined knowingness. On a personal level, Hughes was passionate about the idea of a single black or Negro people defined by common oppression.[85] In *The Big Sea*, he writes about his trip to a generic Africa, where the people are "black and beautiful as the night. The bare, pointed breasts of women in the market places. The rippling muscles of men loading palm oil and cocoa beans and mahogany on ships [for] the white man's world."[86] Hughes was concerned about colonialism in Africa. The narrative notes the role of missionaries and traders, the whip and the gun, in exploiting Africans. He writes, "We brought machinery and tools, canned goods, and Hollywood films. We took away riches out of the earth, loaded by human hands."[87] In Hughes's mind, the injustice in Africa unified African Americans with Africans.

But not everyone felt this way. When Hughes tried to discuss colonialism and black nationalism with Africans on the West Coast, they called him

84. Du Bois, *Souls of Black Folk*, 42.
85. Hughes, *Big Sea*, 102.
86. Hughes, *Big Sea*, 102.
87. Hughes, *Big Sea*, 102.

a white man. He writes, "[I told them that] 'our problems in America are very much like yours . . . especially in the South. I am a Negro, too.' But they only laughed at me and shook their heads and said: 'You, white man! You, white man!'" A Liberian shipmate explained this phenomenon, telling Hughes that "foreign colored men" traveled to Africa as missionaries and as staff for the colonial governments, "so the Africans call them white men."[88] "But I am not white," Hughes responded. The Liberian answered, "You not black either."[89] This laughter and categorization deeply hurt Hughes, who didn't want to make a distinction between Africans and African Americans. What we see here is a knowingness that impeded Hughes from accepting their diverse conceptions of blackness based on citizenship, colorism, and class stratification. This blindness made it impossible for him to predict that these sorts of distinctions would lead to more hurt feelings when Hughes had to deal with upper-class African Americans in Washington, DC. He encountered a different form of knowingness among the black elite, who "drew rigid class and color lines within the race against negroes who worked with their hands, or who were dark in complexion and had no degrees from colleges."[90] He found their repugnance problematic because these African-American aristocrats rejected how he felt about the black folk; growing up alongside poor blacks within shared geography had led to class and cultural identification.

Claude Steele's *Whistling Vivaldi* reveals a comparable motivated ir-rationality, one that emerges out of his childhood experiences bumping up against the color-line at the community swimming pool and golf course. Steele weaves bits of his personal anecdotes into the account of education; both his narrative strategy and his subject matter are concerned with the mind, or "native wit."[91] Steele is also interested in a particular form of dou-ble-consciousness. He investigates how individuals respond to stereotypes that are not explicit but are "threat[s] in the air," lingering "like a balloon over their heads."[92] This "stereotype threat" reveals a class of self-defeating knowingness in which individuals are aware of what others may think about them based on their ascriptive identity:

> Our social identities can strongly affect things as important as
> our performances in the classroom on standardized tests, our
> memory capacity, our athletic performance, the pressure we feel

88. Hughes, *Big Sea*, 103.

89. Hughes, *Big Sea*, 103.

90. Hughes, *Big Sea*, 206.

91. Lear, *Open Minded*, 42.

92. Steele, *Whistling Vivaldi*, 4.

to prove ourselves, even the comfort level we have with different
groups—all things we typically think of as being determined by
individual talents, motivations, and preferences.[93]

In other words, being black—among other identity markers—exerts a strong
influence on the psyche and the way individuals act in different situations,
which can lead to self-defeat when one attempts to accomplish particular
raced-tasks, or when experiencing discomfort in social contexts in which
one might reasonably expect that others might perceive their ascriptive
identity as abnormal, undesirable, or connoting deficiency. *Whistling Vivaldi* suggests that this particular form of knowingness, defined as a stereotype
threat, plagues black men who strive to move beyond the geographies of
their communities, culture, and spheres of influence.

Steele writes about Brent Staples, a columnist for the *New York Times*,
as a case in point. As a young African-American male attending the University of Chicago, Staples would walk around Hyde Park and encounter the
white residents in the area. He writes, "I became an expert in the language
of fear. Couples locked arms or reached for each other's hands when they
saw me. Some crossed to the other side of the street. People carrying on conversations went mute and stared straight ahead, as though avoiding my eyes
would save them."[94] Most rational people would think that a graduate student wouldn't expect to inspire fear in the university's neighbors, but Staples
began to see things otherwise. He explains, "I'd been a fool. I'd been walking
the streets grinning good evening at people who were frightened to death
of me. I did violence to them by just being."[95] In order to deflect stereotypes
about black males being violent and to relieve the fears of passersby, Staples
would whistle classical tunes such as Vivaldi's *Four Seasons.*

Yet, while Staples's whistling might have mitigated white neighbors'
fears, it didn't resolve the stereotype that black males are dangerous. But the
music in itself didn't relieve them. It was a surprising disruption, a meme
from an unexpected cultural domain. While some would argue that it was
disruptive enough to change knowingness into open-mindedness if only
for that moment, I would argue that the minds of Staples and his white
neighbors never opened. The disruption was a temporary distraction that
did not dislodge more significant social categories and judgments. More importantly, however, this scene reveals how black men attempt to manipulate
others by performing their literacy, figuratively and literally.

93. Steele, *Whistling Vivaldi*, 4.
94. Steele, *Whistling Vivaldi*, 6.
95. Steele, *Whistling Vivaldi*, 6.

By demonstrating that identities within the individual are often multiple and fluid, in *Whistling Vivaldi*, Steele attempts to develop wit-oriented strategies for acknowledging the complexity of human identity without falling into identity politics. However, he does not address the individual racial and structural barriers that impede social progress and limit black males' freedom and opportunities. While visiting the University of Michigan at Ann Arbor, Steele began to develop his "new vantage point on a familiar problem, the academic struggles of too many minority students on American college campuses."[96] He would have concluded that students with deficiencies had been admitted to the school in the past. But interviewing myriads of high-achieving students changed his perception. They talked about needing minority-oriented spaces, the low expectations of faculty, the lack of faculty of color, and marginalization. But Steele interpreted their concerns as a function of "something in the air on campus."[97] In other words, in Steele's theoretical framework, one finds academic reasoning equivalent to Oedipus's reliance on his native wit. *Whistling Vivaldi* focuses more on stigma-related contingencies that impede marginalized students' success rather than on actual structural barriers. Tooting classical melody or other Jedi mind tricks are temporary solutions to a long-lasting problem.

Motivated irrationality is lodged at the core of Vershawn Ashanti Young's and Thomas Chatterton Williams's literacy narratives. Young is interested in "the burden of racial performance, the demand to prove what type of black person you are. It's a burden all blacks bear, and it is the core problem of black racial authenticity."[98] The requirement to code-switch from a black urban to a white middle-class identity creates a psychic and social burden equivalent to "racial passing."[99] Yet, Young sees the issue as both a social and personal one.[100] However, this burden reveals a form of knowingness in black individuals and the black community. The expedient response to deploy racial performances defined as black is a "thin 'pragmatism' which purports to offer a solution to any problem."[101] Young urgently needs to address doubts about his masculinity and black authenticity. But like Oedipus, he "is too busy [spinning his wheels] figuring things out."[102] In his self-conscious investment in resolving the conundrum of code-switching,

96. Steele, *Whistling Vivaldi*, 17.

97. Steele, *Whistling Vivaldi*, 23.

98. Young, *Losing My Cool*, 37.

99. Young, *Losing My Cool*, 37.

100. Young, *Losing My Cool*, 39.

101. Lear, *Open Minded*, 51.

102. Lear, *Open Minded*, 51.

Young embodies Toni Morrison's argument that the function of racism is a distraction.

This behavior emerges whenever he participates in family or community gatherings, where his (black) manhood is questioned. Describing one such gathering, Young talks about the quest for black masculinity and literacy performance in a metacognitive manner: "My brothers, male cousins, and brothers-in-law were in the kitchen. I was there too, trying to bond with them, participating in men-talk they found so enjoyable and that I decided I no longer wanted to avoid."[103] This change of heart is significant because, thus far, his family had nicknamed him "Sugar" to signify his effeminacy. Young wants to move beyond having his masculinity and blackness disparaged and marginalized.[104] In the process, he gets in a modern dance contest with Tyrone, a member of the extended family, during which they are called "fags" and "sissies."[105] Because Young is unsure about who is being labeled pejoratively, he pretends that he's tired and drops out. Ironically, Young writes, "I admired [Tyrone], even though I decided right then and there that I wouldn't be caught dead dancing like that again."[106] Here we see Young suppressing his more creative self in order to meet the standards of masculinity needed to pass as a black man. More significantly, he spends less time pondering the meaning behind this labeling.

According to Lear, Aristotle believed that philosophy began in "wonder, or awe."[107] But Young, like Oedipus, "is thinking too hard to experience the terror of abandonment, the awe of fate [regarding race and gender]."[108] Lear helps us understand this phenomenon when he writes, "Philosophy becomes impossible because the originating act of wonder is too terrible."[109] One must move beyond fear-based reasoning and concentrate on gender performance and racial identity to avoid further emasculation or appearing insufficiently black. Motivated irrationalities are grounded in fear. Instead, one must open oneself up to the awe-inspiring and boundless possibilities that reside at the intersection of black and male. Choosing to do otherwise is to unintentionally find oneself moving towards the trauma one hopes to avoid. This harm includes abandonment, marginalization, and rejection.

103. Young, *Your Average Nigga*, 39.

104. Young, *Your Average Nigga*, 39.

105. Young, *Your Average Nigga*, 40.

106. Young, *Your Average Nigga*, 40.

107. Lear, *Open Minded*, 51.

108. Lear, *Open Minded*, 51.

109. Lear, *Open Minded*, 51.

While Williams does not discuss "the burden of racial performance" in theoretical terms, the description of his first year at Georgetown University captures the madness in the politics of black authenticity. He began his undergraduate experience by making stereotyped assessments about college life and black college students that exemplified a form of knowingness. However, Williams's preconceived ideas were disrupted continuously. For example, after arriving, he ignored anyone who was not African American, including his roommates, some of whom he would later find out knew quite a bit about hip-hop. Yet, life experiences had not removed the scales from his eyes.

As a college freshman, Williams behaved as though blackness was connected to geography and the commoditized icons of black manhood circulated in hip-hop culture and American sports. Consequently, the young Williams never questioned the authenticity of a blackness that one could transport from one's bedroom to a college dorm in a suitcase, nor did he question the fact that televised hip-hop culture might exist beyond Union Catholic:

> I arrived there in a backward New Era Yankees cap, Rocawear jeans as stiff as sheet metal, and a pair of brand-new yellow Timberland construction boots. . . . I brought with me stacks of Cash Money, Death Row, and Bad Boy albums, around twenty pairs of tennis shoes, a photo album's worth of pictures of Stacey, and something to prove.[110]

In other words, Williams adhered to a form of blackness that required the necessary accoutrements of credibility and a specific atmosphere. Still, he never interrogated the sources of these criteria for blackness. According to *Losing My Cool*, Pappy had made it clear to Williams and his brother that they were indeed black. Nonetheless, his humiliating childhood experience while riding in a luxury vehicle with his white mother led to confusion about his identity. He had grown up attempting to avoid having another person confuse him with the race of people who had killed Malcolm X's father.

As if mimicking Oedipus, Williams also seemed to believe that his identity was grounded in geography. He imagined himself "a kind of exiled representative of Union Catholic, of New Jersey, of hip-hop culture and blackness."[111] During his first weekend at college, he attended a house party that seemed less like Georgetown—a bastion of privilege—and more akin to

110. Williams, *Losing My Cool*, 82.
111. Williams, *Losing My Cool*, 81.

a high school gym party in the ghetto, where girls gave gratuitous lap dances and guys rolled up things to smoke.[112] He declares, "I was wrong on all counts. The 'hood, however, besieged and dispersed, was alive and kicking [at Georgetown University]."[113] Interestingly, Williams's posture of knowingness led him to prejudge Georgetown's black students, and his superficial knowledge prevented him from pondering the significance of the fact that he had unveiled "the 'hood" within the university's brick buildings, metal gates, and ivy-covered walls. It took him a while to begin to reconsider his assumptions about the meaning(s) and source(s) of his knowingness.

Beyond finding a hip-hop subculture similar to the one in which he participated in New Jersey, Williams anticipated that the black social pecking order at the university would duplicate African-American society, based on knowledge gleaned from Black Entertainment Television.[114] Even more interestingly, if the black community at college were a microcosm of the broader African-American community, then African-American society was an inversion of the white social order, a social order in which Williams admitted he'd never participated. Williams assumed that all African Americans hold to a value system that puts athletes and entertainers on top.[115] Williams had few options on where he might reside in the pecking order among Georgetown's black students. He writes, "At the bottom of the heap were those—mostly males—who didn't rap or sing, who didn't walk and talk like they slung crack rock, who didn't have a wicked jump shot. Which is the same as saying, at the bottom of the pile were those of us who most resembled college students. I was terrified of winning such an ignoble fate."[116] As an adult who graduated and has gone on to a journalism career, Williams is now able to laugh at his self-loathing in the imagined hierarchy of black life that he constructed based on his immature perceptions about a marginalized community he'd experienced from the periphery. But as an undergraduate, his knowingness blinded him from seeing the multiple ways in which African Americans in general, and black men in particular, live their lives. Williams's unawareness and immaturity rendered illegible the broad spectrum of black manhood. With Lear, we can see this self-proclaimed, hip-hop literacy narrative as insinuating a type of knowingness—both cultural and personal—that is contingent upon placing narrow boundaries around black masculinity in a manner that disallows literacy, writ large.

112. Williams, *Losing My Cool,* 83.
113. Williams, *Losing My Cool,* 84.
114. Williams, *Losing My Cool,* 84.
115. Williams, *Losing My Cool,* 84–85.
116. Williams, *Losing My Cool,* 85.

## Conclusion

By reading these narratives through Lear's analysis of modern psychoanalysis and the myth of knowingness, we see how the black male authors and
scholars discussed in this chapter experienced trauma around their racial
identity and then responded to that trauma with their minds. In brief, the
question is not as simple as the one posed by ancient Greek philosophers:
"how do I live?" Instead, it becomes "how do I live as a black man in a racialized society?" Under a racial caste system, events in which race renders one's
humanity opaque precipitate traumatic transformation. If we are to perceive
that the minds of these black men have been and continue to be "everywhere
active and imaginative in the organization of [their] own experience, then
we need to understand the routes of this activity if we are to grasp how the
mind works. This is true whether [those minds are] trying to come to grips
with painful reality, reacting to trauma, coping with the every day, or 'just
making things up.'"[117] He helps us to see how the mind and society are in a
co-productive relationship. In his words, the reasoning is contextual; it begins in the "polis [and moves into the] psyche."[118] In the process of trying to
track trauma and motivated irrationality, what is brought to life is the myth
of knowingness—the denial of tragedy and loss, which is founded on the
idea "that meaning is transparent to human reason."[119] As Sophocles makes
clear in his reading of *Oedipus*, we see that strict rationality is insufficient for
understanding, much less for resolving the issues that come to bear on the
lives of black men. "Oedipus's mistake, in essence, is to ignore unconscious
meaning," Lear explains. "Oedipus attacks the very idea of unconscious
meaning."[120] This line of thought makes evident that more education, more
sociological studies, and more government policies are insufficient to heal
the wounds caused by racial trauma within a racial caste system.

Lear would call African-American males to live open-mindedly and
pursue a narrative understanding of the world through drama and literature. Turning Janus-faced toward Greece during the fifth century BC, an
era that Lear describes as the womb of democracy, he finds in the ancient
proliferation of the Greek tragedy implications for defining and prescribing
open-mindedness. Lear explains:

> This coincidence is not mere coincidence. The tragic theater
> gave citizens the opportunity to retreat momentarily from the

117. Lear, *Open Minded*, 20.
118. Lear, *Open Minded*, 10.
119. Lear, *Open Minded*, 29.
120. Lear, *Open Minded*, 29.

responsibility of making rational decisions for themselves and their society. At the same time, tragedy confronted them emotionally with the fact that they had to make decisions in a world that was not entirely rational, in which rationality was sometimes violently disrupted, [a world] in which rationality itself could be used for irrational ends.[121]

In the case of African-American men, our nation has witnessed a perpetual disruption in the logic of the democratic tenets underwriting our polis—a disruption that either renders black men invisible or marginalizes and sometimes leads to unforeseen and unpredictable murderous acts of violence.

Our political system's illogical racial thinking leads to an understandable irrationality among some black men regarding reading and speaking other than Black Vernacular English. More explicitly, Lear reminds us of the need to remember that self-creation begins first in the polis and then enters into the psyche:

> The members of a community constitute themselves in the creation and maintenance of a social-cultural-political world, the polis. Humans, Plato says, are polis animals. The polis provides the only environment fit for human habitation. That is one reason Socrates refuses to flee Athens, with all its faults: life outside its boundaries would, for him, be meaningless. Indeed, the polis, for Plato, has a deeper claim on humans: they are dependent on it for the very constitution of their psyches. Humans are born with a capacity to internalize their cultural influences.[122]

As I read literacy narratives, I discover that they implicitly challenge us to develop a capacity to live non-defensively and open-mindedly while cultivating a new conception of what it is to be black, male, and literate. This task will require our recognizing that, in a social order that continues to function within a racial caste system, the psyche both engages in and is engaged by "the cultural-political environment, and that both are fundamentally shaped by the movement of meanings from polis to the psyche and back again."[123] Some black men's dilemma is that "literacy" has been historically coded as "white" from the legal perspective and their knowingness orientation. In that case, there is no simple strategy for a black man who is interested in literacy and identifies himself as a specific kind of authentic, conscious, and free human being. On the one hand, he must gain clarity about society's literacy biases. On the other hand, he denies his reality and

121. Lear, *Open Minded*, 29.
122. Lear, *Open Minded*, 58.
123. Lear, *Open Minded*, 10.

persists in a commitment to the literacy myth in his efforts to assimilate and gain inclusion into the broader polis.

The ambivalence that some black men experience around literacy does not fit within existing discourses that implicitly signify an interest in black men's motivated irrationalities. A new discussion would reveal that one cannot easily disaggregate the seeming irrationalities in our nation's sociopolitical neurosis surrounding race. Only then can we begin to see what's worth repeating here: the significance of Lear's belief that "humans are inherently makers and interpreters of meaning. It is meaning—ideas, desires, beliefs—which causes humans to do the interesting things they do."[124] These meanings and interpretations elucidate our deepest yearning: to be autonomous agents who live unencumbered by the narrow definitions of black authenticity and masculinity. Amid racial oppression—from within and without the black community—we still have to grapple with the prerequisite of understanding human complexity and the social world's role in shaping the human psyche to understand the experience of black male literacy.

When we appreciate the complexity of the motivated irrationalities expressed in black male literacy narratives, then we can help ambivalent young men pursue literacy in a manner that acknowledges and fits their self-interest. As black men, our ambivalence contains within it a tendency towards knowingness. Presumption emerges in three forms: (1) what it means to be a black male; (2) a sense of abandonment by the nation-state due to racial injustice; and (3) a surfeit of motivated irrationalities. Prescribed drugs, school counseling, and increased literacy won't resolve this knowingness. We have yet to create a normative context in which black men can ask Socrates's fundamental question in a new way: "How might we live as black men in this particular context and moment?" We must join the citizens of ancient Greece. We must recognize that our world is not wholly rational. We must expect that irrationality unpredictably bursts into our lives. Finally, we must admit that we often deploy our rationality in an illogical manner.[125] This posture will help us see our own irrationality when we try to achieve our goals by native wit. In dispelling the myth of knowingness, we must approach our world and each individual in it with awe and wonder. Only then can we begin to leave behind knowingness. And only then can we begin to ask ourselves non-defensively not just "How do I live?" but also "How do I define literacy and black manhood?"

124. Lear, *Open Minded*, 24.
125. Lear, *Open Minded*, 29.

When I look back on the young African-American boy that I was, posted up against the car in 1979, I can see that the frisking of my body stripped me of my dignity and my manhood in a manner that made me begin to act out a motivated irrationality. All at once, I wanted to be an authentic black man, but more than just an authentic black man in the traditional sense. I would become a man by exploring new territories—geographic, educational, and cultural—beyond Southeast San Diego. During the last two years of high school, I would return to the "classrooms" in my community at Lincoln and Morse High Schools to study among people who esteemed me, allowed me to participate in power, and made me feel safe. My madness, however, involved moving back and forth between the 'hood and more upscale communities in pursuit of a hybrid and more transcendent black self.

My life in the 'hood included reading a number of new things. I began to seek out books by black authors. I hung with older cats—the offspring of black nationalists, gang members, and players—in my free time. Mr. El-Amin dropped science and taught me about being black from the perspective of black nationalist and conspiracy theories. I began to heed my grandparents' Jim Crow wisdom and pursued their respectability politics. At the same time, I sought to transcend it all by being Mr. *GQ* and participating in edgy social settings. Being a black man also involved running through as many women as possible to prove that I was a man. And in serial-monogamous relationships, I tried to prove to the women that I was a man by being an athlete in bed. The fluctuation between good and evil, literate and illiterate, black and a cosmopolitan preppy punk neo-European artiste funkster became overwhelming. Eventually, I gave in to the myths about black manhood, survival, and the streets until I came to understand my soul's logic and began to leave behind self-destructive and self-obstructive behaviors and embrace literacy as a path to becoming more human.

Perhaps I like Louis Armstrong because he's made poetry out of being invisible.

I think it must be because he's unaware that he is invisible. And my own grasp of invisibility aids me to understand his music.

—Ralph Ellison, *Invisible Man* (1952)

Queen Anne, Seattle, Washington (c. 2017)

CHAPTER 7

# Embracing Ambivalence

## *Pedagogy of Transformation*

I OPENED MY EXPLORATION of black male ambivalence concerning literacy with an allusion to Ralph Ellison's *Invisible Man*. The protagonist is smoking reefer and imagining that he is having a conversation with an ex-slave woman who feels double-minded about her former master and her sons' father. "I too have become acquainted with ambivalence," the narrator replies. "That's why I'm here"—high on marijuana, attempting to understand how American racism and black surrogacy inform one's identity and lead to ambivalence and invisibility.[1] Her sons' existence and identity have been foisted upon them due to her rape. Stated differently, these young men literally embody W. E. B. Du Bois's sense of double-consciousness and "twonness—an American, a Negro; two souls, two thoughts, two unreconciled strivings; two warring ideals in one dark body, whose dogged strength alone keeps it from being torn asunder."[2] The narrator's confession about ambivalence in *Invisible Man* captures the motivation for my inquiry into identity performance, literacy ambivalence, and masculinity. My primary goal, thus far, has been to present diverse forms of ambivalence experienced by African-American males. Here, I further explicate the antagonism between black authenticity and mainstream literacy and then devise a framework for embracing the pedagogy of ambivalence as a path towards transformation.

Ellison's connection between ambivalence and invisibility has implications for my ruminations on being black and literate. The narrator argues that being invisible to society leads to a different way of experiencing and

1. Ellison, *Invisible Man*, 10.
2. Du Bois, quoted in Ellison, *Invisible Man*, 10.

being in the world. He elaborates, "Invisibility, let me explain, gives one a slightly different sense of time, you're never quite on the beat. Sometimes you're ahead and sometimes behind."[3] The protagonist's grasp of the meaning of invisibility (blackness), along with an altered state of consciousness resulting from smoking reefer, allows him to understand the relationship between having a belittled racial identity and Louis Armstrong's music. He explains, "Perhaps I like Louis Armstrong because he's made poetry out of being invisible [being stereotyped]. I think it must be because he's unaware that he is invisible. And my own grasp of invisibility aids me to understand his music."[4] The narratives we have examined seek to make poetry or sorrow songs out of their ambivalence about race and literacy.

One's invisibility, being raced, or leading to a conduit or role in black surrogacy, as described in Morrison's *Playing in the Dark*, shapes Ellison's prose, inducing a different notion of time and the historical moments he traverses. Being offbeat similarly informs the authors' ambivalence and anxiety. Being out of sync with one's society (or the self society ascribes to young black men) leads to an extreme sense of one's self-consciousness about literacy and, in some cases, masculinity. Their narratives testify to how blackness and sometimes black masculinity inform the black male author's "sense of time on conscious and unconscious levels." I've sought to use the theorists discussed, so far, in the same manner that Ellison's protagonist uses his reefer to become "aware of [time's] nodes, those points where time stands still or from which it leaps ahead."[5] My work has been focused on unveiling how some black males experience double-consciousness regarding their literacy performances. Ellison's *Invisible Man* lets us see that self-integration requires one being in and out of identities the same way that his narrator is in and out of time. Many black males interpret literacy's significance regarding their own identity when contrasting dominant stereotypes of black males and representations of the black middle-class striving toward assimilation. Hence, endeavoring for the perfect literacy performance in different contexts derails their sense of being coherent in their identity, which one experiences as being offbeat—the last thing a conscious African-American individual committed to a ghetto-oriented vision of blackness wants to be. The lenses that I've used to study these authors reveal that literacy ambivalence results from some black males reacting to racial discrimination and black authenticity in the context of trying to determine what it means to be black, male, and literate.

3. Ellison, *Invisible Man*, 8.
4. Ellison, *Invisible Man*, 8.
5. Ellison, *Invisible Man*, 8.

I have, so far, relied upon several lenses having to do with topics as diverse as education, literary criticism, and politics to make legible diverse forms of anxiety and ambivalence. Ellison enables me to understand the method in my own metaphorical madness in his description of his protagonist's experience with marijuana:

> So under the spell of the reefer I discovered a new analytical way of listening to the music. The unheard sounds came through, and each melodic line existed of itself, stood out clearly from all the rest, said its piece, and waited patiently for the other voices to speak. That night I found myself hearing not only in time, but in space as well. I not only entered the music but descended, like Dante, into the depths.[6]

Although I've avoided descending into the depths of hell, I've tried to develop a new analytical way of listening to each author and allowing each to say his piece. I've used theoretical texts to grasp the narratives' depths regarding the issue at hand. Each scrutinizing lens has had implications for drawing out the sources of ambivalence in each particular black male's literacy experience. Together they allowed us to see how educational metamorphoses, ideologies within the black community, blackness as surrogacy, and motivated irrationality have all played roles in ambivalence.

In the opening to *Invisible Man*, Ralph Ellison establishes the subconscious influence that racial trauma and black authenticity's politics can have upon the black male psyche. While in an altered state of consciousness, he hears a sermon titled "Blackness of Blackness," based on a primordial and polyvalent African-American ideology that informs discourses on black identity and experience, in which the call and response is built on the refrain "black is . . . black ain't."[7] In Ellison's *Invisible Man*, it is in the midst of the sermon on authentic blackness that the narrator begins to talk to the ex-slave woman and confesses his own ambivalence as he grapples with different ideologies. It may seem odd that he would imagine that he is having a conversation with a slave. Still, Ellison helps us visualize the complicated relationship between blacks and whites that goes as far back as joining the two seemingly racially distinct political bodies, so to speak, and how this relationship has created an enduring ambivalence.

6. Ellison, *Invisible Man*, 8–9.
7. Ellison, *Invisible Man*, 10.

## Thinking with Paley and a Pig

While Jonathan Lear's theories lay bare the root of ambivalence in the psyche—a motivated irrationality that leads to knowingness, in reading the narratives of African-American males who experience ambivalence regarding literacy—one discovers that their motivated irrationality originates with a traumatic introduction to their own socially scorned racial identities. Coming to terms with these racialized identities, the men develop anxiety as they attempt to negotiate and reconcile multiple conceptions of black manhood and literacy.

Vivian Paley's work helps me further interpret black male literacy ambivalence. She enables me to reveal a constructive path forward that recognizes these feelings and advocates a more holistic approach to literacy among black men who might experience ambivalence. In 1989, the MacArthur Foundation awarded Paley its prestigious "genius grant" for her oeuvre, which has emerged from four decades of teaching kindergarten and nursery school at the University of Chicago Laboratory Schools. The challenging work of reflecting on teaching children has led her to write thought-provoking books about children's thought life and the educative nature of child's play. To move us beyond the paralysis of ambivalence, I draw on Paley's meditations on her final year of teaching in *The Girl with the Brown Crayon: How Children Use Stories to Shape Their Lives.*

*The Girl with the Brown Crayon* discusses Paley's experience teaching Leo Lionni's classic children's books in a year-long reader's theater. Her kindergartners unconsciously begin to think about their in-school experiences and personal lives, using the characters in Lionni's books as foils. In doing so, the students draw their entire learning community and family members into their process until the boundaries between their human lives and the stories become blurred. In Paley's story, one student in particular stands out. Reeny Willens, a precocious African-American child, helps her classmates and, unexpectedly, Paley uncover the significance of emotions and stories. Paley writes, "Never has there been a child so willing to lead as Reeny. How does she know that the whole point of school is to find a common core of references without blurring our own special profiles?"[8] Reeny embodies the ability that children have to apprehend intractable social issues through stories to illuminate the critical problems in her life and the lives of those around her.

Paley enables us to perceive the implicit relationship among community, family life, history, and literacy. In Reeny's case, the connection

8. Paley, *Girl with the Brown Crayon*, viii.

between her family history, family life, and school is palpable. However, Miss Ettie Willens, Reeny's grandmother, is concerned about Reeny's ability to become a leader in the black community because her authenticity was being "diluted" by attending a predominately white school. She couldn't perceive Paley's ability to cultivate her granddaughter's leadership. During a class visit on Reeny's birthday, Miss Ettie gets snared in the net of Lionni's narratives, however. Through her interaction with his books, the reader begins to understand the root of her concern. Miss Ettie begins to explain the story that she chooses to tell. She says:

> I was going to tell another story today, but when I watched the class do Swimmy, I couldn't help but think about the Harriet I was named after, Harriet Tubman. She was a slave, the same as my grandmother was, and she escaped from the people who owned her, sort of the way Swimmy swam away from the big fish.[9]

As the explanation unfolds, it turns out that Reeny's great-great-grandmother was transported to freedom as a child by Tubman.[10] Miss Ettie wants Reeny to become the modern equivalent of Harriet Tubman in her generation.[11] She tells Paley, "You see Vivian, in any black community, Reeny's family [members] are the pillars, the most respected, and the leaders."[12] Miss Ettie's concerns help us see that she thought about her granddaughter's education or literacy within her family's context and the broader persistent racial background in the United States. In other words, Miss Ettie, too, thinks with race, even in reading the story of Swimmy, the fish. Reeny reciprocates when she reports, "Grandma, you forgot something about Swimmy. He was the leader of red fish. That means black fish could be the leader of another color fish."[13] Here the Willens family demonstrates the ability to maintain narrative continuity between the historical African-American experience and her family's "sustaining narrative."[14] This identity-fostering account is "a touchstone and a guide."[15] Human beings tell themselves these stories about the world to cultivate hope.[16] Miss Ettie recounts the Tubman story to provide her granddaughter with a sustaining identity to inform her literary and

---

9. Paley, *Girl with the Brown Crayon*, 59.

10. Paley, *Girl with the Brown Crayon*, 60.

11. Paley, *Girl with the Brown Crayon*, 64.

12. Paley, *Girl with the Brown Crayon*, 64.

13. Paley, *Girl with the Brown Crayon*, 91.

14. Kihn, "Labeling the Young," 56–58.

15. Kihn, "Labeling the Young," 57.

16. Delblanco, *Real American Dream*, 8.

social ambitions. In reflecting on Paley's encounter with the Willen family matriarch, I find her deployment of a "sustaining narrative" grounded within the tradition of linked fate useful for thinking about ambivalence in black male literacy narratives.

Paley recounts another story about Reeny's family that becomes useful for constructing a black male literacy theory that re-appropriates African-American males' tendency to think *with* blackness in a manner that unintentionally generates ambivalence. Paley reveals how humans can *think with* things—metaphysical ideas, stories, and objects—in a positive way that leads to discovery and learning. This concept parallels Paley's belief in the sustaining power of narratives passed down from generation to generation, which also happens to dovetail nicely with Claude Steele's strategy of "narrative intervention" to support students who might be vulnerable to "highly vigilant-to-threat narratives."[17] Writing about Reeny's creativity, imagination, empathy, and resilience, Paley states, "Miss Ettie has given Reeny the sustaining story out of which to carve her unique talents, among which certainly is the ability to help us recognize who we are and how we are connected."[18] Paley's analysis renders transparent how Miss Ettie has helped Reeny develop a positive sense of her race and gender and a sociopolitical worldview that esteems the community over the individual.

Reading *The Girl with the Brown Crayon* enables one to begin to understand the connections between literacy, history, family life, and community. Recognizing the intersection among these different spheres of human activity helps us discover a pedagogy indigenous to many African-American communities. These encounters unveil a teaching philosophy passed down to Reeny by the child's grandmother and one that I believe will lead us forward.

One day, Mrs. Willens, Reeny's mother, visits Paley's kindergarten class and tells the children a story about how she grew up on a farm in Mississippi, where she attended "a little bitty school that had big and little children all together in one class."[19] Her younger brother Joey had a pet pig named Honey. The two of them were inseparable, which meant the pig attended school alongside her owner. Mrs. Willens explains that the teacher, Reeny's grandmother, "didn't mind a bit having Honey for a visitor. She'd even use Joey's pig for math problems. She'd say, 'How can we find out how many miles Honey walks in a week if Joey brings her to school three times a

---

17. Paley, *Girl with the Brown Crayon*, 91.
18. Paley, *Girl with the Brown Crayon*, 75.
19. Paley, *Girl with the Brown Crayon*, 32.

week?'...Or she'd tell us to write a story about Honey or draw her picture."[20] In telling this story, Mrs. Willens attempts to provide an essential lesson about pedagogy. The lesson is tied to Paley's reliance on Lionni's stories, which Reeny talks about so much that the Willens family cannot distinguish between the characters in the books and her classmates.

Joey talked about Honey in a manner that gets at the underlying rationale informing Miss Ettie's narrative strategy. As a child, Reeny's Uncle Joey was obsessed with his pet pig. "Honey this and Honey that. If Joey was asked how the corn is coming up, he'd answer, 'Honey'll have lots of corn this winter,'"[21] Mrs. Willens reports. Much to his family members' chagrin, Joey thought about everything in terms of Honey. A master storyteller, Mrs. Willens draws her listeners in by playing up her brother's quirky behavior to subvert common assumptions about pedagogy and personalities. All the while, she is preparing the students to hear the positive dimensions of Joey and Honey's supposed problem. She shares a specific instance:

> So one day, Thomas, our oldest brother, got really annoyed at Joey. "Can't your peanut-head think of anything 'cept that stupid pig of yours?"... And our little brother looked Thomas in the eye—mind you, Thomas towered over all of us, so little Joey had to stand on his tippy toes—and Joey snapped back, "Can't your peanut-head see it's Honey that keeps me thinking!"[22]

The hook in Miss Ettie's approach to engaging both her students and children is teaching them to see the world through something they care about from their everyday lives. Joey's life revolved around caring for his pig Honey. In other words, she teaches them to think *with* this object/subject. Joey's thinking with Honey—about math, art, and agriculture—is no different from how African-American males (and females) can make the idea of race an organizing principle in their lives. We must think critically about how to use race in this way to engage black male students and encourage them to acquire mainstream and other forms of literacy.

## The Color-line, Ideology, and the Discourse of Ambivalence

Upon moving north, Frederick Douglass continued to encounter the "artificial distinctions and restraints of mere caste or color."[23] While he had left

20. Paley, *Girl with the Brown Crayon*, 32.

21. Paley, *Girl with the Brown Crayon*, 33.

22. Paley, *Girl with the Brown Crayon*, 32–33.

23. Douglass, *Life and Times*, 887.

slavery behind, he discovered that white Northerners adhered to a racial caste system that implicitly condemned abolitionism:

> In escaping from the South, the reader will have observed that I did not escape from [the] widespread influence [of its racial prejudice] in the North. That influence met me almost everywhere outside of pronounced anti-slavery circles, and sometimes even within them. It was in the air, and men breathed it and were permeated by it often when they were quite unconscious of its presence.[24]

Following this realization, Douglass commits an entire chapter to racial "incidents and events" beyond slavery, suggesting that race is the primary lens that shapes his experience.[25] How could it be otherwise? Douglass's occupations as author and abolitionist overtly reflect that race is his primary analytical framework. He explains, "I might recount many occasions when I have encountered this feeling, some painful and melancholy, some ridiculous and amusing. It has been my mission to expose the absurdity of this spirit of caste and in some measure help to emancipate men from its control."[26] Here Douglass deploys a turn of phrase similar to Steele. "It was in the air, and men breathed it and were permeated by it often when they were quite unconscious of its presence," he explains.[27] This observation makes explicit the pervasive nature of racial thinking and racism, regardless of geography, and the color-line that leads to a preoccupation with one's racial identity.

Concerns about race, racism, and intraracial discrimination are central to Langston Hughes's *The Big Sea*. The poet was fascinated with race as a way of understanding himself, the people he identified with, and society. Racial identity and racism are Hughes's primary lenses of analysis. As a senior at Lincoln College, a historically black university in Chester County, Pennsylvania, Hughes conducted a sociological study to try to understand "[the college's] own peculiar color line . . . the fact that there was an all-white faculty for an all-Negro student body."[28] It bothered Hughes when students believed they were under observation and expressed opinions that implied a belief in black inferiority. During his research, Hughes discovered that 63 percent of the senior class professed that having a white faculty was preferable on many levels. Hughes interpreted this uncritical affirmation of an

24. Douglass, *Life and Times*, 887.
25. Douglass, *Life and Times*, 887–908.
26. Douglass, *Life and Times*, 887.
27. Douglass, *Life and Times*, 887.
28. Hughes, *Big Sea*, 306.

all-white faculty's superiority as implying an internalized racism among the black student body at Lincoln.

Hughes believed that this unspoken policy, uncontested by white professors and black students, was inconsistent with the notion that Lincoln should cultivate leaders for the black community. Yet, more significant than Hughes's sociological findings was that, while at Lincoln, the color-line attracted his attention to such a degree that he decided to do a senior thesis on the topic. He read his own institution of higher learning through the lens of race. Writing a senior thesis on the absence of African-American faculty on his campus has important implications for ambivalence discourse regarding black literacy. The implied internalized oppression of his college colleagues, demonstrated in their preference for white professors, denotes a belief that academic literacy is the domain of white scholars. More importantly, the self-defined research projects reveal that a racial lens encompassed Hughes's social cognition.

Vershawn Ashanti Young's conundrum with performing blackness (and whiteness), black masculinity, and literacy became critical to his quest for knowledge—to his very existence. Young's interest in this problem, on both a personal and societal level, is made clear in his deconstruction of Bill Cosby's "Pound Cake Speech," a talk given on the fiftieth anniversary of *Brown v. Board of Education*.[29] During the speech, Cosby belittled underclass blacks for illegitimacy, teen pregnancy, criminality, and naming practices. More relevant to this project, Cosby underscored the use of the Black English Vernacular in literacy performances, saying, "These people are fighting hard to be ignorant. There's no English being spoken, and they're walking and they're angry."[30] Here again, we see the elite politics of black distinction informing Cosby in his monologue that pits upper-class aspirations in identity performances against lower-class African Americans. The implied clash of cultures is based on their commitment to different ideologies of black authenticity and adherence to racial-uplift policies based on respectability politics. More importantly, it is Young's analysis that enables us to see blackness as Cosby's motivated irrationality.

In analyzing the speech, Young illustrates how the politics of respectability influences expectations for underclass African Americans. In the black past, we used race to demarcate the boundaries of the body politic. Young writes, "The effect that *Brown* was intended to have, but has been prevented from having, would have voided race as a marker of difference that limits

---

29. Young, *Your Average Nigga*, 73–79.
30. Cosby, "Pound Cake Speech," para. 14.

opportunities, especially educational ones, for black people."[31] Yet, a more egalitarian shift in our legal framework could not transform factors residing beyond the political realm.[32] The young black English professor argues that "the full achievement of *Brown* is deferred—because the progress toward making race not matter stopped when the focus shifted from color to [one's cultural and literacy] performance."[33] Following the civil rights movement, dominant society shifted the markers of racial inferiority from skin color to social markers, including the inability to code-switch from the Black English Vernacular. Serendipitously, black youth began to reject the assimilation model implied in the American social [or racial] contract.

In particular, Young notes that Cosby tends to read *Brown* as a racial contract that lower-class African Americans are failing to fulfill, as evidenced by their unwillingness to perform their literacy according to upper-class standards or live according to passé middle-class values for naming children and speech performance strategies to promote social mobility. Cosby says:

> It [black youth] can't speak English. It doesn't want to speak English. I can't even talk the way these people talk: "Why you ain't where you is go ra?" I don't know who these people are. And I blamed the kid until I heard the mother talk. Then I heard the father talk. This is all in the house. You used to talk a certain way on the corner and you got into the house and switched to English.[34]

Young's response to this demeaning tirade from the bully pulpit helps us understand an important facet of African-American males' preoccupation with and ambivalence around literacy. In reading Cosby's speech and throughout *Your Average Nigga*, Young is fascinated with the idea of race, rather than skin color, as a characteristic that one performs. "Thus, language, dialect, and accent must now be understood, at least in regard to black people, in the same way that skin color wrongly used to be (and in some cases still is), as outward signs of inward flaws, as verbal manifestations of inherent inferiority, as faults of character," he argues.[35] Consequently, Young's narrative is concerned not only with the black-white dichotomy but also with the politics of disassociation among blacks. To Young, Cosby's speech is an "attempt to use racial politics and conservative, even racist, views on black speech as the wedge that makes his blackness distinct—better—than that

31. Young, *Your Average Nigga*, 74.
32. Young, *Your Average Nigga*, 74.
33. Young, *Your Average Nigga*, 74.
34. Cosby, "Pound Cake Speech," para. 12.
35. Young, *Your Average Nigga*, 74.

performed by the black lower class. It's another way of saying . . . we may all be black, but we don't all act or sound like we are."[36] In the end, Young's reading of Cosby's social analysis through the lens of class *and* race helps us to see how blackness and literacy are his Honey the pig—that is, a heuristic for self-analysis.

In his writing about black male ambivalence toward literacy, Thomas Chatterton Williams shows that uncertainties about his own race led to a fascination with authentic blackness and *real niggas*—the lens through which he read the world. Whether embracing commercial hip-hop blackness or moving beyond it to pursue a degree in philosophy and hipster cosmopolitanism, blackness (or ideas about being a *real nigga*) provided a framework that allowed him to meditate on his decision to either camouflage or embrace his pursuit of literacy. Besides, Williams thought with blackness about everything from food to sports as a youth. He describes his epiphany about *real niggas* in a Georgetown grocery store. In his BET-informed thinking, authentic black men would not be caught dead eating baguettes and cheese or drinking the kinds of wine found in specialty grocery stores.

Obsession with a narrow conception of black manhood defined Williams's ideas about literacy and his thoughts about his career path. Williams was fixated on basketball until his father helped him to see the futility of pursuing glory on the court. Although Williams decided against pursuing a career in sports or entertainment, his reflection on his alternatives when considering a philosophy major helps us see how hip-hop culture served as his Honey the pig. The narrative implies his need for an authentic black role model or a career aspiration that lined up with the economy of the streets:

> In no way was I immune to such thinking. It is rare that you meet a student who is, even at the best schools—especially at the best schools. We see images of athletes and rappers 24/7, but most of us simply have never seen a black person devoted to the other form of wealth, the life of the mind, and so we do not imagine that it is a feasible—let alone luxurious—way to live. I had seen my father strive to live this way, to live his life inside books, and still, it struck me as an impossible fate to win. Part of me could not relinquish the desire to be a banker.[37]

As a first-year student at Georgetown University, Williams perceived a connection between a street ethos that elevated capital and hedonism and Wall Street's "condescension toward reflective thought, the me-myself-and-I

36. Young, *Your Average Nigga*, 75.
37. Williams, *Losing My Cool*, 150.

world."[38] Believing that he would graduate and join a management team in a big investment firm, he dreamed of returning home a "black Caesar astride a six-figure chariot crammed full of booty and speeding toward Rome—victorious, chrome rims spinning. I would show everyone I wasn't a sucker for having gone off to college."[39] After being ostracized from the black community, though, he began to spend time in the dorms with his white dorm mates. Their companionship allowed him to create a space from which he'd begin to question his hip-hop worldview and embrace his father's love of the book.

Williams writes about this transition in a manner that exposes how a hip-hop-inflected street ethos and an early indoctrination into American racism grounded his worldview in a black-versus-white dichotomy. "The thought that I could make a living *reading* and *thinking* was inspiring and even humbling. Of course, this is a kind of success that you cannot wear on your sleeve. You cannot 'floss' the fruits of intellectual labor, however sweet, in the 'hood the way you floss a Range Rover on dubs [expensive rims]," Williams explains. At Georgetown, he began to recognize that he no longer aspired to live in the ghetto and have children with "real black names." More significantly, he had an additional epiphany. "I didn't realize that once you leave home and see new and more complex things," he writes, "you might lose the desire to measure yourself by the old, provincial standards; they cease to motivate you even when you want to them to; you set your eyes on new and high (though they used to seem lower) sights . . . my point of reference had changed dramatically and definitively."[40] Williams's burgeoning literacy led to his expanding his conception of the relationship between literacy and blackness. Indeed, studying philosophy at Georgetown caused him to develop as a human being.

## Appropriating the Discourse of Ambivalence

Ellison's novel and our authors' stories make it clear that the color-line and racial ideology influence many black males' psyche. It has become impossible to disaggregate beliefs about race, masculinity, sexuality, and literacy performances for many black males and their observers. Because black consciousness, or blackness, is embodied and performed in tangible ways—as whiteness is—how one performs one's linguistic techniques, masculinity, and sexuality are intertwined and often lead to conflict and categorization.

38. Williams, *Losing My Cool*, 150.
39. Williams, *Losing My Cool*, 150–151.
40. Williams, *Losing My Cool*, 151.

African-American males often experience ambivalence due to competing ideologies regarding black authenticity—either assimilative or essential and oppositional—within their communities and broader society. This ambivalence becomes tangible in contexts in which black men encounter society-defined identity contingencies as they move through society.

In *The Girl with the Brown Crayon*, one finds an example of a grandmother who thinks about her granddaughter's identity formation in the context of a family racial heritage traced back to Harriet Tubman. Moreover, in terms of educational psychology, Mrs. Willens's story about her brother suggests that shrewd educators appropriate the ideas/objects/subjects of a child's fascination, using the child's creative energy and love for that thing to increase skill sets and broaden horizons. By combining these two concepts, we can deduce principles to help black males recognize and embrace an inevitable ambivalence for some. *The Girl with the Brown Crayon* and Honey the pig's story teaches us that many black males filter everything through their understanding of blackness. Recognizing this, we should use this habit of mind to (1) cultivate and define identity-suitable notions of literacy, (2) expand our concepts of being black, male, and literate, and (3) develop strategies for assessing and dealing with the inevitable ambivalence.

Paley teaches us that we must expand our notion of literacy. Honey is an archetype of the ideas, objects, and subjects that children, youth, and adults use to think about the world. Because these fascinations are not only lenses but also blinders constraining one's field of interests, the prescient pedagogue would recognize the value of appropriating them. This strategy reminds me of when the homies and I would teach my peers about dealing drugs. They learned how to use the metric system and turn powder cocaine into rock (crack) through the stoichiometry that I learned at university. Afterward, I'd watch this knowledge translate into confidence and enthusiasm in their developing into other areas of social and economic interest. It was amazing how much these young men would learn when they thought about cocaine—chemistry, the metric system, real estate, and business.

I have seen young black men involved in the underground economy research how to open franchises and set up corporations. They functioned as successful entrepreneurs for decades. Today, many have degrees in diverse fields and are pharmaceutical representatives, scientists, detectives, college professors, and entrepreneurs. When I reminisce with them on our pasts, they attribute their success to the lessons we learned dealing drugs. Likewise, blackness, hip-hop, the streets, and masculinity are topics as worthy of study as African-American history, black male autobiography and biography, sociology, and disparities in health and wealth.

Once I was asked to do a workshop on black masculinity in the media at a local high school. The students had dozens of workshops that they could attend, but minority youth packed my room. When I asked them if someone had forced them to come, they said, "No, we wanted to come and talk about manhood." At the end of the first session, one student admitted that he didn't have men in his life and needed to have conversations with a black male adult. He needed a man to help facilitate his academic and personal development. We need to expand our thinking about literacy so that it is broad enough to perceive that our students have long since crossed over from being creatures of nature to creatures of culture. We need to understand the languages used in their discourses in relevant and weighty matters. Suppose we learn to recognize their diverse knowledge and participation in what some might call subcultures. In that case, we can begin to explicate the reasons for their immersion in these parallel worlds and tap into their discourses.

Aware that some young black males care deeply about blackness and masculinity in relation to literacy, writ large, we might help encourage conventional literacy by intentionally developing a canon of relevant texts that expose ambivalence while stretching their understanding of the broader sociopolitical context and implications of black male masculinity. In the process, the educator might help them gain an appreciation for diverse ideas about what it means to be black, a black male, and black and literate within the broader scope of African-American history.

In learning about these varying conceptions of blackness and black masculinity, the student comes to see that black manhood is not some static idea, but one that changes over time. And new texts are coming out every year. When reading these texts with youth, we must help them develop lenses that enable them to discover the ideologies that inform different discourses about blackness and the politics of black authenticity. In doing so, the pedagogical goal is to help them make their perceptions of these ideas elastic enough to encompass diverse forms of literacy.

I believe, however, that it is impossible to ask students to embrace a broader notion of literacy until we begin to see the utility and value of the black vernacular. The Ann Arbor decision (1979) and the Ebonics controversy (1996) concerning the utility and value of Black English Vernacular correspond with a radical departure from traditional pedagogy and the black politics of distinction during the Black Power era. This ideological transformation coincides with research that reveals African-American males have experienced an increasing ambivalence concerning the relationship between race and literacy habits. I have drawn on autobiographies that reveal how recent tensions have led many black males to reject reading,

writing, and speaking Standard English. However, these racialized interpretations and experiences of ambivalence among black males are not new.
Vershawn Ashanti Young, in particular, suggests to us that we would do well
to heed the power of the Black English Vernacular in helping our students
to acquire mainstream literary habits and literacy practices.

Suppose we want to help our students understand their own ambivalence. In that case, we need to help them see the ambivalence that preceding
and future generations of black men have had around their own literacy
and, more recently, around their own masculinity. Although issues connected to masculinity do not always seem immediately relevant in black
males' literacy narratives, the relationship between literacy and manhood in
the minds of black males with a street orientation is prominent enough to
make it a topic for discussion. When speaking of such subjects, the educator must assist students in thinking about their own ambivalence, or lack
thereof, to help them recognize that such a thing exists. While working on
my thesis regarding black make literacy ambivalence, I shared this thought
with an African-American political science professor who studies black political thought. "Most brothers aren't ambivalent," he declared. "They don't
give a damn. They don't want to read. Where's the ambivalence in that?" In
response, I said that many men are simply not talking about the niggling
ambivalence that has led to their seeming rejection of academic literacy.

Stated earlier, these brothers—young and old—lack a lexicon that allows them to discuss this form of cognitive dissonance in a manner that
would help them express this issue. What is more, the social climate disallows their doing so, even if they could; I told the professor that he was a
prime example. A maturing black man, he gained two degrees from prominent higher learning institutions, which he earned after leaving the military. Early on in his career, he punctuated his lectures with expletives—the
F-bomb—while he pranced around in his all-black street gear dressed like
a twenty-first-century Shaft, dipping in his walk like Denzel Washington in
*Devil in a Blue Dress*. Years later, I'd encounter him near his new home on
Alki Beach in West Seattle. He appeared amiable as he informed me that
he belonged to the quasi-secret Black Boulé (Sigma Pi Phi). The Boulé is
America's first black Greek-letter fraternity. Its history related to W. E. B. Du
Bois discouraging black Brahmins from participating in Marcus Garvey's
black nationalist efforts in the early twentieth century. Whether or not the
tale is factual, the narratives predict my secondary marginalization experience when my former professor proclaimed that *Speech Is My Hammer* must
pass muster with the Boulé. In brief, this hip-hop professor embodies the
legacy of ambivalence about the relationship between literacy and race due
to the white gaze.

Two months prior, a high-level university administrator who is now a university president shared a story about her son. She called him a closet reader, a term I have found helpful to describe people like Thomas Chatterton Williams and his father. This administrator's son has done time in prison and is an avid reader but doesn't want anyone to know that he reads. Much like Williams's father—and Williams himself, until he attended Georgetown—this young man hides in the family basement with his books. We must help our students assess, embrace, and find ways to mitigate this inhibiting ambivalence. In many cases, including my own, black men have learned how to signify that we are both "down with" an authentic underclass experience *and* have the pedigree, credentials, and literacy to allow us to function in the academy, mainstream society, and the 'hood. In a society that still uses race, class, and gender as criteria for excluding African-American males, black males will continue to think with these lenses and remain ambivalent about literacy.

I am revising this book during a pandemic and at the beginning of a new presidency while reflecting the existential reality laid bare by police brutality in the killing of George Floyd and Breonna Taylor and deadly disease. My grandmother had taught me that I could not wait for others to acknowledge my humanity. Although she offered books and culture as a path towards the good life and respectability, she knew what critical theorists, lawyers, and philosophers discussed earlier. In a white supremacist society, black skin forecloses dialogues about our humanness and our supposed aspirations for an egalitarian society. Grandmother would jokingly sing the Jim Crow tune, "If you're white, you're alright. If you're brown, stick around, and if you're black, step back." She taught this insight in numerous creative ways to help me digest the painful racial reality that impacted the mental health of Frederick Douglass, W. E. B. Du Bois, and countless other African Americans. I learned this lesson as a young child, though Reginald Dwayne Betts learned it much later in prison. He writes, "My teacher, Ms. Elman, came by and asked me how it went. Nine years, I said, and she shook her head. There weren't any words of encouragement to give. It didn't make any difference that I'd read lots of books, had a high-grade point average or a high school diploma. I was no different from any other black male in the courtroom."[41] Before we begin on a truly egalitarian journey, we must concede that blackness has been designed as a prison, a ruse, a trap.

If we reject distinctions between authenticity and respectability, we can find common ground. Among ourselves, we can create humanizing spaces in response to the broader racial discourse that implicitly and

41. Betts, *Question of Freedom*, 80.

outright dehumanizes black boys and men. Betts describes his reading in a manner that makes this point. Of course, the teenage Betts is hesitant to confront the system, but following incarceration, he reflects on the matter in an illuminating manner when he writes,

> The reading gave peace to all the time I spent awaiting my sentence. I was in jail the first time I read a book cover to cover without stopping. *A Lesson Before Dying* by Ernest J. Gaines. The book was about a young teacher's relationship with a boy who'd been sentenced to death row for a murder he didn't commit. He'd walked into a store right after two men had robbed the place and killed the owner. The teacher mentoring him and the young boy were both black and the point of the mentoring was for the boy to walk to the electric chair knowing he was a man, not a pig and not a killer.[42]

The reference to pig echoes Frederick Douglass's self-description in his slave narrative. A pet pig discussed in *The Girl with the Brown Crayon* created the affective connection that led to little Joey's concern, fascination, and discovery. The teacher offers literacy to the youth condemned to experience capital punishment as a path to existential freedom and transcendence that contradicts our dehumanizing reality that either equates us with a disgusting beast or winks when referring to us as a killer. Betts explains,

> All that was left was the dampened glow that comes with incarceration. The dull night-light that will never go off, that makes you both a prisoner and a child. That's where I began to understand something about what Gaines was saying about humanity. I read under that light, and didn't stop reading until breakfast was served and I read the last page. I thought about what the death penalty meant, and what it meant to go to it as a man, especially for a crime you didn't commit.[43]

By acknowledging the aspirations to intellectual and moral tendencies that can accompany literacy aspirations, one can deploy the appropriate texts to educate black males to recognize, reflect upon, and perhaps even accept their own ambivalence, thus expanding their literacy horizons to define their humanity on their own transcendent terms. More importantly, black men can develop African-American male memoirs as a genre to engage one another in a textual discourse, as a path toward forms of authenticity that leads to black transcendence.

42. Betts, *Question of Freedom*, 56–57.
43. Betts, *Question of Freedom*, 57.

Malcolm X impressed me with his logic and with his disciplined and dedicated mind. Here was a man who combined the world of the streets and the world of the scholar, a man so widely read he could give better lectures and cite more evidence than many college professors.

—Huey P. Newton, *Revolutionary Suicide* (1973)

According to Neal, our uncritical allegiance to the "Strong Black Man," forged in the crucible of racial hatred and historical oppression, obscures the multifaceted range of black masculine expression in reality, in the media, and in artistic production.

—James Braxton Peterson, "Corner-Boy Masculinity"

New Black Man is about resisting being inscribed by a wide range of forces and finding comfort with a complex and progressive existence as a black man in America. As such New Black Man is not so much about conceiving of a more positive version of black masculinity . . . but rather a concept that acknowledges the many complex aspects, often contradictory, that make up progressive and meaningful black masculinity.

—Mark Anthony Neal, *New Black Man*

Union Gospel Mission Summer Camp, Burien, Washington (c. 2018)

# Epilogue

ON THE MORNING OF Marvin Gaye's birthday, as I finished writing *Speech Is My Hammer*, I gathered my children to teach them a lesson about Mr. Gaye. We had a wonderful time listening to his music, which the kids had heard in children's films, and discussing the patron saint of Motown. Later in the morning, I sat alone writing and listening to poignant renditions of "What's Going On" and "What's Happening Brother," remembering with much melancholy when I first heard of his tragic death April 1, 1984. I had smoked my latest sack of imported weed while I drove the entire length of Southeast San Diego up and down Market Street, blasting my well-worn Marvin Gaye cassette on my finely tuned Alpine car stereo and speakers. As I cruised the boulevard, the poignant images in the streets mirrored the art in his lyrics, creating a live music video.

What's going on?

In some instances, it's a casual salutation to an acquaintance or close friend. On other occasions, it's an invitation to a multifaceted and nuanced conversation about the state of black America. The greeting seems to shift with context, current events, and mood. This afternoon, the question caused the present to echo the past as I listened to Gaye's music and began to read Lumumba Seegars's Facebook post. Seegars was a young brother who'd taken an African-American religion course with me at Harvard. He'd posted an online article from *PolicyMic* Harvard, and Stanford graduates Chris Altchek and Jake Horowitz founded the journal to create a democratic online news platform to engage millennials in debates about real issues. As I read an education article posted on Facebook, it became clear that in our post-racial Obama presidency moment, I discovered that African-American educators were still asking their versions of the same question. The headline begged the question, "Is the black community to blame for the black children's performance in school?" The author was Matthew Kevin Clair, a good friend of Seegars. At the time, Clair was a recent Teach for America alum and a

member of the cohort of African-American male undergraduates who were
at Harvard while I was in graduate school.

I was intrigued.

As I read the future Stanford sociology professor's reflections on education and justice—with Marvin blaring in the background—it created a
surreal moment. On the one hand, the young educator evoked Gaye by beg-
ging important cultural and existential questions for black life. Clair began
with the statement about the myriad causes for the current problems of
inner-city black communities—drug abuse, joblessness, mass incarceration,
racism, and welfare policies—he rhetorically asked if we should move from
sociological explanations to developing solutions. This inquiry seemed a
contemporary iteration of the rhetorical statement, "What's going on?"

On the other hand, the article seemed particularly relevant. Clair
seemed to agree with Patrick Welsh's contribution to the Room for Debate
series in the *New York Times* with a problematic title: "Consider Cultural
Differences." The op-ed contributor attributed the nation's low educational
ranking on the Program for International Student Assessment (PISA) tests
to African Americans and Hispanics' underperformance.[1] Welsh argued,
"The overall ranking for the U.S. is lower because of the scores of Hispanic
and African-American students, with Hispanics ranked 41st and black,
non-Hispanics ranked 46th in the reading tests. This situation is unaccept-
able and highlights once again the most intractable problem in many of
our schools." The piece compared black and brown academic performance
to Asian students. Welsh argued that "giving teachers high status is not a
means to an end—i.e., higher test scores for students," and continued, "but
a result coming from parents and children who, as is seen in so many Asian
families, revere learning and are willing to put in the time to do the hard
work involved in learning."[2] In brief, the veteran teacher was invoking the
hackneyed and long-discredited culture of poverty argument. Oscar Lewis
developed and popularized the "culture of poverty thesis" researching the
poor in Mexico City in the fifties.

It, however, was "embraced in America, giving rise to what is arguably
one of the most powerful national discourses on poverty. Politically, attention turned to remediating individual-level cultural values deficiencies, eas-
ing the mounting pressure on the state to address poverty systematically."[3]
Social scientists were sharply critical of Lewis characterization of the poor
and attempted to counteract the monolithically negative stereotype with

1. Welsh, "Consider Cultural Differences," para. 5.
2. Welsh, "Consider Cultural Differences," para. 5.
3. Branch and Scherer, "Mapping the Intersections," 348.

"positive images of the worthy poor, struggling for upward mobility against all odds."[4] Clair, however, decided to construct his ideas on the tiresome, predictable, and discredited argument that reinscribed the color-line when he began to imply that inquiries into the structural sources of educational disparities have been asking the wrong questions. In other words, he tapped into one of the discourses that set me on the road to undertaking this project on literacy ambivalence in black males. I felt that Clair's narrative and implicit respectability politics rendered black males invisible.

I was triggered, of course.

On Marvin Gaye's birthday, I found myself asking what's [really] going on. I thought that Clair's unexpectedly conservative response to Welsh revealed either an honest question or a veiled condemnation: "Is the Black Community to Blame for America's Education Crisis?" Instead, his feigned inquiry suggested the fundamental issue seemed to inhere in the pathological culture of poor blacks who need to learn to bootstrap. I wondered if Clair had ventured into the literature on sociologist and Assistant Secretary of Labor Patrick Moynihan's report on "The Negro Family: The Case for National Action." Branch and Scherer explain my concerns when writing,

> The culture of poverty thesis took on a decidedly racial character in the 1965 Moynihan report. . . . Citing his empirical findings of welfare dependency, unmarried mothers, unemployment, and regressive values among the majority black urban poor . . . suggested that the poor black family was enmeshed in a "tangle of pathology" that creates and reproduces the conditions of poverty. The theory is largely discredited today, both within and outside of the academy, for what many have called a racist, "blame the victim" approach.[5]

I hoped to find that the Harvard-educated Clair had responded, based on his recent TFA experience, in a nuanced manner. Instead, I found something troubling. While seeming unaware of a discourse that is common knowledge in the academy and among conscious black folks in the 'hood and the suburbs, Clair's posture in the article suggests a subtle "rhetorical wink." Jerome G. Miller explains the rhetorical move politicians make when discussing crime and welfare to invoke race while avoiding being charged with racism.[6] "The issues provide the backdrop for the 'rhetorical wink,' whereby [codewords] communicate a well-understood but implicit meaning while allowing the speaker to deny any such meaning," according

4. Branch and Scherer, "Mapping the Intersections," 348.
5. Branch and Scherer, "Mapping the Intersections," 348.
6. Miller, *Search and Destroy*, 150.

to Miller.[7] These coded phrases include crack baby, drug kingpin, housing project, single-parent household, and welfare queen. When the writer or speaker postures towards getting tough on the offending group (i.e., black males), the historically coded nature of the discourse is sure to garner the reader's support, as in the "get tough on crime" discussions leading to the War on Drugs and mass incarceration.[8]

Clair turns to Cosby's "Pound Cake Speech"—black bourgeois politics as minstrelsy—drawing on Cosby's invoking tropes to signal the rhetorical wink and answers to our educational dilemma. Although he concedes that Cosby's rhetoric is vitriolic and divisive, Clair does not pull back from invoking the rhetoric of a romanticized black past and points the reader toward the utility of racial uplift ideology. In his speechifying prose, I could hear the ghost of Booker T. Washington in Clair's rhetoric. He argued that black people should focus on solutions that rest upon personal and community, not institutional, choice. He promoted holding classes on effective parenting in community centers. Echoing Barack Obama, he suggested that racism will not prevent parents from turning off the TV and meeting with teachers regularly. He concluded that Cosby and Welsh both have a point that citizens shouldn't ignore. It's time to work on fixing the black community so that all of America's children can reach their fullest potential, Clair exhorted.

I felt myself bristling, thinking: Isn't that what we've been trying to do since the days of slavery? It's the sole responsibility of us black folks to correct the black community's issues, I thought. The collective, yet divided, ubiquitous black "we" have been trying to fix the black community forever, and I found myself seething. Once again, my ambivalence emerged because I valued the educational experiences and pedigree that gave us a voice in the public sphere. A decade later, I'd read another black male who countered the countered Clair's "insights." Mychal Denzel Smith's memoir argues that our strategies "for resistance became an admonishment toward conformity" that condemns black males for their oppression.[9] Our overreliance on cultural methods to dismantle structural issues fails to encourage black males to "do for self" by promoting a humanizing literacy. The polyvalence mobility of racism foreclosed human possibilities and transcendence. He explains,

> The system of racism invented, and continually adjusts, the rubric to justify its existence. Whether we're talking about the idea that enslaved Africans are a less evolved form of the human

7. Miller, *Search and Destroy*, 150.

8. Alexander, *New Jim Crow*, 46–48.

9. Smith, *Invisible Man*, 206.

species . . . or identifying who isn't a thug based on their fashion choices and patterns of speech [or academic/literacy performance], the underlying context is that black is other.[10]

As I read the young Harvard-educated Clair's more conservative perspective that reiterated respectability politics and compared the ideas, I found myself having a visceral reaction to Clair's implied anti-intellectualism. As his elite talented-tenth predecessors, Clair blamed the victim, suggesting that if African Americans simply turn off the television and roll up our sleeves, we'd regain the idyllic, unified, and respectable black community that preceded post-civil rights integration.

More than ten years later, I pen my final reflection on *Speech Is My Hammer*. I hope that the concepts I have put forth assist individuals like Cosby, Clair, other young black men, and myself to understand how the ideologies that continue to inform racial uplift and black authenticity impact some young black men to develop not only ambivalence but resistance to formal schooling and learning mainstream literacy that can present significant emotional and intellectual barriers. We cannot "fix" black men until we are ready to fix the broader society and go after our sacred ideologies in the black community.

Looking at the past from the perch of the present, I can see how this same ambivalence informed my decision to pursue a degree that would allow me to study the social and cultural foundations of education instead of political science or history science. I was unclear about the subject matter that I'd find most useful for advancing toward an answer to the questions that niggled away at me. My goal was to determine why I felt ambivalent about pursuing post-baccalaureate degrees in fields other than law, business, or medicine—which I believed all smart and prudent African Americans studied.

Clair's argument caused me to remember the essential tension that I felt as an African-American male with origins in the South. It was as if W. E. B. Du Bois and Booker T. Washington were in my head arguing about the Atlanta Compromise all over again. Washington insisted that African Americans should give up political agitation and esoteric knowledge for more humble aims. Black institutions should teach the subject matter and the skills needed to earn a living. Du Bois contended the exact opposite. My grandmother embodied Du Bois's ethos with her love of books, high culture, and the finer things in life, but her work ethic and practical outlook implicitly spoke volumes on Washington's side of things. Neither Du Bois nor Washington had abandoned black respectability. And for all my love

10. Smith, *Invisible Man*, 206.

of the 'hood and ratchet resistance to culture wars within the black community, I grew up believing in black dignity and decency, though through
illegal means, if necessary. In the end, my pragmatic mother pushed me in
Washington's direction. As a result, I would mistakenly feel guilty when I
dreamed about a life of reading books instead of earning money to support
my family and help my mother.

I would eventually learn that Washington, too, desired erudition and
envied Du Bois's cultural and intellectual performances. In his essay on "The
Envy of Erudition," Ernest L. Gibson III excavates the fact that "Washington
was not too different from the paragon of black intellectualism [Du Bois]."
If anything, "for deeper than anything else, the young Du Bois longed to
be viewed as the erudite titan that he would later become. Washington too
wished to rise as an archetype of black erudition."[11] Based on Washington's
early childhood nostalgic recollections of observing children studying in a
paradisical schoolhouse on his intellectual formation, Gibson argues,

> In essence, to become educated for Washington, that is to
> become learned and knowledgeable in the most basic sense,
> marked a way to leave the "hell" and "dystopia" of slavery. This
> exaltation of learning reveals a profound desire for erudition,
> which I employ as an intellectuality that goes beyond funda-
> mental educational training and speaks to what Du Bois has
> called "the object of work of schools—intelligence, broad sym-
> pathy, knowledge of the world that was and is of the relation of
> men to it—this is the curriculum of that High Education which
> must underlie true life. On this foundation we may build bread
> winning, skill of hand and quickness of brain, with never a fear
> lest the child and man mistake the means of living for the object
> of life."[12]

He'd later meet a young black Ohioan who the entire village reverenced
for his literacy. Washington's reflection on their admiration causes him to
confess, "How I used to envy this man!" Gibson underscored Washington's
admission of envy and multifaceted failed pursuit of erudition to revise the
tension between Du Bois and Washington. One might argue that Gibson
reveals Washington's literacy ambivalence. An ambivalence reverberates
among black males well unto the twenty-first century. Had I read Gibson's
essay as a young man, I might have recognized the sources of my envy and
avoided a personal experience with ambivalence as well. But these guilty
feelings about my pursuit of "black erudition" did not merely come from the

11. Gibson, "Envy of Erudition," 66.
12. Gibson, "Envy of Erudition," 54.

fact that Moms needed help at home. Later, I would feel a moral obligation, akin to Washington, to the black community to advance myself as an individual and study in a field that would make me beneficial, in practical terms, to others. And modest work prospects only provided enough to cover rent, student loan payments, and Asian take-out meals.

As a doctoral student at Harvard, I struggled with ambivalence about participating in seminar discussions about "cabinets of curiosities"—early museums—and being isolated from the African-American community when black men were gunning down across the Charles River in the streets of Dorchester and Roxbury. The secret knowledge studied in the history of science that I was learning about race and other matters seemed impossible to communicate to folks in 'hood—at home and in Boston—men whom "life," as Moms would say, had not given the privilege of participating in this elevated discourse. On an almost daily basis, I found myself challenging my colleagues about the "life of the mind" meant for the real world. I took on the persona Kiese Laymon describes in his memoir:

> In class, I spoke when I could be an articulate defender of black people. I didn't use the classroom to ask questions. I didn't use the classroom to make ungrounded claims. There was too much at stake to ask questions, to be dumb, to be a curious student, in front of a room of white folk who assumed all black folk were intellectually less than.[13]

As a professor, I had numerous black males approach me after class to discuss their sense of inadequacy or their sense that their classmates would look to them as spokesmen for the black community. Kiese could function as a black Cartesian. He'd grown up with an academic mother. My challenges were a bit different. I was less frustrated with them than with myself. Meanwhile, my imagined community included a lower socioeconomic African-American people who seemed to grow more and more distant with each day I spent inside Harvard's gilded gates. My connection to Harvard was equally remote.

I'll never forget the day that I almost went "smooth off" in a methods seminar. The distinguished professor leading the class put me on the spot by asking me in his faux-posh accent if I thought racism would endure in the United States. I thought he knew renowned activists on a first-name basis, yet this world-renowned professor made the thoughtless move of asking the only black person (a real one, at that) in the room about race. Hadn't he studied pedagogy? What about multiculturalism 101? Didn't he know that it was the worst practice to make the lone non-privileged student of color the

13. Laymon, *Heavy*, 122.

race spokesperson? I held in my thoughts, gave him a seventies black power scowl, and then answered defiantly to his chagrin, "Yes." This conversation was happening the day after I had learned that police had shot and killed my cousin for resisting arrest. He was less than 135 pounds soaking wet and unarmed. This conversation would lead to asking if we might add a seminar discussion on race, which our refined professor requested that I curate.

One of my colleagues, the son of a famous bioethicist, and physician, gave an abstract talk on race as a black box in which Home Depot was a model (or something like that). The son of privilege, he had ancestors who'd come over with the earliest settlers to New England. My other colleague and panelist was an intellectual property lawyer who had retired early to pursue her doctorate. Her cousin, it turned out, was one of Darwin's top biographers, the mercurial and suspicious James Moore, who was teaching at Harvard that term. In brief, I was out of my league. She decided to give a talk titled, "Why talking about race makes historians of science stupid" or something to that effect. I was incredulous and humiliated (and it turns out that she graduated to work on gender and race).

By that time, I'd already learned that in that particular Ivory Tower, no one was allowed to bring their lives into the academy. It just wasn't done at Harvard. To do so, I would evoke certain racial stereotypes, the kinds of stereotypes that Clair and Cosby cared so much about either castigating or submerging. In the end, I had to try to divorce emotions and mind from my Ivy League reality. The professor probably thought I was stupid, and I thought he—a good friend of Coretta Scott King and Bayard Rustin— was equally lacking in judgment. I wasn't one of those "bougie" black folks whom he was "down with" in his social struggles in the academy.

I felt unsettled about not responding to his discriminatory questions and comments. When I thought about my cousin's death and my graduate school struggles, I wanted to "go smooth off" on my colleagues and professor to let them know I was a *real nigga*. I learned about a side of life that mattered to the actual black folks suffering beyond Harvard's gates and the Ivory Tower—real things that it seemed the culture at Harvard refused to let in unmediated by academic discourse. Moreover, I'd happened upon Henry Rosovsky's *Black Studies at Harvard: Personal Reflections Concerning Recent Events* (1969) and learned about the effort to appease radical students, and then their efforts to dismantle the program, once social foment had flattened.

More importantly, the people and situations I cared about could only enter the discourse after being turned into statistics, numbers, and theories that need new polysyllabic terms and theories by scholars. Often, my concerns came to campus as academic entertainment, as when the Kennedy

School hosted a panel on *The Wire*. That night, my ghetto ethos worked. When a police officer stopped me at the front door, I sneaked in through a different entrance. I made a convoluted journey through back passages in the auditorium just as I had done back in the day at back alleys, clubs, concerts, and criminal inhabited neighborhoods. I needed to connect with "my people": the black actors who portrayed my drug-dealing days in Washington, DC.

Before leaving Cambridge, I began to experience more ambivalence. I'd earn admission into three different programs and earn two graduate degrees. During my last two years, I'd teach in the lowest-performing public school in Boston and then become a teaching fellow at Concord Academy, all the while doing manual labor—moving furniture and raking leaves—to help make ends meet. In the Boston Public Schools, I identified with the urban students who rose to the challenges I placed before them. These students negotiated a commute that required them to avoid being shot or stabbed on the way to school in Back Bay. They'd wear hats and t-shirts that memorialized the unfortunate casualties of street violence.

On the other hand, at Concord Academy, I found myself resenting the scholarship students who felt obligated to kowtow to their benefactors—faculty and staff—at the school. Moreover, the white scholarship students and their parents often resented my credentials and feared that I'd somehow lord my pedigree over them. I perceived subtle coercion to inflate white students' grades and deflate those of non-whites. I resisted as much as I could. My eccentric colleagues seemed hip, not collegial, and ignorant about how to relate to blacks as their peers. The African-American peers that I had were biracial with white partners and committed to respectability politics. It was a terrible time.

During this period, I came to appreciate the comments made when a benevolent African-American professor in the graduate school of education described me as privileged and underprivileged. For the first time, I began to see my predicament. While decades older than Mychal Denzel Smith, my literacy narrative implied searching for a role model that inhibited a middle space. He writes, "My nostalgia for a time period that I didn't live through had me wishing I grew up with Malcolm X, Huey P. Newton, H. Rap Brown, Amiri Baraka, Stokely Carmichael (turned Kwame Ture), or Fred Hampton around to show me how black rage could be harnessed as a weapon for revolution."[14] Smith had looked to hip-hop artists to define black masculinity for him, but their actual and lyrical misogyny created ambivalence. He confesses,

14. Smith, *Invisible Man*, 52–53.

These black men were guides through the minefield of identity when faced with racism. I was attracted to the bravado, to the reclamation of black excellence. I wanted to absorb their performance of black arrogance as a corrective to self-loathing. But what I hadn't considered was how that ego was gendered. I spent my childhood passively absorbing white supremacist ideas of invisibility, then unconsciously shrinking from the world. Everything I read, listened to, and learned validated my right to existence as a black man in America. But that wasn't the whole equation. [Black masculinity was] only within the confines of a patriarchal definition of masculine identity.[15]

Eventually, Smith discovered such a figure in Kanye West. In Smith's mind, West resided between a hustler and street-focused rap narratives and the underground rappers who took the baton from the neo-black nationalist who'd defined the golden age of hip-hop. In *The College Dropout*, Smith found in West an "in-rhyme biography [he] could relate to while still enjoying the music."[16] He, however, had no plans of abandoning his education in pursuit of a path towards black masculinity. Nevertheless, he did need someone to guide him towards authenticity. "Kanye was able to locate the space in the middle of all that [conscious and gangster rap], where sped-up soul samples, ego-tripping, self-reflection, an indictment of racism coexisted in harmony, all from an ostensibly middle-class perspective, while desperately seeking 'hood validation," according to Smith.[17] As a role model, West synthesized the tensions inherent in old-school black respectability politics and "keeping-it-real" black authenticity.

In *Invisible Man*, Smith confides to the reader that he'd experienced anger and solitude in his inability to communicate with others about social issues and appropriate responses, which I read as his need to find a path towards black authenticity, liberation, and transcendence. His epiphany occurred following Hurricane Katrina when West proclaimed, "George Bush doesn't care about black people."[18] Where others judged West as arrogant and infantile for his egotistical statements at the 2004 American Music Awards, after losing, and the Grammy Awards, after winning for Best Rap Album, Smith found something else. He admired "the perfect, unabashed celebration of his black genius self—and by extension, my black genius [or

15. Smith, *Invisible Man*, 29.
16. Smith, *Invisible Man*, 45
17. Smith, *Invisible Man*, 45.
18. Terry, "10 Years Ago Today."

literate] self."[19] During my generation, the raunchy gender-bending Prince performed a similar function in my masculinity formation. Moreover, West was a wealthy entertainer and music mogul; I couldn't afford his instability and volatility, though it was there. I tried to bottle that anger and rage to cobble together a bricolage revolutionary ideology to raise my "negronese" children to change the system.

As a black father with a growing family, I faced tensions between both ideological and practical issues. As Smith argued when engaging the rapper Mos Def's riff on Ralph Ellison's *Invisible Man*, "being invisible to these systems [of power] has real material consequences."[20] I abhorred strategies needed to render myself visible. My race, gender, and class led individuals and institutions to respond to me in one way. Still, my pedigree had empowered me to get in the door and resist those forces with a modicum of authority and efficacy. Smith explains my challenge when writing, "But if we look back to what politics of respectability was initially meant to describe, it's still an insufficient philosophy. Part of the reason why a new generation of thinking and activists rejected respectability politics is that it's by necessity a politics of exclusion."[21] I hated that I had to rely on my "pedigree privilege" to be treated as a citizen, a professional, a human being. But I did that time and time again—at hospitals, schools, and other places—to make sure I could meet my family's needs. I'd do it, but I would feel ambivalent about it. In the end, the race and class privilege of others would trump my credentials. The H bomb had limited power. I mean, I wasn't a member of the black Brahmins or the Boulé.

In the spring of 2010, when I graduated with a doctoral degree in educational leadership and policy studies, the ambivalence remained as I began teaching a course at the University of Washington called "Reading While Black: Thinking about Black Male Literacy in the Age of Hip-Hop." Initially, I thought I'd partner with Dr. Eddie Moore, who put on the annual White Privilege Conference and served as a diversity officer at the posh Bush School. We named the course after Vershawn Ashanti Young's book *Your Average Nigga: Performing Race, Literacy, and Masculinity.* Interestingly, a black admissions officer complained to the administration after the Comparative History of Ideas program sent out my flyer to advertise the course to the campus. The ambitious young admissions administration was concerned that its existence would give white fraternity guys the license to use the course title's offending word. His concerns led to a meeting with the

19. Smith, *Invisible Man*, 126.
20. Smith, *Invisible Man*, 126.
21. Smith, *Invisible Man*, 201.

provost and two vice provosts; all three administrators were people of color. During our conversation, I had an epiphany: I had grown up with a myth regarding academic freedom when in reality, higher education has functioned under a conservative regime. Our intense conversation confirmed the need for the book *Speech Is My Hammer*.

I had gleaned a new insight through studying our literature, literary analysis, and reflection. This knowledge has allowed me to understand anew my earliest ruminations on what it means to be black, male, and literate in the United States. In constructing a black male canon for the course, I began developing increased gratitude for my literacy narrative and the community members, educators, intellectuals, and writers who have nurtured me as a literate human being. I sought to balance the tension between being an academic and more relatable (real) black male, or at least I thought so. On the first day of class, I let my students know that I had high academic standards and social expectations regarding collegiality. I had designed the course to promote a realness I felt the material required. I didn't want my students to feel the hidden requirement to code-switch and "perpetrate fraud," as they'd say in Southeast San Diego. Dr. Vershawn A. Young was right: I, and other black scholars, had been relying on code-meshing in our literacy performances.

During our next meeting, as we plowed through a discussion of Jane Roland Martin's *Educational Metamorphoses*, we began to experience a breakthrough that I did not expect to happen until much later. My students began to demonstrate that they wanted to actively participate in the class by sharing their authenticity and ambivalence crises. These students included a thirty-something-year-old African-American male graduate student and a black female undergraduate from the rough side of Tacoma, Washington. One standout was a young white mother of several biracial children who had moved to Seattle from the South. Once in the Northwest, she had begun to identify with our regional African-American population based on similarities in culture and food. She kept it real, it seemed.

Based on the course's rigor (lots of reading and writing expectations), a part of the group dropped the seminar. It wasn't going to be an academic voyeuristic experience. I imagine that my code-meshing confused more than a few (white) students. On day two, my students began to open their hearts and minds in a manner that let me know—both implicitly and explicitly—that I had created a safe space where some felt comfortable discussing their connection to the material and their ambivalences. It seemed that the sky was the limit. In the end, my experience teaching on black masculinity at the University of Washington would include earnest undergraduate students generating insights beyond their academic training and others who seemed to enroll in these courses with pretensions intent on disrupting the flow of our discussions. In short, my academic literacy did not translate into racial transcendence.

As I wrote this epilogue, I was in the process of closing one chapter in my life and opening a whole new chapter. A month later, I passed my dissertation defense. I participated in commencement, fulfilling my grand-mother's dream. I planned on carrying her scarf and my mother's baby picture with me on that platform to take them along with me on the very last leg of this long and convoluted journey. The photograph made it. While I'm ambivalent about the race and class politics that create the context for secondary marginalization, I have always been. I will continue to be an advocate of mainstream literacy. What's different today is that I'm aware of the burden that it places on underclass black men who grow up speaking the Black English Vernacular in socially isolated ghettos. The men in their lives tend to promote hyper-masculinity out of a desire to avoid domination by white and black upper-class notions of what it means to be an intelligent and manly human. Moreover, I am much more conscious and respectful of the differences that exist among African Americans in terms of culture and ideology, recognizing that in many ways, most seek to resist hegemonic culture while at the same time being complicit in their own domination.

My grandmother used to say that the essential thing in life was to gain an "understanding." Before I learned the concept from a scholarly book, Grandma taught me the linked fate concept. Yet, now as I read Huey P. Newton's *Revolutionary Suicide*, I begin to understand the soil from which my politics of literacy emerged. Newton writes, "There is an old African saying, 'I am we.' If you met an African in ancient times and asked him who he was, he would reply, 'I am we.'"[22] As I listened to Marvin Gaye on YouTube and watched the audience listen pensively, I recognized that his questions—what's going on? What's happening, brother?—hold within them a multifaceted inquiry with nuances that seek not so much to find definitive answers to restore a notion of "I am we" or linked fate, *and* cultivate a discourse of trauma, empathy, reflection, and understanding. Robert Birt argues as much in "Blackness and the Quest for Authenticity":

> Black authenticity [should] mean choosing and affirming one-self as black, choosing and affirming solidarity and community with one's black sisters and brothers, and affirming our legacy of struggle and the universal worth of liberating values emerging from that legacy. And while this striving for authentic existence and liberated subjectivity must be a movement of resistance to

22. Newton, *Revolutionary Suicide*, 359.

dehumanizing reification and denied transcendence, resistance
does not exactly exhaust our quest. It is also a question of expanding the sphere of possibilities wherein human creativity—
especially self-creation—can thrive.[23]

Over the years, existential blackness has devolved from the pursuit of liberating subjectivities to a cultural straitjacket and fodder for academics,
creatives, and black public intellectuals to debate. For me, one response to
resolving our contemporary discontents is to reflect on the philosophy and
poetry in African-American music. In "What's Going On," Gaye describes a
tangible misunderstanding between the generations based on judgments on
appearance and diverging youth culture. Gaye responds to social fragmentation with a call for an increase in understanding and healing in response
to the escalation in social disharmony within our borders and a devastating
war abroad.

The soul singer's lyrics contain questions and rhetorical statements
that are loving invitations to (re)begin a conversation about oneself, about
the black community, and broader society—because in the imagined black
community, the shared experience of anti-blackness intertwines individuals
in a collective existential reality. Gaye's words might express a version of the
African-American adaptation of the primordial philosophical questions:
How do I live? How might we live well while navigating a racist system?
African-American males might probe into new terrain with the following questions: Does literacy make a difference? How do we read African-
American literacy narratives with empathy and compassion? How do we
move from a politics of respectability (and distancing) to what critical-race
theorist Regina Austin labels as a "politics of identification"?[24] Suppose we
don't ask ourselves these questions in every generation. In that case, we will
continue to find ourselves stuck in a place of ambivalence about the relationship between literacy, humanity, masculinity, and blackness. We must
teach each generation of African-American female and male readers to look
to the canon, peers, and mentors and ask the two most important questions:
"What's going on? What's happening, brother and sister?"

23. Birt, "Blackness and the Quest," 271.
24. Austin, "Black Community," 290–301.

# Bibliography

Alexander, Bryant Keith. *Performing Black Masculinity: Race, Culture, and Queer Identity*. Lanham: AltaMira, 2006.

Alexander, Michelle. *The New Jim Crow: Mass Incarceration in the Age of Colorblindness*. New York: New Press, 2010.

Anderson, Benedict. *Imagined Communities: Reflections on the Origin and Spread of Nationalism*. London: Verso, 2006.

Anderson, Elijah. "The Code of the Streets." *Atlantic Monthly* (May 1994) 81–94.

Ashcroft, Bill. "Ambivalence." In *Post-colonial Studies: The Key Concepts*, edited by Bill Ashcroft, Gareth Griffiths, and Helen Tiffin, 10–11. New York: Routledge, 2007.

————."Cultural Diversity/Cultural Difference." In *Post-colonial Studies: The Key Concepts*, edited by Bill Ashcroft, Gareth Griffiths, and Helen Tiffin, 53–54. New York: Routledge, 2007.

————. "Hybridity." In *Post-colonial Studies: The Key Concepts*, edited by Bill Ashcroft, Gareth Griffiths, and Helen Tiffin, 108–11. New York: Routledge, 2007.

Austin, Regina. "'The Black Community,' Its Lawbreakers, and the Politics of Identification." In *Critical Race Theory: The Cutting Edge*, edited by Richard Delgado and Jean Stefancic, 290–301. Philadelphia: Temple University Press, 2000.

Bassard, Katherine Clary. "Gender and Genre: Black Women's Autobiography and the Ideology of Literacy." *African American Review* 26 (1992) 119–29.

Bergonzi, Bernard. "Black Cartesian." *Hudson Review* 22 (1969) 508–12.

Betts, Reginald Dwayne. *A Question of Freedom: A Memoir of Learning, Survival, and Coming of Age in Prison*. New York: Penguin, 2009.

Beliveau, Ralph, and Laura Bolf-Beliveau. "Posing Problems and Picking Fights." In *The Wire: Urban Decay and American Television*, edited by Tiffany Potter and C. W. Marshall, 91–106. New York: Continuum International Group, 2011.

Bey, Dawoud. "Swagger." In *Black Cool: One Thousand Streams of Blackness*, edited by Rebecca Walker, 147–54. Berkeley: Soft Skull, 2012.

Bhabha, Homi. "Of Mimicry and Man: The Ambivalence of Colonial Discourse." *October* 23 (1984) 125–33.

Birt, Robert E. "Blackness and the Quest for Authenticity." In *White on White/Black on Black*, edited George Yancy, 265–73. Lanham: Rowman & Littlefield, 2005.

Blackmon, Douglas A. *Slavery by Another Name: The Re-Enslavement of Black Americans from the Civil War to World War II*. New York: Doubleday, 2008.

Bobo, Lawrence D., and James R. Kluegel. "Status, Ideology, and Dimensions of Whites' Racial Beliefs and Attitudes: Progress and Stagnation." In *Racial Attitudes in the 1990s: Continuity and Change,* edited by Steven A. Tuch and Jack K. Martin, 93–120. Westport: Praeger, 1997.

Branch, Enobong Hannah, and Mary Larue Scherer. "Mapping the Intersections in Resurgence of the Culture of Poverty." *Race, Gender, and Class* 20 (2013) 346–58.

Brown, William Wells. *Clotel, or, The President's Daughter.* Armonk: M. E. Sharpe, Inc., 1996.

Cheney, Charise L. *Brothers Gonna Work It Out: Sexual Politics in the Golden Age of Rap Nationalism.* New York: New York University Press, 2005.

Coates, Ta-Nehisi. *The Beautiful Struggle: A Father, Two Sons, and an Unlikely Road to Manhood.* New York: Spiegel & Grau, 2008.

———. "How the Obama Administration Talks to Black America: 'Convenient Race-Talk' from a President Who Ought to Know Better." *Atlantic,* May 20, 2013. https://www.theatlantic.com/politics/archive/2013/05/how-the-obama-administration-talks-to-black-america/276015/.

Cohen, Cathy J. *The Boundaries of Blackness: AIDS and the Breakdown of Black Politics.* Chicago: University of Chicago Press, 1999.

Collins, Patricia Hill. *From Black Power to Hip Hop: Racism, Nationalism, and Feminism.* Philadelphia: Temple University, 2006.

Cosby, Bill. "Pound Cake Speech." *American Rhetoric On-line Speech Bank,* May 17, 2004. http://www.americanrhetoric.com/speeches/billcosbypoundcakespeech.htm.

Dancy, T. Elon, II, and Bryan K. Hotchkins. "Schools for the Better Making of Men? Undergraduate Black Males, Fraternity Membership, Manhood." *Culture, Society & Masculinities* 7 (2015) 7–21.

Davis, Ossie. "Our Shining Black Prince." In *Malcolm X: The Man and His Times,* edited by John Henrik Clarke, 128–31. New York: MacMillan, 1969.

Dawson, Michael C. *Behind the Mule: Race and Class in African-America.* Princeton: Princeton University Press, 1995.

———. *Black Visions: The Roots of Contemporary African-American Political Ideologies.* Chicago: University of Chicago Press, 2001.

Delblanco, Andrew. *The Real American Dream: A Meditation on Hope.* Cambridge: Harvard University Press, 2000.

Douglass, Frederick. *Autobiographies: Narrative of the Life of Frederick Douglass, an American Slave; My Bondage and My Freedom; Life and Times of Frederick Douglass.* Edited by Henry Louis Gates Jr. New York: Penguin, 1994.

Du Bois, W. E. B. "Of Mr. Booker T. Washington and Others." In *The Souls of Black Folk,* edited by Nathan Hare and Alvin F. Poussaint, 79–96. New York: New American Library, 1982.

———. *The Souls of Black Folk.* Edited by Nathan Hare and Alvin F. Poussaint. New York: New American Library, 1982.

Dumas, Michael. "Critical Thinking as Black Existence." In *Critical Thinking and Learning,* edited by Danny Weil and Joe Kincheloe, 155–59. Westport: Greenwood, 2004.

Edmonds, Ennis. "Dread 'I' In-a Babylon: Ideological Resistance, and Cultural Revitalization." In *Chanting Down Babylon: The Rastafari Reader,* edited by

Nathaniel Samuel Murrell, William David Spencer, and Adrian Anthony McFarlane, 23–35. Philadelphia: Temple University Press, 1998.

Ellison, Ralph. *Invisible Man.* New York: Vintage, 1990.

Eldred, Janet C. "Narratives of Socialization: Literacy in the Short Story." *College English* 53 (1991) 686–700.

Eldred, Janet Carey, and Peter Mortensen. "Reading Literacy Narratives." *College English* 54 (1992) 512–39.

Ferguson, Ann A. *Bad Boys: Public Schools in the Making of Black Masculinity.* Ann Arbor: University of Michigan Press, 2000.

Foucault, Michel. *"Society Must Be Defended": Lectures at the Collège de France, 1975–76.* New York: Picador, 2003.

Faulkner, William. *The Sound and the Fury.* New York: Vintage, 1984.

Favor, Martin J. *Authentic Blackness: The Folk in the New Negro Renaissance.* Durham: Duke University Press, 1999.

Forman, Murray. *The 'Hood Comes First: Race, Space, and Place in Rap and Hip-Hop.* Middletown: Wesleyan University Press, 2002.

Freud, Sigmund. *The Uncanny.* New York: Penguin, 2003.

Gates, Henry Louis. *America Behind the Color Line: Dialogues with African Americans.* New York: Warner, 2004.

———. *The Classic Slave Narratives.* New York: Signet Classic, 2002.

———. *The Signifying Monkey: A Theory of African-American Literary Criticism.* Oxford: Oxford University Press, 2014.

Geronimo, India. "Systemic Failure: The School-to-Prison Pipeline and Discrimination against Poor Minority Student." *Journal of Law in Society* 13 (2011) 281–98.

Gibson, Ernest L., III. "The Envy of Erudition: Booker T. Washington and the Desire for a Du Boisian Intellectuality." *Black Scholar* 43 (2013) 52–68.

———. "'For Whom the BELL Tolls': The Wire's Stringer Bell as Tragic Intellectual." *Americana: The Journal of American Popular Culture* 10 (2011). https://www.americanpopularculture.com/journal/articles/spring_2011/gibson.htm.

Gershenhorn, Jerry. *Melville J. Herskovits and the Racial Politics of Knowledge.* Lincoln: University of Nebraska Press, 2004.

Greene, Deric M., and Felicia R. Walker. "Recommendations to Public Speaking Instructors for the Negotiation of Code-Switching Practices among Black English-Speaking African American Students." *Journal of Negro Education* 73 (2004) 435.

Grimes, William. *Life of William Grimes, the Runaway Slave.* New York: Oxford University Press, 2008.

Gutmann, Amy. *Identity in Democracy.* Princeton: Princeton University Press, 2003.

Herskovits, Melville J. *The Myth of the Negro Past.* Boston: Beacon, 1990.

Higginbotham, Evelyn Brooks. *Righteous Discontent: The Women's Movement in the Black Baptist Church, 1880–1920.* Cambridge: Harvard University Press, 1993.

Hobbs, Allyson Vanessa. *A Chosen Exile: A History of Racial Passing in American Life.* Cambridge: Harvard University Press, 2014.

Hohle, Randolph. *Black Citizenship and Authenticity in the Civil Rights Movement.* New York: Routledge, 2013.

hooks, bell. *We Real Cool: Black Men and Masculinity.* New York: Routledge, 2004.

Hughes, Langston. *The Big Sea.* New York: Hill and Wang, 1993.

————."The Negro Artist and the Racial Mountain." In *African American Literary Theory: A Reader*, edited by Winston Napier, 27–30. New York: New York University Press, 2000.

Ice T. "Foreword." In *Inside the Crips: Life inside L.A.'s Most Notorious Gang*, by Colton Simpson, xv–xxiii. New York: St. Martin's, 2005.

Iwamoto, Derek. "Tupac Shakur: Understanding the Formation of Hyper-Masculinity of a Popular Hip-Hop Art." *Black Scholar* 33 (2003) 44–49.

Jackson, Mitchell S. *The Residue Years: A Novel*. New York: Bloomsbury, 2013.

Jenkins, Candice M. "A Kind of End to Blackness." In *From Bourgeois to Boojie: Black Middle-Class Performances*, edited by Vershawn Ashanti Young and Bridget Harris Tsemo, 261–86. Detroit: Wayne State University Press, 2011.

Johnson, E. Patrick. *Appropriating Blackness: Performance and the Politics of Authenticity*. Durham: Duke University Press, 2003.

Jones, Suzanne W. *Crossing the Color Line: Readings in Black and White*. Colombia: University of South Carolina, 2000.

Kennedy, Randall. *Nigger: The Strange Career of a Troublesome Word*. New York: Vintage, 2003.

Kihn, Paul. "Labeling the Young: Hope in Contemporary Childhood." In *Labeling: Pedagogy and Politics*, edited by Glenn M. Hudak and Paul Kihn, 55–74. New York: Taylor & Francis, 2001.

Kim, Catherine Y., Daniel J. Losen, and Damon Hewitt. *The School-to-Prison Pipeline: Structuring Legal Reform*. New York: New York University Press, 2010.

Laymon, Kiese. *Heavy: An American Memoir*. New York: Scribner, 2008.

Lear, Jonathan. *Open-Minded: Working Out the Logic of the Soul*. Cambridge: Harvard University Press, 1998.

Majors, Richard, and Janet Billson. *Cool Pose: The Dilemma of Black Manhood in America*. New York: Lexington, 1992.

Malcolm X. *The Autobiography of Malcolm X*. Westminster: Random House, 1999.

Martin, Jane Roland. *Educational Metamorphoses: Philosophical Reflections on Identity and Culture*. Lanham: Rowman and Littlefield, 2007.

Miller, Jerome. *Search and Destroy: African-American Males in the Criminal Justice System*. Cambridge: Cambridge University Press, 1997.

Morris, Errol, dir. *The Fog of War*. Sony Pictures Classics, 2003. DVD.

Moore, Darnell L. *No Ashes in the Fire: Coming of Age Black and Free in America*. New York: Bold Type Books, 2018.

Moore, Madison. *Fabulous: The Rise of the Beautiful Eccentric*. New Haven: Yale University Press, 2018.

Morrison, Toni. *The Nobel Lecture in Literature, 1993*. New York: A. A. Knopf, 1993.

————. "The Official Story: Dead Man Golfing." In *Birth of a Nation'hood: Gaze, Script, and Spectacle in the O. J. Simpson Case*, edited by Toni Morrison and Claudia Brodsky Lacour, vii–xxvii. New York: Random House, 1997.

————. "On the Backs of Blacks." In *What Moves at the Margins*, edited by Carolyn C. Denard Jackson, 145–48. Oxford, MS: University of Mississippi, 2008.

————. *Playing in the Dark: Whiteness and the Literary Imagination*. Cambridge: Harvard University Press, 1992.

————. *Tar Baby*. New York: Vintage International, 2004.

Murch, Donna. "The Campus and the Street: Race, Migration, and the Origins of the Black Panther Party in Oakland, CA." *Souls: A Critical Journal of Black Politics, Culture, and Society* 9 (2007) 333–45.

Mills, Charles W. *The Racial Contract*. Ithaca: Cornell University Press, 1994.

Neal, Mark Anthony. *Looking for Leroy: Illegible Black Masculinities*. New York: New York University Press, 2013.

———. "'A Man without a Country': The Boundaries of Legibility, Social Capital, and Cosmopolitan." *Criticism* 52 (2010) 399–411.

Newton, Huey P. *Revolutionary Suicide*. New York: Penguin, 2009.

Norris, Keenan. *Street Lit: Representing the Urban Landscape*. Lanham: Scarecrow, 2014.

Ogbar, Jeffrey O. G. "'Real Niggas': Race, Ethnicity, and the Construction of Authenticity in Hip-Hop." In *Hip-Hop Revolution: The Culture and Politics of Rap*, 37–92. Lawrence: University Press of Kansas, 2007.

Oliver, Valerie Cassel. "Through the Conceptual Lens: The Rise, Fall, and Resurrection of Blackness." In *Double-Consciousness: Black Conceptual Art Since 1970*, edited by Johanna Burton, 72–80. New York: Distributed Art, 2005.

Paley, Vivian. *The Girl with the Brown Crayon*. Cambridge: Harvard University Press, 1997.

Pareles, Jon. "Prince, an Artist Who Defied Genre, Is Dead." *New York Times*, April 21, 2016. https://www.nytimes.com/2016/04/22/arts/music/prince-dead.html.

Poe, Edgar Allen. *The Raven and Other Poems*. New York: Penguin, 2013.

Rainwater, Lee, and William Y. Yancey. *The Moynihan Report and the Politics of Controversy*. Cambridge: MIT Press, 1967.

Read, Jason. "Stringer Bell's Lament: Violence and Legitimacy in Contemporary Capitalism." In *The Wire: Urban Decay and American Television*, edited by Tiffany Potter and C. W. Marshall, 122–34. New York: Continuum International Group, 2011.

Ross, Andrew. "The Gangsta and the Diva." In *Black Male: Representations of Masculinity in Contemporary Art*, edited by Thelma Golden, 159–66. New York: White Museum of American Art, 1994.

Salvino, Dana N. "The Word in Black and White: Ideologies of Race and Literacy. In Antebellum America." In *Reading in America*, edited by Cathy N. Davidson, 140–56. Baltimore: John Hopkins University Press, 1989.

Sawyer, Michael. *Black Minded: The Political Philosophy of Malcolm X*. London: Pluto, 2020.

Stoler, Ann Laura. *Carnal Knowledge and Imperial Power: Race and the Intimate in Colonial Rule*. Berkeley: University of California Press, 2002.

———. *Race and the Education of Desire: Foucault's History of Sexuality and the Colonial Order of Things*. Durham: Duke University Press, 1995.

Steele, Claude M. *Whistling Vivaldi: And Other Clues to How Stereotypes Affect Us*. New York: W. W. Norton & Company, 2010.

Stepto, Robert B. *From behind the Veil: A Study of Afro-American Narrative*. Urbana: University of Illinois, 1991.

Simpson, Colton. *Inside the Crips: Life inside L.A.'s Most Notorious Gang*. New York: St. Martin's, 2005.

Skitolsky, Lissa. *Hip-Hop as Philosophical Text and Testimony: Can I Get a Witness?* Lanham: Rowman & Littlefield, 2020.

Smith, Mychal Denzel. *Invisible Man, Got the Whole World Watching: A Young Black Man's Education.* New York: Nation Books, 2016.

Strayhorn, Terrel L., and Derrick L. Tillman-Kelly. "Queering Masculinity: Manhood and Black Gay Men in College." *Spectrum* 1 (2013) 83–110.

Tatum, Alfred. *Reading for Their Life: (Re)building the Textual Lineages of African American Adolescent Males.* Portsmouth: Heinemann, 2009.

Terry, Josh. "10 Years Ago Today, Kanye West Said, 'George Bush Doesn't Care about Black People.'" *Chicago Tribune*, September 2, 2015. https://www.chicagotribune.com/redeye/redeye-kanye-west-katrina-telethon-george-bush-black-people-20150902-htmlstory.html.

Tucker, Linda. *Lockstep and Dance: Images of Black Men in Popular Culture.* Jackson: University Press of Mississippi, 2007.

Twain, Mark. *Adventures of Huckleberry Finn.* New York: Dover, 1994.

Vidler, Anthony. *The Architectural Uncanny: Essays in the Modern Unhomely.* Cambridge: MIT Press, 1992.

Washington, Booker T. *Up from Slavery.* New York: Signet Classics, 2000.

Wiener, Jonah. "A$AP Rocky's Hard Knock Life." *Rolling Stone* (March 2013) 44–47.

Welsh, Patrick. "Consider Cultural Differences." *New York Times,* March 27, 2011. https://www.nytimes.com/roomfordebate/2011/03/27/how-to-raise-the-status-of-teachers/consider-cultural-differences.

Williams, Thomas Chatterton. "Black Culture, Beyond Hip Hop." *Washington Post*, May 28, 2007, A17.

———. *Losing My Cool: Love, Literature, and a Black Man's Escape from the Crowd.* New York: Penguin, 2010.

———. *Self-Portrait in Black and White: Family, Fatherhood, and Rethinking.* New York: W. W. Norton & Company, Ltd., 2019.

Wright, Richard. *Black Boy (American Hunger): A Record of Childhood and Youth.* New York: Perennial Classics, 1998.

———. "Foreword." In *Pan-Africanism or Communism?: The Coming Struggle for Africa*, edited by George Padmore, 11–14. London: Dobson, 1956.

———. *The Outsider.* New York: Harper & Row, 1953.

———. *White Man Listen!* Garden City: Anchor, 1964.

Yancy, George. *Backlash: What Happens When We Talk Honestly about Racism in American.* Lanham: Rowman & Littlefield, 2018.

Young, Vershawn Ashanti. *Your Average Nigga: Performing Race, Literacy, and Masculinity.* Detroit: Wayne State University Press, 2007.

# About the Author

A NATIVE SOUTHERN CALIFORNIAN, Dr. Max Hunter spent his formative years experiencing the urban deterioration associated with Southern California and Washington, DC, in the late sixties, seventies, and eighties. After dropping out of college to traffic cocaine, he went on to earn his PhD in educational leadership and policy studies and a master's degree in bioethics from the University of Washington and two master's degrees in history of science and education from Harvard University. As a professor and professional coach, Hunter developed curricula focused on anti-blackness, equity, health disparities, inclusion, and the social determinants of health. He was appointed to serve as a diversity-affairs liaison to the Association of American Medical Colleges (AAMC). Dr. Hunter seeks to promote health justice and undermine the factors that perpetuate literacy ambivalence among black men. A renowned omnivore and soccer dad, he enjoys eating his daughter's cooking, dining out, watching his children play soccer, and walking down Alki Beach with his family in Seattle, WA.

**August and Smith Hunter (c. 2007)**